FUTURES MARKETS: THEIR ESTABLISHMENT AND PERFORMANCE

Futures markets are an increasingly important feature of the world's major financial centres. Much attention has been given to the speculation and returns to traders aspects of these markets. Increasingly, however, attention is being given to the ability of futures markets to reflect information and their consequent role as an efficient forward pricing mechanism. This reflects a general interest by economists in the study of risk, uncertainty and information. In addition, attention is being given increasingly to feasibility, that is the analysis of conditions under which futures markets are likely to emerge and develop, in an attempt to provide a more general framework of analysis. This book discusses many important aspects of the theory and practice of futures markets. It concentrates on areas of current concern such as feasibility, forward pricing and returns as well as the modelling of price determination in these markets. Evidence is drawn from twenty-five different commodities representing all the major commodity groups; and from all the world's major centres of futures trading.

FUTURES MARKETS:

THEIR ESTABLISHMENT AND PERFORMANCE

Edited by
Barry A. Goss

NEW YORK UNIVERSITY PRESS
Washington Square, New York

First published in 1986 in the U.S.A. by
New York University Press, Washington Square,
New York, N.Y. 10003

Library of Congress Cataloging-in-Publication Data

Future markets.
Bibliography: p.
Includes index.
1. Commodity exchanges. I. Goss, Barry A.
HG6024.A3F88 1986 332.64′4 86-8466
ISBN 0-8147-3009-4

Manufactured in Great Britain

CONTENTS

ACKNOWLEDGEMENTS

This volume began with some very good research papers submitted by students taking my graduate course 'Hedging and Uncertainty' at Monash University. At least that is how the papers by Veljanovski, Harrison and Rainbow began. The remaining papers resulted from invitations to other researchers in the area of futures markets to contribute to this volume.

While most of the papers in this book are published here for the first time, acknowledgement is made to the editor of *Quarterly Review of Economics and Business* for material from C.F. Lee and R.M. Leuthold, 'Investment horizon, risk, and return in commodity futures markets: an empirical analysis with daily data', published in that journal; to the Chicago Board of Trade for permission to reprint D.J.S. Rutledge, 'Trading volume and price variability: new evidence on the price effects of speculation', *International Research Seminar Proceedings*, 1978; to the Royal Statistical Society for permission to reprint S.J. Taylor, 'Conjectured models for trends in financial prices, tests and forecasts', *Journal of the Royal Statistical Society*, A, 1980; and to the editor of Chapman and Hall for permission to reprint B.A. Goss, 'The forward pricing function of the London Metal Exchange', *Applied Economics*, 1981, a revised version of which appears as Chapter 7.

In addition, thanks are due to Gulay Avsar for her careful assistance in compilation of the index and checking the proofs, to Franca Goodwin and Philippa Geurens who typed the manuscript so well, and to Margaret Watts and Jenny Francis who checked it.

I would like to acknowledge also the help and co-operation I have received from the editorial and production staff of Croom Helm. This book is published with the assistance of a grant from the Monash University Publications Committee.

B.A. Goss

INTRODUCTION: FEASIBILITY AND THE CONSEQUENCES OF USING INFORMATION IN FUTURES MARKETS

Barry A. Goss

1. Conditions for the Establishment of Futures Markets

Originally the conditions for the establishment of futures markets were treated as a list of commodity prerequisites based on generalizations from past experience, such as price variability, ability to specify a standard grade, storability, deliverability, etc. (e.g. Houthakker, 1959; see the discussion in Section 1 of Chapter 7 of this volume). Gray (1966) distinguished between the feasibility of a futures market and its success, and referred to contractual characteristics which may hinder success, such as where delivery provisions favour one side of the market.

Such a list of prerequisites, however, is not an economic theory and lacks predictive ability. In particular it was unable to predict the development of markets trading in commodities which are virtually non-storable (such as live beef cattle) or which are both non-storable and non-deliverable (such as trading in share price indices).[1] As Veljanovski points out in this volume (Chapter 1), this list of prerequisites focused on local examples of economic variables such as the possibility of delivery, rather than the economic variables themselves, such as transactions costs or costs of arbitrage.

Telser and Higinbotham (1977) addressed the hypothesis that trading is most active in those contracts where the net benefits are greatest. Net benefits were related (directly) to price variability, liquidity, turnover and commitments. It was found *inter alia*, first, that the most actively traded commodities had the most variable prices; second, margin and commission costs vary inversely with turnover (but directly with open interest and average contract price); third, the standard deviation of market clearing prices (which varies inversely with liquidity) was found to vary inversely with turnover, as predicted.

In Telser and Higinbotham the existence of futures trading is predetermined, but in Veljanovski the market penetration of futures trading is an endogenous variable as is the contractual form itself. Veljanovski brings together emphasis on transactions costs and the concept of property rights to argue that futures markets develop because they are more efficient, in terms of transactions costs, than spot and forward markets in transferring certain bundles of property rights attached to price. Within this framework, he uses the property rights concept to explain the tendency to self-regulation in futures markets, and the concentration of trading in a few market locations is explained in terms of liquidity benefits. Indeed Veljanovski suggests that increasing returns favour the existence of a few large exchanges.

2. Performance of Futures Markets

The literature contains no comprehensive framework for analysing the performance of futures markets; nevertheless, there is probably a reasonable degree of agreement on the functions of these markets, and in the view of the present editor, these may be stated as follows:

(i) Futures markets provide facilities for risk management, because they provide opportunities for hedging.
(ii) They perform a forward pricing function, and they thus facilitate the intertemporal allocation of resources.
(iii) They collect and disseminate information.
(iv) As Working (1953) showed, in the case of commodities with continuous inventories (especially where those inventories are seasonal), they facilitate the holding of inventories in private hands.

The real difficulty is that there exist no clearly agreed criteria for evaluating the performance of futures markets in these functions. Still less are these criteria integrated into a coherent framework. Nevertheless, some criteria have been developed for analysing the performance of futures markets in some of these individual functions.

Over 30 years ago several papers were published which investigated the routine hedging performance of futures markets. For example, Yamey (1951) and Graf (1953) considered whether profits and losses resulting from price movements were smaller with hedging than without. This question was generally answered in the affirmative, especially when spot price changes were large.

It was argued strongly that agents in these markets pursue the joint objectives of uncertain profit and risk reduction (Working, 1953). The important question of the ratio in which agents hold spot and futures contracts was analysed from a portfolio theoretic viewpoint by Stein (1961, 1964), Johnson (1960) and Ward and Fletcher (1971). Some economists addressed the difficult task of modelling and estimating the outcomes for these portfolio type hedgers (see Rutledge, 1972 and Dusak, 1973). The optimum proportion of a commitment to be hedged from a portfolio viewpoint has also been discussed by Ederington (1979), Kahl (1983) and Schneeweis (1982).

This volume contains no chapters on the outcomes of hedging, although Yamey (Chapter 3) offers a critique of current views of the motives for hedging, including the relative importance of risk-avoidance hedging. In particular Yamey discusses the pecuniary and non-pecuniary benefits of hedging, and attempts to place in perspective the non-pecuniary benefits, especially risk reduction. In this he seeks support in the finding of Telser and Higinbotham (1977) that future markets are more active the greater the degree of price volatility.

Returns to traders in futures markets have received attention from time to time during the past 60 or so years. Keynes's theory of normal backwardation (1930) (developed on the assumption that hedgers are net short and speculators net long) contains the obvious returns implication that speculators will receive a risk premium from hedgers. Indeed Keynes's statement in the *Manchester Guardian* in 1923 suggests that speculators may expect substantial returns from being persistently long (see Keynes, 1923, 1930). Houthakker (1957) and Rockwell (1967) estimated returns to various groups of traders using open position and price change data, and found that (individually large) professional speculators gained sometimes at the expense of large hedgers, but mostly at the expense of small traders.

The question of returns to traders has also been addressed by analysing daily price change data, an analysis which has implications also for market efficiency (see below). Rainbow and Praetz in this volume (Chapter 9) investigate which function best fits the distribution of returns in this sense for Australia's longest trading contract — that for merino wool. They concluded that the Student t distribution is the best fit, as against various rival hypotheses including the alternative that futures prices are stable Paretian (infinite variance) in distribution (as claimed by Mandelbrot, 1963). They refer to studies of share prices where the data also have favoured the Student model (e.g. Blattberg and Gonedes, 1974).

Dusak (1973) examined the returns to holders of selected futures contracts (in wheat, corn and soybeans) relative to the return on 'wealth in general' (represented by the Standard and Poor index), using the Sharpe (1964)-Lintner (1965) Capital Asset Pricing Model. She found the systemic risk premium so defined, to be close to zero. In this volume Lee and Leuthold (Chapter 5) examine the returns, in the sense of proportionate price changes in futures contracts, to investment horizons ranging from 1 to 22 days. They also investigate the systematic risk between futures contracts and shares, for a range of grains, livestock, precious metals and financial futures. Their result, that there is little systematic risk between futures and shares, has implications for holders of shares.

Futures markets, by forming prices relating to forward delivery dates, project their prices into the future. These prices are used by agents to plan future production, to price forward contracts for the supply of commodities, and to tender for forward contracts. Agents need not transact on futures exchanges to use futures prices in this way, and the information contained in such prices is an externality to them. Agents may also use futures markets in deciding whether to store a commodity (using the forward premium as an indicator of whether storage is expected to be profitable). In addition, futures markets may help agents to decide the timing of input purchases and of processing activities according to the expected outcome of hedging. Agents in these latter two categories are of course transactors on futures markets. Thus, futures markets perform a forward pricing function, and in these ways futures prices facilitate the allocation of resources between present and future uses (see Hicks, 1953).

The process of price determination in futures markets has received attention in the literature, and Peston and Yamey (1960), Stein (1961, 1964), Telser (1958) and others have provided theoretical models of the determination of spot and futures prices. In this volume the chapter by Goss and Giles (Chapter 4) presents a model of the intertemporal allocation of supply and the determination of spot and futures prices using data from the Australian wool market. Subsequent work by these authors has investigated this question using United States corn and soybeans data (Giles, Goss and Chin, 1985).

The formation of spot and futures prices has also been modelled in experimental markets by Friedman, Harrison and Salmon (1983, 1984) and Plott and Sunder (1982). Friedman, Harrison and Salmon (1983) found that spot prices converged to equilibrium more rapidly with experienced agents and futures markets operating, than without futures markets, or with inexperienced agents. Plott and Sunder (1982) conducted experiments in which dividends on securities depended on the state of nature drawn at random at the start of each 'year', where some traders were given inside information. The authors found that where the price initially reflected the prior information of non-insiders, and the rational expectations equilibrium (REE) differed, then agents revised their expectations and prices converged to the REE.

In the series of experiments reported in this volume, Harrison (Chapter 2) investigates the effects of event uncertainty on the formation of spot and futures prices, and on hedger behaviour, both with and without inside information.

Economists have discussed for some time whether futures prices are anticipations of delivery date spot prices, and if so whether they are unbiased anticipations. Keynes (1930) argued that under 'normal' conditions the futures price would be less than the expected spot price by an amount equal to the marginal risk premium of speculators. If agents' expectations are correct, then the futures price will be a downward biased anticipation of the subsequent spot price.

Working was not fond of interpreting futures prices as predictions of later cash prices. Instead he favoured the view that the spread between various futures prices, and also between futures and cash prices, reflected the cost of carrying the commodity between the relevant dates (1942, p. 44). New information would be expected to affect the whole spectrum of prices. Nevertheless, Working believed that all prices are forecasts in the sense that they embody information including expectations (1948, pp. 14-15).

Many economists have addressed empirically the hypothesis that futures prices are unbiased anticipations of delivery date cash prices. The hypothesis is based upon the assumptions that current prices reflect relevant information, including agents' expectations, as fully as possible, that new information is random, and that agents are risk neutral. It also assumes, in the view of this editor, that there are no systematic differences between cash and futures contracts, with respect to the options of agents under those contracts. Empirical investigation of this hypothesis most frequently has taken the form of regression of delivery date cash prices on lagged futures prices, so that the unbiasedness hypothesis is tested appropriately by a joint test of zero intercept and unit slope.[2]

The unbiasedness hypothesis has been supported for a wide range of commodities including corn, soybeans and coffee in the USA, the pound sterling and the French franc against the US dollar, and Australian wool. On the other hand, the hypothesis has been rejected for potatoes in the USA, for live cattle in the US and Australia (with lags greater than three months), for US Treasury Bills, and for the Deutsche Mark against the US dollar (see for example, Tomek and Gray, 1970; Kofi, 1973; Hansen and Hodrick, 1980; Leuthold, 1974; Hamburger and Platt, 1975; Giles and Goss, 1981). In the chapter by Goss in this volume (Chapter 7) the unbiasedness hypothesis generally is supported for non-ferrous metals on the London Metal Exchange, although the case of zinc is marginal.

Rejection of this hypothesis has been variously accounted for in terms of the additional valuable options of sellers of futures contracts, the presence of a risk or liquidity premium, the absence or discontinuity of inventories, and the comparative youthfulness of some contracts, etc. (see also Breeden, 1982, Gray, 1972). Whatever the economic ground sought to account for rejection, it should be stressed that rejection of the unbiasedness hypothesis does not imply that the market under review is informationally inefficient, because of the jointly conditional nature of the hypothesis (see also Gregory and McCurdy, 1984; Yamey, 1984).

The conditions which must be satisfied for market prices to 'fully reflect' all information are so stringent that they are unlikely to be satisfied in the real world. These requirements include risk neutrality of agents, zero transactions costs, the agreement of agents on the implications of current information and also that information is costless to acquire. Nevertheless, for the purposes of empirical study, a working definition of market efficiency may be obtained if we interpret these conditions in a slightly more realistic fashion. For example, if we assume that transactions costs are small in relation to the value of the contract, that any disagreement among agents about the implications of information is not interdependent, and that costly information is utilized so as to maximize returns from its acquisition, etc., then we shall have an approximation to market efficiency. Any test of the efficient markets hypothesis with such a model, of course, is a joint test of that hypothesis and the validity of the other assumptions.

If current prices in a particular market fully reflect the information in own past prices, then the expected return to a trading strategy based on that information set (only) is zero. If such information is fully utilized the market is said to be weak form efficient, and Fama (1970) has surveyed *inter alia* the research on this version of the efficient markets hypothesis in securities markets. Research on this issue in the area of futures markets has employed techniques similar to those used in the securities area, and this form of the hypothesis is usually made operational by assuming that prices follow a random walk. This in turn has been addressed by runs tests, serial correlation tests, filter tests and spectral analysis. Many authors have investigated the random walk hypothesis with futures market data, including Larson (1960), Stevenson and Bear (1970), Leuthold (1972), Praetz (1975) and Cargill and Rausser (1975). Generally, some evidence of dependence in past prices has been found, and some authors have used this to reject the strict random walk hypothesis. Most would agree that it is unlikely that significant profits could have been made on the basis of such information, taking into account transactions costs. Significant filter profits on some contracts do not imply that the whole series is non-random. In any case, rejection of the random walk hypothesis does not necessarily mean that the market is weak form inefficient, because this hypothesis, which requires that price changes are independently and identically distributed, is a special case of weak form efficiency.

The efficiency of futures markets with respect to publicly available information has been investigated by two main methods. One approach has utilized the information in the immediately prior forecast errors[3] of related commodities, thus defining these forecast errors as the relevant set of publicly available information. Any systematic relationship between the current forecast error of the commodity under review and the elements of this information set would require rejection of the semi-strong version of the efficient markets hypothesis. On the other hand, inability to reject this hypothesis does not necessarily imply that the market is efficient, but may simply reflect an inappropriate specification of the information set. This method has been used by Hansen and Hodrick (1980) for currencies and Goss (1983) for non-ferrous metals (revised estimates for the latter study are included as an appendix to Chapter 7 of this volume).

An alternative approach has deployed an economic model to forecast the cash price of the relevant commodity, this forecast being compared with that contained in the futures price. If the economic model outperforms the futures price as a predictive medium, this version of the efficient markets hypothesis must be rejected, because the model contains information not incorporated in the futures price. On the other hand, inability to reject this hypothesis (because the futures price outperforms the model) does not necessarily imply that the market is efficient but may arise from an inadequate model. This method has been used by Hamburger and Platt (1975) for Treasury Bills, Leuthold and Hartmann (1979) for hogs, Brasse (1986) for tin, and Rausser and Carter (1983) for the soybean complex. In this volume Taylor (Chapter 10) tests the random walk hypothesis against a rival price-trend hypothesis for a wide range of commodities, and Weston and McDonnell (Chapter 8) consider the response of three international gold markets to external events, and also the weak form efficiency of these markets.

Finally, Arrow (1982) has suggested that futures markets place undue emphasis on the most recent information, and hence exhibit excessive price fluctuations. In Chapter 6 of this book Rutledge examines whether incremental speculation accentuates price variation on futures markets, or responds to that variation. He reaches the conclusion for a sample of US commodity and financial futures, that speculation essentially responds to price variation.

Notes

1. It is the view of the present editor that the literature on futures markets is starved of published feasibility studies for new markets. Such studies are usually prepared as consulting reports, and offer the prospect of commercial advantage to the firm which commissions the report. Publication is therefore out of the question until such advantage is realized, and then the minds of the promoters are usually occupied with other matters. Nevertheless, students of this area of economics

would probably benefit if these studies were published, even some time after the establishment of the market in question. (Sandor, 1973, is a notable exception.)

2. Ordinary least squares may not be an appropriate estimator. If serial correlation is present, instrumental variable estimation is preferred in the interests of consistency. The use of overlapping observations is likely to result in serial correlation in this context.

3. A forecast error is defined here as the difference between a lagged futures price and the delivery date cash price.

References

Arrow, K.J. (1982) 'Risk Perception in Psychology and Economics', *Economic Inquiry*, 20, 1-9.

Blattberg, R. and N. Gonedes (1974) 'A Comparison of the Stable and Student Distributions as Statistical Models for Stock Prices', *Journal of Business*, 47, 244-80.

Brasse, V. (1986) 'Testing the Efficiency of the Tin Futures Market on the LME', in K. Tucker and C. Baden Fuller (eds.), *Firms and Markets: Essays in Honour of Basil Yamey*, London: Croom Helm.

Breeden, D.T. (1982) 'Statement [On Researchable Issues]', *Review of Research in Futures Markets*, 1(2), 175-8, Chicago Board of Trade.

Cargill, T.F. and Rausser, G.C. (1975) 'Temporal Price Behaviour in Commodity Futures Markets', *The Journal of Finance*, 30(4), 1043-53.

Dusak, K. (1973) 'Futures Trading and Investor Returns: An Investigation of Commodity Market Risk Premium', *Journal of Political Economy*, 81(6), 1387-406.

Ederington, L.J. (1979) 'The Hedging Performance of the New Futures Markets', *Journal of Finance*, 34(1), 157-70.

Fama, E.F. (1970) 'Efficient Capital Markets: A Review of Theory and Empirical Work', *Journal of Finance*, 25, 383-417.

Friedman, D., G.W. Harrison and J.W. Salmon (1983) 'The Informational Role of Futures Markets: Some Experimental Evidence', Chapter 6 in M.E. Streit (ed.), *Futures Markets: Modelling, Managing and Monitoring Futures Markets*, Oxford: Blackwell.

Friedman, D., G.W. Harrison and J.W. Salmon (1984) 'The Informational Efficiency of Experimental Asset Markets', *Journal of Political Economy*, 92, 349-408.

Giles, D.E.A. and B.A. Goss (1981) 'Futures Prices of Forecasts of Commodity Spot Prices: Live Cattle and Wool', *Australian Journal of Agricultural Economics*, 25, 1-13.

Giles, D.E.A., B.A. Goss and O.P.L. Chin (1985) 'Intertemporal Allocation in the Corn and Soybeans Markets with Rational Expectations', *American Journal of Agricultural Economics*, 67, November (in press).

Goss, B.A. (1983) 'The Semi-Strong Form Efficiency of the London Metal Exchange', *Applied Economics*, 15, 681-98.

Graf, T.F. (1953) 'Hedging — How Effective Is It?', *Journal of Farm Economics*, 35, 398-413.

Gray, R.W. (1966) 'Why Does Futures Trading Succeed or Fail: An Analysis of Selected Commodities', *Futures Trading Seminar*, vol. III, MIMIR, Madison.

— (1972) 'The Futures Market for Maine Potatoes: An Appraisal', *Food Research Institute Studies*, 11(3), 313-41.

Gregory, A.W. and T.H. McCurdy (1984) 'The Unbiasedness Hypothesis in the

Forward Foreign Exchange Market: A Cross Country Specification Analysis', University of W. Ontario Discussion Paper No. 566.
Hamburger, M.J. and E.N. Platt (1975) 'The Expectations Hypothesis and the Efficiency of the Treasury Bill Market', *Review of Economics and Statistics*, 57(2), 190-9.
Hansen, L.P. and R.J. Hodrick (1980) 'Forward Exchange Rates as Optimal Predictors of Future Spot Rates: An Econometric Analysis', *Journal of Political Economy*, 88, 829-53.
Hicks, J.R. (1953) *Value and Capital*, London: Oxford University Press.
Houthakker, H.S. (1959) 'The Scope and Limits of Futures Trading', in M. Abramovitz *et al.*, *The Allocation of Economic Resources*, Stanford, California, Stanford University Press.
— (1957) 'Can Speculators Forecast Prices', *Review of Economics and Statistics*, 39(2), 143-51.
Johnson, L.L. (1960) 'The Theory of Hedging and Speculation in Commodity Futures', *Review of Economic Studies*, 27(3), 139-51.
Kahl, K.H. (1983) 'Determination of the Recommended Hedging Ratio', *American Journal of Agricultural Economics*, 65(3), 603-5.
Keynes, J.M. (1923) 'Some Aspects of Commodity Markets', *Manchester Guardian Commercial: European Reconstruction Series*, Section 13, 29 March.
— (1930) *A Treatise on Money*, vol. 2, London: Macmillan.
Kofi, T.A. (1973) 'A Framework for Comparing the Efficiency of Futures Markets', *American Journal of Agricultural Economics*, 55(4), 584-94.
Larson, A.B. (1960) 'Measurement of a Random Process in Futures Prices', *Food Research Institute Studies*, 1, 313-24.
Leuthold, R.M. (1972) 'Random Walks and Price Trends: The Live Cattle Futures Market', *Journal of Finance*, 27.
— (1974) 'The Price Performance on the Futures Market of a Nonstorable Commodity: Live Beef Cattle', *American Journal of Agricultural Economics*, 56(2), 313-24.
— and P.A. Hartmann (1979) 'A Semi-strong Form Evaluation of the Efficiency of the Hog Futures Market', *American Journal of Agricultural Economics*, 61(3), 482-9.
Lintner, J. (1965) 'Security Prices, Risk, and Maximal Gains from Diversification', *Journal of Finance*, 20, 587-615.
Mandelbrot, B. (1963) 'The Variation of Certain Speculative Prices', *Journal of Business*, 36, 394-419.
Peston, M.H. and B.S. Yamey (1960) 'Inter-temporal Price Relationships with Forward Markets: A Method of Analysis', *Economica*, 27, 355-67.
Plott, C.R. and S. Sunder (1982) 'Efficiency of Experimental Security Markets with Insider Information: An Application of Rational Expectations Models', *Journal of Political Economy*, 90(4), 663-98.
Praetz, P.D. (1975) 'Testing the Efficient Markets Theory on the Sydney Wool Futures Exchange', *Australian Economic Papers*, 14(25), 240-9.
Rausser, G.C. and Colin Carter (1983) 'Futures Market Efficiency in the Soybean Complex', *Review of Economics and Statistics*, 65, 469-78.
Rockwell, C.S. (1967) 'Normal Backwardation, Forecasting, and the Returns to Commodity Futures Traders', *Food Research Institute Studies*, 7, Supplement, 107-30.
Rutledge, D.J.S. (1972) 'Hedgers' Demand for Futures Contracts: A Theoretical Framework with Applications to the United States Soybean Complex', *Food Research Institute Studies*, 11(3), 237-56.
Sandor, R.L. (1973) 'Innovation by an Exchange: A Case Study of the Development of the Plywood Futures Contract', *Journal of Law and*

Economics, 16, 119-36.

Schneeweis, T. (1982) 'Statement [On Researchable Issues]', *Review of Research in Futures Markets*, 1(2), 127-9. Chicago Board of Trade.

Sharpe, W. (1964) 'Capital Asset Prices: A Theory of Market Equilibrium Under Conditions of Risk', *Journal of Finance*, 19, 425-42.

Stein, J.L. (1961) 'The Simultaneous Determination of Spot and Futures Prices', *American Economic Review*, 51(5), 1012-25.

— (1964) 'The Opportunity Locus in a Hedging Decision: A Correction', *American Economic Review*, 54(5), 762-3.

Stevenson, R.A. and R.M. Bear (1970) 'Commodity Futures: Trends or Random Walks?', *Journal of Finance*, 25, 65-81.

Telser, L.G. (1958) 'Futures Trading and the Storage of Cotton and Wheat', *Journal of Political Economy*, 66(3), 233-55.

— and H.N. Higinbotham (1977) 'Organized Futures Markets: Costs and Benefits', *Journal of Political Economy*, 85(5), 969-1000.

Tomek, W.G. and R.W. Gray (1970) 'Temporal Relations Among Prices on Commodity Futures Markets', *American Journal of Agricultural Economics*, 52(3), 372-80.

Ward, R.W. and L.B. Fletcher (1971) 'From Hedging to Pure Speculation', *American Journal of Agricultural Economics*, 53(1), 71-8.

Working, H. (1942) 'Quotations on Commodity Futures as Price Forecasts', *Econometrica*, 10(1), 39-52.

— (1948) 'Theory of the Inverse Carrying Charge in Futures Markets', *Journal of Farm Economics*, 30, 1-28.

— (1953) 'Futures Trading and Hedging', *American Economic Review*, 43, 314-43.

Yamey, B.S. (1951) 'Hedging in an Organized Produce Exchange', Manchester School, 19, 305-19.

— (1984) 'The Economic Performance of Futures Trading', *Three Banks Review*, March, 33-43.

1 AN INSTITUTIONAL ANALYSIS OF FUTURES CONTRACTING

Cento G. Veljanovski*

> This figment of delivery ... is a vestigial remnant of an age old custom, a slender strand of gossamer that is easily severed, freeing the two [spot and future prices] to go where they will in fulfilling their destiny. The Gordian knot is severable once the secret is known.[1]

Paradoxically, even though economics is primarily concerned with the study of markets, it does not possess a theory of markets. The entire subject of the institutions that have been developed to facilitate the trading and distribution of commodities has been eliminated from contemporary economics — markets are just assumed to exist. In the futures trading literature the issue of market development and innovation had been tackled in a rather crude way. Initially, a commodities approach had been adopted. The emergence of futures trading was explained by reference to a set of feasibility conditions relating mainly to the common physical characteristics of commodities that have been successfully traded on organized futures exchanges. The inadequacy of this approach is shown by a contraction in the number of common characteristics as futures trading has expanded. In short, there does not exist a satisfactory and comprehensive theory of futures markets.[2]

In this chapter I propose to sketch the rudiments of a theory of futures contracting that has predictive power.[3] The theory is based on the hypothesis that new contracts and institutions evolve to facilitate trade in order to maximize the wealth of individuals and in particular to reduce the direct costs of transacting.

1. Brief Review of Feasibility Conditions

A futures market is an organized exchange dealing in standardized contracts for forward delivery or settlement. Futures markets are widely held to serve several functions ranging from the transfer of the risk of price fluctuations to those better able to bear them (hedging), as guides to future cash prices and market expectations (thus assisting inventory control and business planning) and as a forum for speculation. Economists have devoted most of their attention to modelling the process and performance of futures trading and relatively little to developing a theory of why futures markets develop in one commodity rather than another. In my view this neglect can be attributed to two principal factors — the economists' general preoccupation with pricing behaviour, and the bad image acquired by institutional analysis among North American economists due largely to the legal economics of John R. Commons (1934) and his followers.[4] It is now firmly recognized among many economists, however, that the study of institutions is not only amenable to economic analysis but crucial to the understanding of economic activity. This recognition has spawned a new field of study, law-and-economics,[5] and much work has been undertaken on the economic aspects of contract.[6]

In the textbook model of perfect competition, where the same physical commodities are sold and consumed on different dates, it is assumed that there exists a 'universal regime of futures markets, ... extended to all times and all commodities' (Arrow, 1981, p. 4; Radner, 1970). The real world is a radical departure from this theoretical ideal — there are in fact very few commodities traded in organized futures markets.

The question naturally arises as to what are the factors which determine the feasibility of futures trading. In the past economists have attempted to answer this question by listing a set of so-called 'feasibility conditions'. That is, a set of conditions that are seen to be necessary for a commodity to be eligible for futures contracting. The list of conditions changes with the authority consulted, but a modest list representative of this approach is provided by Goss (1972). In addition to price volatility and a spot market commitment on the part of the potential hedger, Goss (1972, pp. 4-6) lists five preconditions:

(1) The commodity must be homogeneous or, alternatively, it must be possible to specify a standard grade and measure deviations from that grade.
(2) Delivery of the commodity must be possible under the contract.
(3) Storage of the commodity must be possible.

(4) There must be a speculative element present which is net short or net long respectively to take up the balance of open positions.

(5) There must be sufficient liquid assets to facilitate market settlement.

Conditions (1) to (3) reflect the commodity emphasis of the feasibility approach; that the feasibility of futures contracting depends on the characteristics of the physical commodity traded.

The commodity approach to futures trading feasibility has proved unsatisfactory. As futures trading has expanded, the number of preconditions has contracted in size. The extension of trading to financial futures, which has witnessed an explosive growth in recent years, indeed severs futures from any necessary connections with physical commodities. Most of the other conditions have been rendered redundant. Some time ago Houthakker (1959a, p. 158) wrote: 'The mainspring of futures trading, ... is the need to finance inventories in the face of fluctuating prices. A pre-requisite for sustained trading, therefore, is the existence of considerable inventories.' Yet in the US, in 1964, trading started in live beef futures and has since been extended to fresh eggs, live hogs and fresh broiler chickens, all of which are not stored. Gray and Rutledge (1971) note that the extension of futures trading to these commodities was facilitated by a *contractual innovation*; that of changing the delivery instrument from the conventional warehouse receipt to one that was 'a call on production'. Delivery of the commodity in settlement of a futures contract has always been regarded as crucial. Goss and Yamey (1978, p. 11) provide the orthodox rationale for this condition: 'the possibility of settlement by delivery binds together the two (spot and futures) market prices'. In February 1982 this condition was also violated when the Kansas City Board of Trade began trading a contract on the Value Line Index of 1,700 stocks. The stock index future accepts the radical principle of cash settlement, i.e. instead of the possibility of obtaining the physical commodity, or in this case the stocks on which the index is based, in settlement, the contract can be closed by a pure cash transfer. Five other stock index futures have also been authorised in the US (Lascelles, 1982).

That the commodity approach to futures trading feasibility has proved to be unsatisfactory should not be surprising. It is after all *ad hoc*, proceeding on the assumption that the characteristics of commodities successfully traded on organized futures exchanges in the past provide a guide to the class of commodities that are susceptible to futures trading. Clearly to the extent that the feasibility conditions do provide a guide it is because they are correlated with other factors that economize on the costs of transacting.

2. Theoretical Framework

Nature of Exchange

The conventional view of exchange is trade in physical commodities. This characterization of exchange is acceptable so long as the analysis is limited to transactions involving homogeneous contractual obligations. Once the inquiry is extended to consider the choice of market, or, more correctly, the bundle of contractual obligations, the standard approach no longer suffices.

Instead of treating the physical commodity as the primary object traded in markets the *transaction* is substituted as the basic unit of analysis. Every transaction involves a contract, whether an explicit legally enforceable set of promises or an implicit understanding, and a transfer of contractual obligations.[7] As Commons (1934, p. 58) emphasizes '[T]ransactions ... are not the exchange of commodities in the physical sense of "delivery", they are the alienation and acquisition of future ownership of physical things'. All exchange apart from barter involves future obligations – contracts are executory, they involve promises to do things in the future. The value of commodities is determined by the bundle of rights transferred in transactions, and markets are places where such rights are transferred.

Transactions give rise to transaction costs which can be defined as the costs of defining, transferring and enforcing contracts. The central hypothesis advanced here is that the organization of exchange is governed by transaction costs and that institutional arrangements are matched to activities so as to economize on transaction costs (Williamson, 1979).

The central role of transaction costs in understanding institutional innovation has been emphasized by Coase (1937, 1960). In a world in which trade is costless, there would be no need for futures markets since all trades would be adequately governed by fully specified contingent claims contracts (Shavell, 1980). In actual markets, contracting and information are both costly, so that such contracts rarely exist. Instead other types of contracts and institutions will arise to economize on transaction costs. This simple proposition was suggested by Coase (1937) many years ago, when he argued that the produce exchange is 'a technique for minimising contract costs'.

To explain institutional innovation, the standard economic assumption of self-interested maximizing behaviour is adopted. Individuals or groups of individuals are assumed to take advantage of new opportunities for enhancing their wealth. Institutions will evolve and be fashioned to facilitate wealth maximization. That is, it is assumed that the structure of institutions in society is determined by economic forces.

In the face of positive and differential transaction costs, the choice of contractual mode will affect the wealth of individuals, whether through its impact on expected benefits or on the magnitude of transaction costs. At any one time an individual will hold a portfolio of contractual obligations (Crocker, 1973). The optimal portfolio will be determined by the usual maximizing rules. Suppose that different contractual arrangements alter the variance of expected wealth and that individuals exhibit risk aversion. Following Cheung (1969a, 1969b), the choice of contract will be governed by comparing their relative benefits in terms of risk reduction with their transaction costs. The individual will choose that contract, or, more specifically, that risk-sharing arrangement that maximizes expected utility.

If the (expected) variance of income is used as a measure of risk, risk averse individuals will prefer a lower variance. The variance of income can be lowered for the individual by alternative contractual arrangements designed to share the risk of price changes. For example, in the case of agricultural land leases, fixed-rent leases place the bulk of the risk of price fluctuations on the leasee, whereas a sharecropping contract shares the risk of price changes between lessor and lessee. Forward contracts are analogous to fixed-rent leases in that if the commodity price increases, those who have sold forward lose; if it falls they gain. On the other hand, both futures and sharecropping contracts share the risk of price fluctuations and hence tend to lower the variance of expected returns to hedgers.[8]

In order to determine whether a contractual arrangement with a low variance is preferred to one with a higher variance, the transaction costs of using the respective contracts must be considered.

Suppose an individual has a choice between two contractual arrangements that differ in terms of their expected benefits and that these benefits decline with the individual's usage of each contract. In Figure 1.1, the marginal expected present value curves for two contracts, 1 and 2, are drawn and labelled as MB_1 and MB_2 respectively. The marginal transaction costs of using each contract differ but are assumed to be constant.

If the choice between these two contracts were mutually exclusive the individual would choose contract 2 since its *net* present value (NMB_2) is greatest; area $HP_2O > IP_1O$. The additional gain associated with contract 2 can be separated into two effects; AFEB due to its greater ability to maximize the individual's return and CFGD attributed to its lower transaction costs. In fact, an individual would be willing to pay a sum up to these two amounts (AGDCE or HP_2P_1I) to use contract 2. If contract 1 were a forward contract and contract 2 a futures contract, the area AGDCE can be viewed as a payment that hedgers would be will-

Figure 1.1

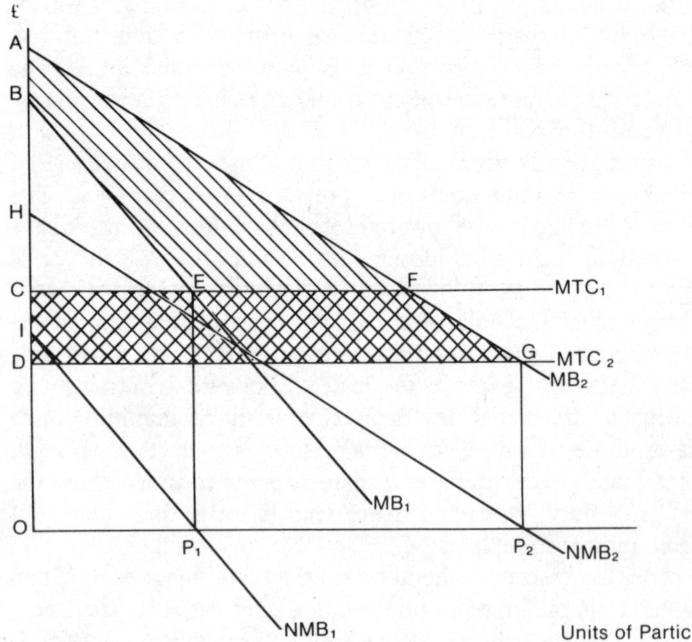

ing to transfer to brokers and speculators for the superior ability of futures contracts to maximize net benefits. These benefits need not necessarily be limited to risk reduction but would embrace other attractive attributes of futures trading such as improved business planning.

Alternatively, if both contracting modes can be used simultaneously the individual will use both contracts. The profit maximizing portfolio of contracts 1 and 2 will be determined by the usual marginal equivalences. Partial hedging of stocks and inventories will be a rational strategy. Moreover transactional efficiency alone is capable of explaining trading in futures contracts. Assume that the MB curves for both contracts are identical at MB_1, but that marginal transaction costs still differ. In this case even though futures contracts do not enhance marginal benefits they lower transaction costs which is sufficient to encourage futures trading.

An institutional equilibrium of the type depicted in Figure 1.1 can be disturbed by exogenous changes in either benefits or costs (Davis and North, 1971). Three categories of factors may change the cost-benefit ratio; market, institutional and transaction technology.

First, alterations in market opportunities brought about by changes in technology, demand and other market conditions may lead to changes in the method of organizing transactions. For example, the increasing capital intensity of production may lead to greater use of forward contracts as a way of ensuring demand and/or supply.

Second, legal and political changes can alter the cost-benefit ratio of various institutional and contractual arrangements by prescribing limitations, prohibitions or expanding the scope of permissible arrangements. This has been an important source of change in futures market development, particularly with the early association of futures trading with gambling.[9] The breakdown of the Bretton Woods Agreement and consequent exchange rate instability, which has led to significant growth in foreign exchange futures, is another example of the way institutional factors can promote futures trading.

Third, changes in the transaction costs of organizing and operating various institutional arrangements due to technological innovations may decrease the costs of information, e.g. telegraph, teleprinters, telephone and computers.

Sources of Transaction Costs

Transaction costs arise from a variety of sources. Perhaps the most important factors giving rise to transaction costs are search activity, bounded rationality and opportunism.

In a market with incomplete information, buyers and sellers will have to search each other out. The costs of such search activity will differ and will be greater the more geographically dispersed and heterogeneous are buyers and sellers. Search costs will not only raise the costs of activities, being equivalent often to a proportional tax, but may preclude otherwise value-maximizing transactions from taking place. Many devices have arisen to economize on costly search; brand names, advertising, centralized produce exchanges, marketing boards, etc.

Bounded rationality precludes parties from drawing up contracts that fully define the relationship between them. Bounded rationality refers to the cognitive limits of individuals in formulating and solving problems and processing information (Williamson, 1979). It leads to contract incompleteness. Thus many matters that could alter the value of a transaction will not be covered by explicit terms in the contract negotiated by the parties.

The performance difficulties occasioned by opportunism raise the costs of transacting.[10] Each party is confronted by what can be termed a reliability risk — the risk that the other party will default either on the whole transaction or on individual terms in a way that decreases the expected wealth of the non-defaulting party. Reliability risk is an important source of transaction costs because it will pay individuals to guard against opportunism and contract breach. Acquiring information on the reliability of those with whom one transacts yields benefits in the form of reduced losses due to default and incomplete or inferior performance. As Ben-Porath (1980, p. 5) states:

> They [transaction costs] arise because the parties to transactions are different individuals with asymmetric information, divergent motives and mutual suspicions, and because expenditure of resources can reduce the gap in information and protect the parties against each other.

Impersonal and Personal Markets

Transactions generally take place in two types of markets: impersonal and personal markets. The textbook model of the competitive market is the archetypal impersonal market where standardized commodities are traded between parties whose identities are of no economic relevance. Faceless buyers and sellers meet to consummate bargains in discrete perfectly replicable transactions. Such markets can be expected to function smoothly if there are a large number of buyers and sellers and information regarding market opportunities is easily gained. Personal markets are those in which the identity of the trading parties is important. As Telser and Higinbotham (1977, p. 970) note, most market transactions display the characteristics of a barter economy where the identity of the parties — their reliability, credit-worthiness, promptness, reasonableness, etc. — is important. Personal markets arise because of transaction idiosyncracies which diminish the relevance of market information in assisting the parties to particular transactions and involve transaction-specific investments.

The uniqueness of personal market transactions increases both the reliability risk and the costs of default. Individuals will tend to invest resources in establishing their own and determining the other party's reliability and reputation. The incentive for such experience rating is enhanced by the fact that personal markets involve transaction-specific investments that have low scrap value. The absence of perfect replicability of personal market transactions has the effect of 'locking' the parties into the relationship. Moreover, investing resources in establishing and determining reliability is a sunk cost. Personal markets are therefore characterized by decreasing costs and exhibit a tendency to specialization by identity to take advantage of scale economies.

Governance Structures

Governance structures are market and institutional devices designed to eliminate or reduce reliability risk (Williamson, 1979). They range from market sanctions such as price adjustments and loss of custom to formal legal penalties imposed by the courts.

In impersonal competitive markets, price adjustments will be a relatively efficient means of regulating and compensating for reliability risk (Klein and Leffler, 1981). If the probability of default is perceived as non-trivial, a seller will demand a price premium and the buyer a price discount. Governance by price premia/discounts in impersonal markets is virtually self-enforcing. If the risk comes from sellers, buyers will either turn to other sellers or reduce their demand for the product. The unreliable seller will then be forced to improve his services or go out of business. Market governance will tend to be most effective the more competitive the market, which in turn depends on the degree of product homogeneity and flow of information between buyer and seller.

In personal markets, governance will generally occur through reputation and experience rating. The desire to retain the goodwill associated with a reputation of being reliable and reasonable in adapting to contract difficulties may discourage opportunism. However, opportunism is not necessarily deterred by the prospect of a bad reputation or the existence of goodwill. As Telser (1980, p. 36) points out:

> The accumulation of a fund of goodwill of a buyer toward a seller that depends on past experience stands as a temptation to the seller to cheat the buyers and convert the goodwill into ready cash. It is the prospect of the loss of future gain that deters and the existence of past goodwill that invites cheating.

Reliability risk can be reduced by non-market forms of governance ranging from vertical integration and self-regulation to legal penalties under contract law.

Opportunism can be reduced by undertaking the production and distribution of intermediate tasks, thus subjecting all transactions to the authority relation, i.e. principal-agent rather than market relations. The firm is one such device (Alchian and Demsetz, 1972), a futures exchange another. Group self-regulation can also be used to reduce opportunism and reliability risks. Such governance is common among the professions and in commodity futures exchanges. Although self-regulation may introduce monopoly elements into the market, it can also remedy information problems by ensuring the integrity of traders and imposing minimum quality standards.

3. The Organization of Futures Trading

Before investigating the transaction cost economizing features of futures contracts, it will be helpful to discuss the nature and process of futures trading.

Hedging Theory

The futures literature presents the following characterization of futures trading. The commercial demand for futures contracts is seen as coming from hedgers and speculators. A potential hedger is one who is confronted by price volatility and a 'price risk' — the chance that the price will move in an unfavourable direction. The hedger enters the futures market in order to transfer the price risk to another party. In doing this the hedger replaces the price risk with a basis risk — that spot and futures prices will not move in parallel. If the price spread between spot and futures prices is constant at the time the contract is sold, and when it is bought the hedge is said to be perfect, then the risk (both price and basis) is eliminated.

A short hedger is one who sells a futures contract and incurs a liability to deliver the 'commodity' during the maturity month of the contract at the price prevailing when the initial transaction took place. If the contract is settled by delivery, the net change in the value of the asset is the original futures price minus the spot price during the delivery month. Typically the seller of a futures contract will offset his obligation to deliver by the purchase of a futures contract, thus extinguishing his net obligations to the market. If this is done, the net change in the value of the asset due to futures trading is the difference in the two futures prices. A long hedger or buyer of a futures contract confronts the mirror-image of these changes.

The extent to which the price of a forward futures contract can exceed the spot price (called a contango) is limited by arbitrage. The maximum difference cannot exceed the marginal cost of storage until maturity plus delivery costs. A larger contango would give arbitrageurs a riskless profit by buying in the spot market and simultaneously selling futures. The extent to which the spot price exceeds the futures price, called a backwardation, is not necessarily constrained by arbitrage. To take advantage of a large backwardation requires that the arbitrageur simultaneously sell spot and buy futures. The ability to do this obviously depends on the volume of stock held by traders willing to take advantage of the backwardation. If the stock is limited, a large backwardation may result. Thus a short hedger has a limited basis risk whereas the long hedger has a potentially larger basis risk, though not an unbounded one because, as the futures contract nears maturity, future and spot prices will converge.

The Natures of Futures Contracts

The object traded in a futures market is not the actual commodity but a futures contract. Typically there is one standard contract per commodity relating to a large quantity and specified quality of the commodity. All the terms of each contract except the price are determined by the rules of the exchange so that the only term that is negotiated during trading is the sale price of the contract. Trading in futures contracts is centralized on the floor of the exchange (the 'pit'), is limited to specified hours and to a restricted number of accredited members of the exchange. Trading is by 'open outcry' — an auction system where buyers shout out their bids and motion with their hands to sellers who do likewise. The settlement of futures contracts is handled by the exchange or a clearing house which interposes itself between buyers and sellers. The exchange members' obligations are to the clearing house not to each other and members are liable to the clearing house.

Futures markets have several other unique characteristics. First, a futures contract has a *limited and short life.* A buyer of a futures contract usually must liquidate his position in a relatively short time. The life of the longest futures contract is only 18 months (although quotations up to two years ahead are not unknown). Second, *for every short position in the market there is a long position.* So if hedgers are net short, speculators must be net long and vice versa. Consequently on the day of a price change 50 per cent of positions lose and 50 per cent gain. Third, futures contracts are *highly leveraged.* One can usually trade on a margin of 10 per cent of the value of the contract. These margins are in the nature of a security deposit that protects the broker and principal from losses against adverse price movements. In all US futures exchanges, daily limits are placed on the fluctuation of prices. This, plus the brokers' additional margin call, gives the buyer of a futures contract time to reassess the situation and liquidate his position if desired. Fourth, futures markets *operate on a 'no debt basis'.* All trading gains and losses are settled through the clearing house before the commencement of the next day's business. Finally, futures markets are highly organized self-regulated markets. The exchange oversees the conduct of business, designs trading rules and contracts, either it or the clearing house ensures that all contracts are settled according to their terms and it has the power to discipline members of the exchange who breach the rules. Although the hectic and competitive nature of futures trading has led many to refer to it as the 'last frontier of capitalism', it is none the less highly regulated capitalism, both in the form of self-regulation, as in the UK, or government regulation administered by the Commodities Futures Trading Commission (CFTC) in the US (Gemmill, 1982; Rock, 1982).

4. Applications

The Evolution of Contract

Risk and uncertainty in the form of price volatility and opportunism are major factors giving rise to futures trading. The economic significance of the distinguishing features of futures contracts is initially best discussed by comparing futures with spot and forward contracts.

Although the historical development of futures trading has been well researched, few of the insights distilled from this work have been incorporated into the theory of futures markets.[11] The origin of organized futures trading in its modern form can be traced back to the New York produce exchanges which appeared in 1752. This, however, obscures the iterative nature of futures evolution. Futures trading evolved out of autonomous forward contracting by merchants, dealers and processors which was designed to increase business efficiency. Irwin (1954) points out that futures trading evolved out of time contracts of the delivery type. Indeed, early futures markets were viewed as delivery markets in which transactions were facilitated by the provision of uniform rules on grade and delivery terms, and the security provided by the clearing houses in guaranteeing individual contracts.

This evolution from spot, to forward, to futures contracts suggests a progressive adaptation of institutions to more efficient methods of dealing with price risk. For example, it is frequently argued that a precondition for futures trading is a well-developed cash market and the breakdown of forward contracting. The latter is too rigid a precondition. For example, in 1969 trading began in plywood futures contracts, a commodity that did not have a history of forward contracting (see Sandor, 1973, pp. 131-2). The observation, however, that a breakdown in forward contracting has frequently preceded futures contracting in the past indicates that the latter has become an inefficient means of dealing with price risk.

Futures markets develop because they are a more efficient means of transferring those contract rights attached to price. For reasons that will be explored later, spot and forward contracting may become too costly. However, these three contracting modes are *not* mutually exclusive ways of transacting. Indeed the development of futures markets will improve the efficiency of spot and possibly of forward contracting. It is perhaps best to view futures markets as 'side' markets designed to deal with price volatility that is poorly handled by spot and forward markets. The transactional superiority of futures markets comes mainly from their transaction-cost reducing attributes.

In dealing with price risk, futures contracts have several transactional advantages relative to spot and forward contracts. Sequential spot contracts, that is spot contracts where the terms of the contract are renegotiated as events unfold, do not inject any certainty into the transaction. Such a method of contracting is particularly liable to the hazards of opportunism and may deter investment because of the relatively high probability that the contract will be breached.

Forward and futures contracts inject some certainty into the transaction. Both share the property that the parties agree to perform the terms of the contract at some future date. Arrow (1974, p. 8) has argued that time-dated contracts are generally costlier to enforce than spot contracts. This is due to the absence of the self-enforcing, near simultaneous exchange of value for value characteristic of spot transactions and the greater uncertainty attached both to the eventual outcome and each party's compliance with the terms of forward contracts.

Forward and futures contracts differ, however, in their susceptibility to opportunism, especially in their role of reducing price risk. First, forward contracts that cover all feasible contingencies are costly to devise. The information and transaction costs will thus preclude a fully specified forward contract and this contractual incompleteness will give rise to enforcement and execution difficulties. Incomplete contracting has a clear economic justification. Given the cost of tailoring the contract to the particular needs of the parties, it will usually be cost-effective to use standard form contracts. In this regard, organized forward and futures contracting have identical properties. Nevertheless, enforcement and execution difficulties can be expected to pose a more serious problem for forward contracts. This is so for several reasons. First, in forward contracting, individuals will have to incur the expense of determining the reliability risk of the opposite party. To the extent that there are scale economies in such specialization by identity, forward contracting will be more expensive than organized futures contracting where the exchange ensures the integrity of its members and trading practices. Forward contracts also are subject to high enforcement costs where personal market sanctions are weak. The penalty rules of contract law are costly to enforce and may not deal effectively with all types of breaches.

A further disadvantage of forward contracts is that they are *tied transactions.* The forward contract transfers rights relating to quantity, quality and price. The last, however, may best be separated, especially when the parties are risk averse and their access to insurance markets limited. Moreover, as Wachter and Williamson (1978, p. 55) have stressed, price changes have an unfortunate zero-sum quality that increases the likelihood of opportunism. Thus while forward contracts may inject certainty into the quantity and possibly quality dimensions of future transactions, it is not clear that they are the least-cost adaptation to price risk. Depending on the transaction costs in alternative markets, and the strength of governance in each, it may be desirable for both risk-spreading and opportunism-reducing reasons to separate price risk from the other aspects of time-dated transactions.

The view suggested here is that spot, forward and futures markets deal in different bundles of rights among different individuals. In particular, rights can be divided between those relating to quantity and quality, and those concerning certainty of profits and costs. Forward contracts, especially in personal markets, are best suited to ensuring that contract terms relating to the former are complied with, whereas futures contracts deal with price volatility.

Futures contracts permit the price risk to be separated from the reliability risk by removing the former from the set of factors giving rise to opportunism. The governance structure supplied by the exchange authority effectively eliminates reliability risk from futures trading. The seller of a futures contract incurs a liability not to the buyer, but to the clearing house, and likewise the buyer acquires an asset from the clearing house. The clearing house in effect guarantees all transactions. In addition the exchange rules, especially regarding its members' conduct, severely limit their ability to behave opportunistically. Organized exchanges greatly reduce default and reliability risk from futures contracts. This is achieved by transferring transactions over price risks from a personal to an impersonal market through standard form futures contracts traded in a self-regulated market place.

Contract Standardization

Futures contracts are standard form contracts with only one negotiable term: price. The standardization of futures contracts has significant implications for transaction costs. This is so for several reasons. First, contract standardization eliminates the costs of bargaining over non-price terms and of enforcing contract provisions. Second, it reduces monitoring costs that are generally incurred in principal-agent relationships. The principal only needs to give his broker instructions as to price and quantity which are easily observed. The monitoring costs in the futures market are therefore significantly lower than those in the spot market, where numerous other matters require attention and provide the broker with opportunities to take advantage of the principal. Third, contract standardization makes all futures contracts of a particular maturity month perfect substitutes. The fungibility of futures contracts is not a property shared by forward contracts and, as Houthakker (1959a) and Telser (1981a) have noted, likens futures contracts to money. Provided that the volume of trade is sufficient, there will be a highly elastic excess demand for individual futures contracts, enabling transactions to take place in a rapid and continuous manner, thus significantly reducing the risks to market makers.

The liquidity and competitive nature of futures trading will also reduce the waiting costs of brokers and speculators for acceptable bids and offers. One component of the transaction costs of futures trading is the ask-bid spread which, in a competitive situation, is directly correlated with the search costs of finding acceptable bids and offers. Demsetz's (1968) study of trading on the New York Stock Exchange postulates that waiting costs, that is the time cost of waiting for acceptable exchange prices, is an important determinant of the ask-bid spread. Working's (1967) study of 'thin' futures markets suggests a similar relationship; that for inactive markets, scalpers must take wider margins because of the greater time period between trades and the greater uncertainty associated with slower trading. Thus a positive relationship exists between the waiting cost and the ask-bid spread, and an inverse relationship between the volume of transactions and average transaction costs.

As in all economic activities, specialization leads to increased efficiency and greater net benefits. The existence of specialists with differential search and information costs is an important factor in explaining both why large speculators consistently make profits and why commodity exchanges tend to minimize transaction costs.

Following Alchian (1970, pp. 30-2), the determination of the ask-bid spread can be illustrated with the aid of Figure 1.2. In Figure 1.2 the curve P_oP_t represents the expected maximum contract price that can be found in period t. The curve relates maximum expected price to the level of search effort. Speculators in futures markets would be willing to offer a price greater than P_o at t_o if they expect the discounted re-sale value of a futures contract (net of search costs) will increase faster than the rate of interest. The highest bid price can be shown by constructing an iso-present value curve, P*P*, which shows the gross expected present value of a futures contract. It is positively sloped due to the assumption that more intensive search generates knowledge about higher return trading opportunities. Brokers and speculators, however, incur search and information costs that decrease their net return. The schedule N_o is the return net of search costs and the difference P^*P_1 is the ask-bid spread, where P_1 is the expected

Figure 1.2: Determination of Ask-bid Spread

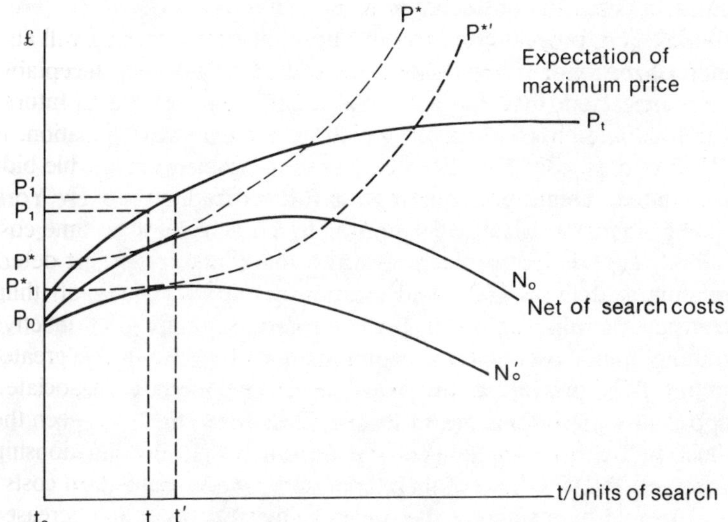

future selling price. Obviously the greater the search costs the greater will be the margin required by brokers and speculators to engage in trading. For example, in a market with higher search costs, the next expected present value schedule will be depressed to No′ and the ask-bid spread will increase to P^*P_1'.

The importance of market liquidity arises not only because it reduces waiting costs, but also because it ensures that competitive pressures exist to keep waiting costs to a minimum for any volume of trade. Competition among futures traders will have the effect of weeding out those with excessive search costs and poor forecasting ability. Studies (e.g. Rockwell, 1967) tend to support the view that large professional speculators make consistent profits whereas smaller traders make losses. Houthakker (1959b) attributes this to superior access to information. Speculators do better in near futures (those close to maturity), the prices of which depend on spot market conditions, i.e. stocks, location of deliverable grades, etc., about which smaller traders would find it difficult to acquire information. Moreover in 'thin' futures markets monopolistic elements may arise in speculative behaviour that increase the costs of hedging. Gray's (1960) finding that thin markets display the largest bias is consistent with this view.

Contract Design

Although not emphasized in the theoretical literature, in practice contract design is considered to be crucial to the success of futures trading.[12] A poorly designed contract that does not reflect commercial reality or favours one group of traders will lack the necessary appeal and will fail to attract a sufficient volume of trade. Contract design is a matter for the exchange which, as Silber (1981) notes, confronts a basic marketing problem: how to translate the economic prerequisites for futures trading into contract specifications with sufficient appeal to both hedgers and speculators. The design problem centres on contract specifications relating to delivery grade and locations, contract size, number of contract months, units for price quotations, daily price limits, trading hours and margin requirements. Silber's (1981) study found a surprising sensitivity of a new contract's success to apparently minor changes in its specifications. This is graphically illustrated by the simultaneous appearance of four similar gold contracts in 1975. Two of these contracts called for the delivery of 100 oz gold bars whereas the others called for 3 kg and 1 kg bars.

The 100 oz contracts succeeded despite the fact that the 3 kg contract was offered on the more capitalized floor of the Chicago Board of Trade. The popular explanation is that the round figure of a 100 oz simplified calculations, enabling arbitrageurs to respond more rapidly to price discrepancies.

Futures contracts relate to a specified grade of the commodity or to a prescribed list of deliverable or substitutable grades. Since only one grade can govern the futures price, it is important that the contract specify the grade that will best reflect price movements of the hedged commodity.

The delivery options of futures contracts typically have the following features. In addition to the contract (or basis) grade and delivery locations, a difference system is used that imposes contractual premia or discounts for non-contract grades or delivery at different locations. Two difference systems are used to deal with the delivery of non-contract grades; the commercial difference system and the fixed difference system. The commercial difference system permits non-contract grades to be delivered at premia and discounts as determined daily by the intergrade differences prevailing in the spot market. The fixed difference system, which is more common, specifies the exact amounts to be paid if a non-contract grade is delivered. Finally, the seller has the options as to grade, place and date (within the maturity month) of delivery. The seller's option over these matters was originally introduced to prevent corners and squeezes in the market.

The standardization of futures contracts makes them ill-suited as delivery instruments, and generally less than 1 per cent of futures contracts are settled by delivery. The usual method of 'closing-out' a futures contract is by reversing the transaction through the purchase or sale of an offsetting contract. Seller's options and contract standardization make delivery of the commodity a potentially costly affair for the long hedger, although for the short hedger it may reduce the number of transactions since both spot and futures commitments can be closed with the one transaction.

Contract standardization may also diminish the hedging properties of a contract if there are marked disparities between price movements in the contract grade and the actual grade traded by the hedger in the spot market and/or anomalies in the difference system. This problem could be avoided if several contracts were offered that reflected more closely the particular needs of groups of hedgers. All things being equal, such individualization would improve the hedging ability of futures trading for the individual hedger. This problem has been addressed by Working (1967), who puzzled over the question of why contract standardization occurred when some degree of contract heterogeneity would seem more appealing to a market where traders' requirements differed. Working's answer was in terms similar to the analysis of this chapter: that is, the trade-off between transaction costs and the benefits derived from contract heterogeneity. According to Working, if two contracts, each with differing specifications, were traded, the less active one would require an increased margin by scalpers, which would raise the hedging cost, leading to further concentration in the more active contract and an eventual demise of the more costly contract. Contract heterogeneity raises transaction costs by reducing market liquidity. As Working concludes '... it is understandable that many hedgers should prefer a "poor" hedge that is cheap to a more perfect hedge that is relatively expensive'. Working's analogy with insurance, that the choice is between coverage for all risks at high cost or for only serious loss at lower cost, is particularly apt.

McManus and Acheson (1979) provide a different analysis of the impact of standardized delivery options and commodity specifications on the hedging property of futures contracts. McManus and Acheson (M-A) contend that futures contracts are inferior to spot (or forward) contracts (as delivery instruments) because the impersonal nature of futures trading leads to potential distortions in product quality that need to be deterred by a backwardation which, in turn, reduces the attractiveness of futures contracts as a hedge.

The M-A thesis is based on the following reasoning. Futures contracts provide objective and incomplete descriptions of the commodity. This encourages a potential deterioration in the quality of goods that will be supplied to settle futures contracts. The sellers of futures contracts will have an incentive to deliver the lowest quality goods that satisfy the contract description in as much as those quality attributes omitted from the description, but valued in the spot market, will be less intensively provided. Incomplete objective commodity description creates incentives for the production of contract goods, i.e. goods designed for delivery against a futures contract. This distortion will not, however, be reflected in the actual production of inferior quality contract goods but in a backwardation in futures prices sufficient to deter their production. This implies that the futures price must lie below the expected spot price by at least the difference in the price of contract and the 'spot' commodities. Contract incompleteness thus generates a backwardation which increases with the extent to which the commodity is incompletely specified in the futures contract. The futures price will increase as the contract nears maturity, reflecting the higher costs of producing contract goods.

McManus and Acheson characterize this as a moral hazard problem that is exacerbated by the impersonal nature of futures trading. They suggest that the subjective evaluation of quality in personal spot markets is cheaper and superior to trade by objective commodity description.

The following comments can be made on the M-A thesis. First, to the extent that commodity quality can be fully and objectively described, the M-A thesis does not apply. Futures trading in gold, silver, metals, foreign exchange and financial futures, therefore, is not subject to the problem of potential quality deterioration. Moreover, the monitoring of quality attributes that can be objectively defined will be provided at lower cost through a centralized exchange than by individual traders in the spot and forward markets. Second, the M-A thesis assumes that the alternative to futures trading is personalized spot or forward market transactions, where specialization by identity and subjective quality evaluation are a cheaper means of monitoring and preventing quality deterioration. This assumption is obviously inapplicable when the relevant forward market may also be impersonal and rely on objective or imperfect commodity description. A more serious criticism, however, is the assumption that subjective quality evaluation is cheaper and as finely tuned in personal markets as M-A believe. Several empirical studies (e.g. Macaulay, 1964) have stressed that in long-term personal contracting, the parties tend to be flexible and respond to variation in the quality of performance in reasonable and accommodating ways. Wilson's (1980) study of personal contracting in the New England fish market suggests that the subjective evaluation of quality is extremely crude. The information and monitoring costs encountered in the loose and ill-defined long-term contracts characteristic of personal markets makes subjective quality evaluation extremely difficult. 'As a result', concludes Wilson (1980, pp. 503-4) 'implicit product quality standards often tend to approximate a simple "acceptable" or "unacceptable" state and actual product falls to the lowest level consistent with acceptability.' Which is to say that precisely the identical difficulty is encountered in the spot market when product quality is not objectively definable.

Margins

So far it has been argued that the organization of futures trading eliminates reliability risk. This in fact is not entirely true. The governance supplied by the exchange removes the risk of default in the settlement of futures transactions by holding members of the exchange liable to the clearing house, and protects the clients of brokers from loss due to the latter's insolvency or dishonesty. The broker, however, still faces the risk that his client will default. To the extent that the risk of client default is present, the brokerage costs of futures trading will rise to cover expected losses.

The problem of client default has been handled by futures exchanges by requiring clients to pay their brokers a deposit margin, usually between 1 per cent and 5 per cent of the value of the contract (Telser, 1981b). These margins serve to protect the broker from losses that may result from adverse changes in the customer's net balances. Margins are a security deposit that cushions the broker from losses arising from client default. Margins also economize on transaction costs by substituting a simple 'price rule' for the customer's legal liability to the broker that would require costly legal proceedings to enforce. The practice of additional margin calls, when there has been an adverse movement in the customer's account, plus daily price limits, both serve to reduce the probability of loss due to customer default. Thus, unlike a customer's liability rule, margins are finely tuned responses designed to minimize customer default and hence transactions costs in futures markets.

Centralization of Trading

There is a strong tendency for futures trading to take place not only in one contract but also in one exchange. The centralization of trading in futures tends to increase market liquidity. As Telser (1981a) has argued, there are increasing returns to market liquidity due to the effect of increases in the volume of trade on the variance of market clearing prices. If the distribution of market clearing prices is asymptotically normal, a 1 per cent increase in the volume of trade will reduce the variance by half a per cent.

Thus a single market will be twice as liquid as two markets each half its size. Silber's (1981) comprehensive study of contract innovation by US exchanges finds that the liquidity of the larger established exchanges is important for the success of new contracts. The success rate of new contracts for the largest five exchanges in the US was over two times that for the rest of the industry (30.2 per cent compared to 13.6 per cent). He also found that the chances of the competitive coexistence of two contracts in the same commodity is greater if they are traded on the same exchange.

These findings indicate that there are increasing returns to futures trading and a tendency for natural monopoly markets to form. In the US the futures industry is highly concentrated. There are 14 exchanges and the three-firm concentration ratio is nearly 90 per cent (measured in number of contracts traded). Despite this concentration, the rivalry between exchanges is fierce and the big three are responsible for most contractual innovations. Although much more work needs to be done on this issue, there appears to be strong competition between exchanges, thus minimizing the likelihood that any exchange will be able to exercize monopoly power.

Exchange Governance

Futures markets are generally owned by their members and operated as non-profit institutions. They, like the firm, can be viewed as private proprietary markets as opposed to a 'non-owned' market where autonomous contracting takes place. Non-owned or public markets tend to suffer from common property inefficiencies where transaction costs are significant. This is because no one individual has an interest in the efficient operation of the market as such. If the inefficiencies of public markets become large enough, individuals will have the incentive to privatize the market by establishing property rights in its operations.

The members of a futures exchange have a property right in its activities, and the value of their property right depends on its efficiency. The governance mechanism provided in futures markets thus has several characteristics that reflect this fact. First, although the interests of exchange members will be diverse, it is reasonable to assume that the rules of the exchange will be fashioned to maximize the collective profit of its members. Thus exchanges will act to promote futures trading, reduce reliability risk and maintain the general integrity of its operations and members. Thus, unlike most other forms of regulation, self-regulation by the exchange will tend to be economically motivated and wealth maximizing. It is of course true that self-regulation can promote monopolistic abuses, especially given the strong tendency for natural monopolies to arise in futures trading. However, the scope for monopolistic practices is greatly limited by potential competition from other futures exchanges. Moreover, members of the exchange have a common interest in ensuring the good name of the exchange; their business depends on it, as does the value of their seat on the exchange. Thus each has an interest in the survival and reputation of the other, as evidenced by arrangements designed to assist members in financial difficulties.

The nature of futures markets seems to provide endogenous forces that cause market regulation to be efficiency-based. Since the *raison d'être* of futures trading is transaction costs economies, it should not be surprising to find that most of the regulations devised by the industry reflect this fact. Regulations that did not reduce transaction costs and reliability risks simply would not survive.

This view of exchange governance and inter-exchange competitive pressures gives rise to a testable prediction. It suggests that government regulation of futures exchanges may be detrimental to their performance and efficiency. In the US, futures trading is subject to government regulation whereas in the UK the industry is largely self-regulated (Gemmill, 1982). One test of this aspect of the theory, suggesting that exchanges govern efficiently, is to investigate whether regulation in the US has led to increased trade on UK (and other self-regulated) futures markets (Gemmill, 1982).

5. Feasibility Conditions Reconsidered

Equipped with the model developed above, a few final comments can be made concerning the generally accepted feasibility conditions.

First, it should now be fairly obvious that the 'commodity approach' misses the essential factors that limit futures trading. For example, homogeneity or near homogeneity of the commodity is not a condition *per se*, but refers to the fact that as heterogeneity increases so too do the transaction costs of trading in futures. As a rule of thumb this feasibility condition may be adequate, but one should not be surprised to see it violated as the cost-benefit ratio changes as a consequence of technological developments or changing market structure.

Another condition that can be cast in a different light is that of the necessity of possible delivery of the commodity in settlement of the futures contract. We have seen that the economic rationale for this condition is to bind futures and spot prices. Yet the extension of futures trading to stock market indices and financial instruments is assailing the logic of this argument and it could well be that delivery options are in large part a device to avoid the legal inference that futures contracts are gambling contracts.

The necessity of delivery needs to be reappraised. In this chapter futures markets have been characterized as side markets which provide valuable services, whether it be price insurance, price determination or an aid to business planning, for which the hedger is willing to pay a price. Spot and futures markets perform different functions. They trade in different property rights attached to physical commodities. The spot market is a delivery market where rights to specific lots of the commodities are traded. The futures market is where hedgers take a position of temporary zero ownership, transferring the rights to commodities for a specified period to people willing to trade in those rights in the expectation of gain.

If this view is taken, there is no logical necessity why delivery is a necessary condition. The mechanism that permits futures markets to exist is the relative efficiency with which they transfer property rights. If a futures market performs this task at too great a cost, it fails. It is not delivery that binds the two markets, but the competitive forces in the futures market that keep the benefits of the services provided equal to their marginal costs.

A similar view has been expressed by Henry Bakken, who asserts that futures trading is not circumscribed by certain physical features of the commodity, particularly the 'figment of delivery'. According to Bakken, the primary purpose of futures trading is price determination, although the logic of his argument does not depend on this view of the function of futures. Bakken (1960, p. 50) concludes on an especially prophetic note that bears repetition: 'It is even possible, in my way of thinking to conceive of a universal contract rather than to have many commodity contracts tied to specific commodities. Under this concept one would really engage in trading on the basis of index numbers.'

Houthakker's (1959a) comment that the possibility of delivery makes futures analogous to banknotes under a convertible currency regime can be turned on its head by asserting that non-delivery makes futures analogous to banknotes by fiat. The fact that the latter have no effective commodity backing does not imply that they are worthless or tend to bear no relationship to reality. To use Bakken's term, contracts would still create 'net possession utility' in the form of wealth-increasing potential.

Notes

*Wolfson College, Oxford. This chapter is a substantially revised version of my paper 'An Institutional Analysis of Futures Trading' completed as part of Barry Goss's graduate course in hedging and uncertainty at Monash University in 1975. I am grateful to Dr Goss for his comments on the original paper.

1. Bakken (1960).
2. Goss and Yamey (1978, p. 45) comment: 'we have not provided a systematic analysis or analytical framework from which the necessary conditions for the feasibility and success of futures trading can be derived. This lack of such a firm framework is a deficiency in the theory of futures trading.'
3. Several recent articles on futures trading have also adopted such a transaction cost approach. In particular Telser and Higinbotham (1977); Burns (1979); McManus and Acheson (1979). The earlier work of Houthakker (1959a) and Working (1953a,b) also emphasizes the transaction cost-reducing aspects of organized futures trading.
4. In Houthakker's (1959a, p. 134) opening paragraph he states: 'The economic analysis of institutions is not highly regarded or widely practised among contemporary economists. The very word "institution" now carries unfavourable associations with the legalistic approach to economic phenomena that was respectable during the first three decades of this century. There is little reason to regret the triumphant reaction that swept institutionalism from its dominant place.'
5. This literature is surveyed in Veljanovski (1982).
6. See, for example, the readings collected in Kronman and Posner (1979).
7. This position is also taken by modern economic property rights theorists. Furubotn and Pejovich (1972, p. 1139) stress that '[T]hough sometimes forgotten, there should be no confusion about the fact that both trade and production involve contractual arrangements. These activities exist not so much to accomplish the exchange of goods and services but to permit the exchange of "bundles" of property rights. Permission to do things with goods and services is at issue ...'
8. Studies generally indicate that the risk per unit of unhedged commodity is greater than hedged stock due to the close correlation of spot and futures prices. Gray and Rutledge's (1971, p. 80) survey finds that 'in virtually every study "basis risks" were found to be smaller than price risks'.
9. According to Bakken (1960), 330 Bills were introduced in the US Congress during the period 1884-1953 designed to regulate, investigate, limit, prohibit and otherwise obstruct trading in futures contracts.
10. The definition of (ex post) opportunism differs among authors. For

example Muris (1981) does not contemplate breach as opportunistic. According to Muris (1981, p. 521) opportunism occurs 'when a performing party behaves contrary to the other party's understanding of their contract, but not necessarily contrary to the agreement's explicit terms, leading to a transfer of wealth from the other party to the performance'. I adopt a wider definition in the text.

11. AAAPSS (1911); Dumbell (1927); Irwin (1954); Bakken (1960, 1966).

12. There are only a few studies of futures contracts specifications: Jesse and Johnson (1970), Powers (1967), Sandor (1973) and Silber (1981).

References

AAAPSS (1911) 'American Produce Exchange Markets', *Annals of the American Academy of Political and Social Science*, 38, 319-64.

Alchian, A.A. (1970) 'Information Costs, Pricing and Resource Unemployment' in E.S. Phelps (ed.), *Micro-economic Foundations of Employment and Inflation Theory*, New York: Norton & Co.

Alchian, A.A. and H. Demsetz (1972) 'Production, Information Costs and Economic Organization', *American Economic Review*, 62, 777-95.

Arrow, K.J. (1974) 'Limited Knowledge and Economic Analysis', *American Economic Review*, 64, 1-10.

— (1981) 'Futures Markets: Some Theoretical Perspectives', *Journal of Futures Markets*, 1.

Baer, J.B. and O.G. Saxon (1948) *Commodity Exchanges and Futures Trading*, Madison: Harper Bros.

Bakken, H.H. (1960) 'Historical Evaluation and Legal Status of Futures Trading in American Agricultural Commodities', *Futures Trading Seminar*, vol. 1, Madison: MIMIR.

— (1966) 'Futures Trading — Origin, Development and Economic Status', *Futures Trading Seminar*, vol. III, Madison: MIMIR Pub. Inc.

Barzel, Y. (1979) 'Measurement Cost and the Organization of Markets', *Journal of Law and Economics*, 25, 47-8.

Beale, H. and T. Dugdale (1975) 'Contracts Between Businessmen: Planning and the Use of Contractual Remedies', *British Journal of Law and Society*, 2, 45-60.

Ben-Porath, Y. (1980) 'The F-Connection: Families, Friends and Firms and the Organization of Exchange', *Population Development Review*, 6, 1-30.

Burns, J.M. (1979) *A Treatise on Markets — Spots, Futures and Options*, Washington: American Enterprise Institute.

Cheung, S.N.S. (1969a) 'Transaction Costs, Resource Allocation and the Choice of Contractual Arrangements', *Journal of Law and Economics*, 12, 23-42.

— (1969b) *Theory of Share Tenancy*, Chicago: University of Chicago Press.

Coase, R.H. (1937) 'The Nature of the Firm', *Economica*, 4, 386-405.

— (1960) 'The Problem of Social Cost', *Journal of Law and Economics*, 3, 1-44.

Commons, J.R. (1934) *Institutional Economics*, New York: Macmillan.

Crocker, T.D. (1973) 'Contractual Choice', *Natural Resources Journal*, 13, 561-77.

Davis, L.E. and D.C. North (1971) *Institutional Change and American Economic Growth*, New York: Cambridge University Press.

Demsetz, H. (1968) 'The Cost of Transacting', *Quarterly Journal of Economics*, 82, 33-53.

Dumbell, S. (1927) 'The Origin of Cotton Futures', *Economic History*, 1, 259-67.

Furubotn, E.G. and S. Pejovich (1972) 'Property Rights and Economic Theory: A

Survey of the Recent Literature', *Journal of Economic Literature*, 10, 1137-62.
Gemmill, G. (1982) 'Regulating Futures Markets: A Review in the Context of British and American Practice', paper presented at Conference on Futures Markets, Florence, 11-13 March.
Goss, B.A. (1972) *The Theory of Futures Trading*, London: Routledge & Kegan Paul.
Goss, B.A. and B. Yamey (eds.) (1976) *The Economics of Futures Trading*, London: Macmillan.
Gray, R.W. and J.S. Rutledge (1971) 'The Economics of Commodity Futures: A Survey', *Review of Marketing and Agricultural Economics*, 39, 59-108.
Gray, R.W. (1959) 'The Characteristic Bias in Some Thin Futures Markets: Survey', *Food Research Institute Studies*, 1 (3), 298-312.
Hieronymous, T.A. (1971) *The Economics of Futures Trading*, Commodity Research Bureau Inc.
Houthakker, H.S. (1959a) 'The Scope and Limits of Futures Trading', in M. Ambramovitz (ed.), *Allocation of Economic Resources*, California: Stanford University Press, 135-59.
— (1959b) 'Can Speculators Forecast Prices?', *Review of Economics and Statistics*, 34, 143-51.
Irwin, H. (1954) *Evolution of Futures Trading*, Madison: MIMIR.
Jesse, E.V. and A.C. Johnson Jr. (1970) 'An Analysis of Vegetable Contracts', *American Journal of Agricultural Economics*, 52, 545-53.
Johnson, L.L. (1957) 'Price Instability, Hedging and Trade Volume in the Coffee Futures Markets', *Journal of Political Economy*, 65, 306-21.
Klein, B. and K. Leffler (1981) 'Non-Governmental Enforcement of Contracts: The Role of Market Forces in Guaranteeing Quality', *Journal of Political Economy*, 89, 615-45.
Kronman, A.T. and R.A. Posner (eds.) (1979) *The Economics of Contract Law*, Boston: Little, Brown.
Lascelles, D. (1982) 'US Stock Index Futures — A New Hedge for Investors', *Financial Times*, 23 June, p. 8.
Lovell, M.C. and R.C. Vogel (1973) 'A CPI-Futures Market', *Journal of Political Economy*, 81, 1009-12.
Macaulay, S. (1964) 'Non-contractual Relations in Business: A Preliminary Study', *American Sociological Review*, 28, 55-69.
McManus, J. and K. Acheson (1979) 'The Costs of Transacting in Futures Markets', Carleton University, manuscript.
MacNeil, I.R. (1974) 'The Many Futures of Contract', *Southern California Law Review*, 47, 691-816.
Muris, T.J. (1981) 'Opportunistic Behavior and the Law of Contracts', *Minnesota Law Review*, 65, 521-90.
Powers, M.J. (1967) 'Effects of Contract Provisions on the Success of a Futures Contract', *Journal of Farm Economics*, 49, 833-43.
Radner, R. (1970) 'Problems in the Theory of Markets Under Uncertainty', *American Economic Review (Papers and Proceedings)*, 60, 454-60.
Rock, C.A. (1982) 'Regulatory Control Over the United States, Canadian and United Kingdom Futures Markets', *Business Lawyer*, 37, 613-36.
Rockwell, C.S. (1967) 'Normal Backwardation, Forecasting and the Returns to Speculators', *Food Research Institute Studies*, 7, 107-30.
Sandor, R.L. (1973) 'Innovating by an Exchange: A Case Study of the Development of the Plywood Futures Contract', *Journal of Law and Economics*, 16, 119-36.
Shavell, S. (1980) 'Damage Measures for Breach of Contract', *Bell Journal of Economics*, 11, 466-90.

Silber, W.L. (1981) 'Innovation, Competition and New Contract Design in Futures Markets', *Journal of Futures Markets*, 1, 117-22.
Telser, L.C. (1980) 'A Theory of Self-enforcing Agreements', *Journal of Business*, 53, 27-44.
— (1981a) 'Why There Are Organized Futures Markets', *Journal of Law and Economics*, 24, 1-22.
— (1981b) 'Margins and Futures Contracts', *Journal of Futures Markets*, 1, 225-54.
Telser, L.G. and H.N. Higinbotham (1977) 'Organized Futures Markets: Costs and Benefits', *Journal of Political Economy*, 85, 969-1000.
Veljanovski, C.G. (1982) *The New Law-and-Economics*, Oxford: Centre for Socio-Legal Studies.
Wachter, M.L. and O.E. Williamson (1978) 'Obligational Markets and the Mechanics of Inflation', *Bell Journal of Economics*, 9, 549-71.
Williamson, O.E. (1979) 'Transaction Cost Economics: the Governance of Contractual Relations', *Journal of Law and Economics*, 22, 549-71.
Wilson, J.A. (1980) 'Adaptation to Uncertainty and Small Numbers Exchange: the New England Fresh Fish Market', *Bell Journal of Economics*, 11, 491-504.
Working, H. (1953a) 'Futures Trading and Hedging', *American Economic Review*, 43, 316-43.
— (1953b) 'Hedging Reconsidered', *Journal of Farm Economics*, 35, 544-61.
— (1967) 'Test of a Theory Concerning Floor Trading on Commodity Exchanges', *Stanford Food Research Institute* (supplement), 7, 5-48.

2 EXPERIMENTAL FUTURES MARKETS

Glenn W. Harrison*

1. Introduction

This chapter studies in detail the behaviour of three experimental futures markets. The separate and joint effects of 'event uncertainty' and 'inside information' on the performance of spot and futures markets are also examined.

This section discusses the general experimental methodology employed here and the relationship of this chapter to the existing literature. Section 2 introduces the specific experimental design, and Section 3 provides a series of theoretical equilibrium predictions concerning observable behaviour in these markets. The experimental results are presented in Section 4, in two stages: first there is an account of the observed performance of *each* market relative to theoretical predictions, followed by an analysis of the *comparative* performance of markets with certain controlled differences. Finally, Section 5 draws several general conclusions and provides suggestions for further research.

Experimental auction markets involve recruited subjects who are induced, by means of controlled market trading schedules and standard incentive structures, to display real-time market behaviour. Experimental control of market conditions, the 'treatment variables', allows one to design groups of such experiments to gauge the effects of those variables on observed behaviour (e.g. the strength of equilibrium tendencies, efficiency of market outcomes and the variability of price movements). Each of the hypotheses to be studied involves the specification of well-defined, and hence *replicable*, sets of trading rules, informational imperfections and other institutional features. Smith (1982) and Plott (1982) provide excellent general statements of the advantages of an experimental methodology, several features of which are relevant here.

The first methodological point is that the experimental approach *does* provide evidence on 'real-world' markets. The fact that these experiments typically involve small numbers of traders, that they deal with homogeneous commodities and that the experimenter can control the notional trading schedules, does *not* render these markets irrelevant. They are indeed special, but so are the institutional trappings of most organized exchanges. The main point, however, is the *purpose* for which such markets are conducted: to provide evidence on general theories. *If a theory or economic principle is general, it should cover special cases.*

The second methodological point follows from the first: if we *cannot* confirm or reject general theories in the context of controlled environments *designed* for the purpose of testing the theory, then the theory cannot be regarded as operational in any useful respect. Moreover, it is often difficult to 'control' for all conceivably relevant influences on market behaviour with econometric methods and actual market data; see Leamer (1978, 1983) for a clear statement of the methodological weaknesses of standard econometric practice here.

An example from the futures market literature may illustrate the significance of this last point. Conventional empirical tests of the hypothesis that futures markets induce 'unwarranted and undesirable' spot price fluctuations involve comparisons of estimates of spot price dispersion statistics for time periods associated with, and then without, the presence of active futures trading in the good. The evidence for this class of tests has been noticeably mixed: see, for example, the results of Cox (1976) and his survey of other studies using this empirical approach. Aside from the frequent lack of a theoretical model to specify the tests and interpret the results, the long time periods involved imply almost certain violations of the implied *ceteris paribus* assumption. Since we have the ability to specify the theoretical models for our experimental markets, we *know* the underlying market structure. Thus the tests of the influence of futures trading on the informational efficiency of asset markets reported in Friedman, Harrison and Salmon (1983, 1984) do not involve *joint hypotheses* about market structure and market efficiency.

A final methodological point relates more particularly to the use of the experimental technique to analyse the role of information in futures market performance. One common difficulty with analytic models of the informational aspects of markets is the precise definition of 'the information set' of traders. Our experiments allow very detailed knowledge of that set; for instance, they provide the ability to control which traders know what information.

The relevance of this point will be apparent in Sections 3 and 4.

Our experiments represent a synthesis of recent work by Forsythe, Palfrey and Plott (1982a), Friedman, Harrison and Salmon (1983) and Plott and Sunder (1982), hereafter referred to as FPPa, FHSa and PS, respectively.[1] All of these studies employed a continuous double oral auction for multiple units of a single good (the 'asset') traded against cash. They differ primarily in their treatment of two critical elements of asset valuation: time and uncertainty.

PS focused on uncertainty: their asset expired after a single period but had trader-specific marginal values that depended on an exogenous 'state of nature'. Trade typically occurred before the state of nature was revealed, although in some cases certain agents ('insiders') had advance information. They found that equilibrium prices usually revealed the inside information after several repetitions of the market, at least when that information was conclusive as to the true state of nature.

FPPa focused on time: their asset derived its value from cash dividends paid over two periods, but each trader knew his own dividend schedule with certainty. Inasmuch as traders did not know others' schedules and therefore did not initially know what prices would be available to them, there existed an endogenous type of uncertainty that we may refer to as *market uncertainty*, in contrast with the exogenous *event uncertainty* of PS. FPPa found that asset prices approached 'Rational Expectations' values after several repetitions of the market.

FHSa also focused on time: they employed a three-period design, and examined trader experience and the presence of futures markets as separate treatment variables in a setting with no event uncertainty. FHSa confirmed the importance of both variables in speeding convergence towards more informationally efficient prices. They also found that spot prices were less volatile when futures markets operated.[2] We discuss the precise nature of the futures contracts in the next section.

Friedman, Harrison and Salmon (1984), hereafter FHSb, conducted six experiments combining the three-period and futures market features of FHSa with the event uncertainty and inside information features of PS. The markets examined in the present chapter are drawn from the three FHSb experiments with futures markets.[3] FHSa and FHSb study the role of futures markets by comparing experiments that have them with experiments that do not; that is, by isolating the presence of futures markets as a treatment variable. FHSb conclude that: (i) asset market outcomes tend to evolve towards strong-form informationally efficient equilibria, whether or not futures markets and/or event uncertainty are present; (ii) the presence of futures markets clearly stabilizes spot prices; (iii) the presence of futures markets tends to speed the evolution of asset markets to more efficient equilibria when there is event uncertainty; and (iv) futures markets promote the 'leakage' of inside information, with strong-form predictions outperforming semi-strong-form predictions.

The present study is not concerned with the role of futures markets in the above sense. Rather, it is concerned with the detailed performance of asset markets with futures markets, relative to theoretical equilibrium predictions, and with the effects of event uncertainty and inside information on spot and futures market performance. The results presented here, therefore, complement the analysis of these experiments contained in FHSb.

2. Experimental Design[4]

The participants in the experiments, referred to as *traders*, were recruited primarily from MBA classes at the UCLA Graduate School of Management — as likely a habitat for *homo economus* as we could think of. After distributing and reviewing the instruction sheets (available on request), double oral auction markets were opened. Any trader was free to announce bid and offer prices and accept the bids or offers of others[5] providing he or she did not violate any budget constraint, as discussed below. Transacted prices were publicly recorded. The assets traded were called certificates; they yielded returns, called dividends, to traders who possessed them at the end of each trading period.

Each experiment consisted of a series of 'Market Years', which can be thought of as Hicksian Weeks. Within each Market Year there were three trading periods, referred to as Periods A, B and C. Trading Periods A and B lasted for five minutes and each trader could buy or sell one certificate at a time. Lot sales, short sales (i.e. short spot positions and 'naked' short futures positions) and negative cash positions were prohibited.[6] At the beginning of each Market Year each trader was endowed with two certificates and an interest-free loan of 20 dollars. The loans were sufficiently large that the liquidity constraint was never an impediment to trade.

Incentives for exchange among traders were provided by varying the per certificate dividends across individuals as well as across periods. There were three trader types, with individuals randomly assigned to each group; Table 2.1 provides details of the parameterizations for each experiment. The underlying period-specific certificate returns were identical across Market Years — identical in the aggregate and for each individual.[7] Thus the markets were repetitively stationary from year to year. Note that traders were not informed of this stationarity; they had to *learn* about it in 'real time'. Each individual was carefully monitored so that his/her private dividend profile was not observed by any other trader. Possibilities for explicit collusion were effectively nil.

To motivate the experimental set-up one can think of the traders as grain merchants trading in warehouse certificates which have a par value of zero but provide each trader with a finite time profile of convenience yields. Of course, in these experiments traders actually received a cash 'dividend' for each certificate held at the end of each trading period, and the certificates expired after the Market Year ended.

In Experiment 1, trading in Periods A and B consisted either of an immediate exchange of cash for certificates at accepted bid or offer prices (i.e. spot transactions) or a futures transaction. The futures contract consisted of the delivery of a certificate in Period C. Futures contracts as well as spot contracts could be written in both Period A and Period B. In Periods A and B dividends were paid as usual for each (spot) certificate held at the end of that period. No transactions were allowed in Period C, but deliveries previously contracted for were performed. An individual with a net long (short) futures position was required to take (make) delivery of the certificates, and then Period C dividends distributed. A natural interpretation of Period C is that it corresponds to the day after the last trading day in the delivery month of a futures contract. Note that an agent had ample opportunity to offset futures positions during Periods A and B. However, because of the restriction on short sales, agents' short futures positions were limited to the quantity of inventoried spot certificates at any point in time. For a given net short position an agent's spot sales were also constrained.

In all experiments traders were given a small trading commission of 1 cent per transaction. Such commissions are a standard

Table 2.1: Induced Experimental Market Parameters

Experiment	Experienced Traders?	Event Uncertainty?	Insiders?	Agents Type	Agents ID#	Dividend Profile Period A X	Period A Y	Period B X	Period B Y	Period C X	Period C Y
1	Yes	No	No	I	5,7,9	0.75		0.20		0.10	
				II	1,3,6	0.40		0.45		0.45	
				III	2,4,8	0.15		0.30		0.80	
2	Yes	Yes	No	I	1,6,9	0.25	0.75	0.10	0.60	0.50	1.00
				II	3,5,8	0.20	0.20	0.80	0.80	0.30	0.30
				III	2,4,7	0.50	0.30	0.60	0.30	1.00	0.70
3	Yes	Yes	Yes	I	1,4*,9	0.45	0.30	0.35	0.35	0.35	0.25
				II	3,5,7*	0.15	0.50	0.30	0.60	0.45	0.30
				III	2*,6,8	0.20	0.40	0.40	0.45	0.30	0.70

Notes: (i) In Year 5 of Experiment 1 a random reassignment of agents to trader type occurred. Trader type I consisted of Agents 1, 3 and 5; type II of Agents 4, 6 and 8; and type III of Agents 2, 7 and 9. The parameters shown here pertain to all other market years.

(ii) In Experiment 3 an asterisk beside an Agent ID# denotes an insider.

feature of most experimental market studies; the usual rationale for their inclusion is to overcome subjective transaction costs which might be especially relevant when transacted prices are very close to a market-clearing price. At the end of each experiment we paid our traders in cash for all profits accrued from dividends and trading.

The distinguishing feature of Experiments 2 and 3 compared with Experiment 1 is that in the former each trader's dividend profile is specific to a 'state of nature'. Two different states, called X and Y, were possible. At the beginning of the experiment all traders were told that we would flip a fair coin at the end of each Period A trading round: if the coin came up heads then state X occurs and if the coin showed tails then state Y occurs for that Market Year.

At the beginning of Period A in Experiment 2 all traders had *common* prior beliefs about the ultimate realization of states X or Y, based on *public knowledge* that each state had a 50 per cent probability of occurring for each Market Year. Trading during Period A occurred under this well-defined event uncertainty. The uncertainty was then resolved as advertised,[8] so Period B represented a posterior trading round in which agents had the opportunity to revise their portfolio of certificate holdings under conditions of *no* event uncertainty, as in Experiment 1. The futures market in Experiments 2 and 3 operated in the same manner as in Experiment 1, except that, in Period A, trading for Period C futures certificates was subject to the same event uncertainty as spot trading.

Some care was taken in selecting the dividend profiles in Experiments 2 and 3. Note, however, that one state always had a higher pay-out distribution over a complete Market Year (in both experiments this state was Y). Thus the market faced a situation of social risk. One can think of our events as a 'good crop' versus 'bad crop' alternative.

The distinguishing feature of Experiment 3 compared with Experiment 2 is that, in the former, one trader of each trader type was randomly selected to receive conclusive information about which state would occur *before* Period A trading took place for each Market Year.[9] This was accomplished by the experimenter leaving the room before the start of the experiment, flipping a coin and then writing down the results on three out of nine cards. Cards which read either 'No Information' or 'State ___' were put into envelopes and passed out to the traders. The six non-insiders therefore did *not* have prior knowledge about the identity of the insiders. The experiment then proceeded in the same manner as Experiment 2 in terms of the resolution of the event uncertainty at the end of Period A trading.

3. Equilibrium Concepts and Predictions

Following FHSa and FHSb, the various equilibrium concepts applied to our experiments are defined in terms of the information set that traders are assumed to have available and to act upon. There are two fundamental 'pieces' of information of relevance in our experiments: the market structure of dividends conditional on each state of nature, and the actual state of nature. By design, the latter piece of information is public knowledge in all three experiments in Period B and (trivially) in the Period A of Experiment 1. It is also shown, by design, to insiders in Period A in Experiment 3. At all times and/or for all other traders, the state of nature is information that must be 'discovered' during trading. The former piece of information, the market valuation of the asset in each period, must be 'discovered' by all traders.

The four equilibrium concepts developed by FHSb as operational benchmarks to measure informational efficiency are:

(1) *Expected Private Information (EPI) equilibrium.* Prices and allocations reflect only the private structure of expected dividends; neither piece of information is reflected in market behaviour.

(2) *Private Information (PI) equilibrium.* Prices and allocations reflect the private structure of dividends relevant to the actual state of nature; market behaviour only reflects the second piece of information.

(3) *Uninformed Rational Expectations (URE) equilibrium.* Prices and allocations reflect the expected market dividend structure; market behaviour reflects only the first piece of information.

(4) *Perfect Foresight (PF) equilibrium.* Prices and allocations reflect the market dividend structure relevant to the actual state of nature; both pieces of information are reflected in market behaviour.

Clearly the EPI and URE equilibria do not apply to Experiment 1. Note also that we define the 'expected dividend structure' as the 'actual dividend structure' for the actual state of nature revealed in Period B in Experiments 2 and 3.

Tables 2.2 and 2.3 list the various equilibrium predictions for prices and allocations. In Table 2.2 we employ the following notation: $d_i^k(z)$ denotes the per-certificate dividend of trader type i (i = 1,2,3 referring to trader types I, II and III respectively) in Period k (k = 1,2,3 referring to Periods A, B and C respectively) when state of nature z obtains (z = X or Y; we drop the index z when discussing Experiment 1), $\pi(z)$ denotes the probability of state of nature z, and $Z = \{X,Y\}$ denotes the set of possible states of nature. The term 'leakage' is used to refer to the dissemination of inside information (concerning the true state of nature) to the market. In terms of our experimental design, $\pi(z) \equiv 0.5$ for each z and each trader in Experiment 2 and for the outsiders in Experiment 3. Referring back to Table 2.1, we see for example that $d_i^k(z) = d_1^2(X) =$ \$0.10 in Experiment 2; in words, the per-certificate dividend of trader type I in Period B is \$0.10 if the state of nature is X.

The rationale behind the various equilibrium concepts can be most easily appreciated by working through several specific numerical examples. Consider Experiment 1, in which there is no event uncertainty to complicate matters. Consider further the market valuation of each Period C *futures* certificate given the private dividends of each trader type in Table 2.1. Ignoring resale possibilities, and assuming non-co-operative bidding between the three agents of each trader type, it is clear that trader type III will end up paying \$0.80 for each Period C futures certificate. If the three type III agents colluded they could hold prices down to \$0.30, just enough to induce trader types I and II to sell their supply of certificates (recall the 1 cent commission). We shall assume throughout an absence of collusion. Thus \$0.80 is the *reservation price* for type III traders with respect to futures certificates: they will profit by any purchases at a lower price and any sales at a higher price. Similarly, \$0.45 is the reservation price for type II traders and \$0.10 for type I traders. Thus we obtain the predictions in Tables 2.2 and 2.3, noting that Period C is the final period of each year and that PI and PF predictions coincide.

Now consider the market valuation of Period B *spot* certificates in Experiment 1. We shall assume that the (PI = PF) equilibrium

Table 2.2: Equilibrium Price Predictions

Experiment		Weaker Efficiency		Stronger Efficiency
1	p(A|PI)	$= p(C\|PI) + \max_i (d_i^1 + d_i^2) = \$1.75$	p(A|PF)	$= \sum_{k=1}^{3} \max_i d_i^k = \$2.00$
	p(B|PI)	$= p(C\|PI) + \max_i d_i^2 = \$1.25$	p(B|PF)	$= \sum_{k=2}^{3} \max_i d_i^k = \$1.25$
	p(C|PI)	$= \max_i d_i^3 = \$0.80$	p(C|PF)	$= \max_i d_i^3 = \$0.80$
2	p(A|EPI)	$= p(C\|EPI) + \max_i [\sum_{k=1}^{2} \sum_{z \varepsilon Z} \pi(z) d_i^k(z)] = \$1.85$	p(A|URE)	$= \max_i \{\sum_{z \varepsilon Z} \pi(z)[d_i(z) + p(B\|PF,z)]\} = \$2.30$
	p(B|PI,z)	$= \max_i \sum_{k=2}^{3} d_i^k(z) = \$1.60$ (X or Y)	p(B|PF,z)	$= \max_i d_i^2(z) + p(C\|PF,z) = \$1.80$ (X or Y)
	p(C|EPI)	$= \max_i [\sum_{z \varepsilon Z} \pi(z) d_i^3(z)] = \$0.85$	p(C|URE)	$= \sum_{z \varepsilon Z} \pi(z) p(C\|PF,z) = \$1.00$
	p(C|PI,z)	$= \max_i d_i^3(z) = \$1.00$ (X or Y)	p(C|PF,z)	$= \max_i d_i^3(z) = \$1.00$ (X or Y)
3	With Leakage	: p(A|PI,z) = $1.15(X) or $1.55(Y)	With Leakage	: p(A|PF,z) = $1.30(X) or $1.80(Y)
	No Leakage	: p(A|EPI) = $1.225	No Leakage	: p(A|URE) = $1.45
	p(B|PI,z)	= $0.75(X) or $1.15(Y)	p(B|PF,z)	= $0.85(X) or $1.30(Y)
	With Leakage	: p(C|PI,z) = $0.45(X) or $0.70(Y)	With Leakage	: p(C|PF,z) = $0.45(X) or $0.70(Y)
	No Leakage	: p(C|EPI) = $0.50	No Leakage	: p(C|URE) = $0.575

Table 2.3: Equilibrium Allocation Predictions

		Weaker Efficiency				Stronger Efficiency		
		A	B	C		A	B	C
Experiment	Concept	X or Y	X or Y	X or Y	Concept	X or Y	X or Y	X or Y
1	PI	I	II	III	PF	I	II	III
2	EPI	II	—	III	URE	I	—	—
	PI	III or I	III or I	III or I	PF	III or I	II or II	III or I
3	EPI	III	—	III	URE	I	—	—
	PI	I or III	II or III	II or III	PF	I or II	III or II	II or III

price of Period C futures certificates has been established at \$0.80 in Period A and Period B trading. Thus *all* traders know the *market* valuation of a Period C certificate in Period A and Period B, and can incorporate that valuation in the computation of their Period B reservation prices.[10] Again assuming non-co-operative bidding behaviour between agents of each trader type, these reservation prices are \$1.00 (= \$0.20 + \$0.80), \$1.25 (= \$0.45 + \$0.80) and \$1.10 (= \$0.30 + \$0.80) for types I, II and III respectively. We therefore predict that Period B certificates will be held by type II agents and that they will pay \$1.25 for each one they buy.

A similar logic implies Period A spot certificate *Private Information* reservation prices of \$1.75 (= \$0.75 + \$1.00), \$1.65 (= \$0.40 + \$1.25) and \$1.25 (= \$0.15 + \$1.10) for types I, II and III, respectively. Thus we predict a PI equilibrium price of \$1.75 based solely on traders' private information about Period A and B dividends *and* the *public* knowledge of the Period C futures certificate *market* value. Note that we recursively employ the Period B reservation prices for each trader type when computing the Period A reservation prices. Note, also, the role of a Period C futures market operating during Period A and Period B in the computation of the Period B reservation prices. In the absence of a futures market, traders would have to observe spot Period C market prices over several Market Years in order to feel confident that the market valuation of a Period C certificate is \$0.80.

After several years traders will realize that Period B spot certificates have a *market* valuation of \$1.25, and will adopt *Perfect Foresight* reservation prices of \$2.00 (\$0.75 + \$1.25), \$1.65 (\$0.40 + \$1.25) and \$1.40 (\$0.15 + \$1.25), respectively. Thus we predict a PF equilibrium price of \$2.00 for Period A spot certificates. Note that the PI and PF allocation predictions in Experiment 1 coincide; FHSb provide a hypothetical numerical example in which both price and allocation predictions differ.

Essentially the same logic applies in Experiments 2 and 3 except for the complication of event uncertainty and inside information. The PI and PF equilibrium concepts are exactly identical, and assume that the actual state of nature is known (either because it is publicly revealed before Period B trading or is 'leaked' in Period A trading by insiders). The EPI (URE) equilibrium concepts assume that traders know the *conditional* PI (PF) equilibria and have common prior probabilities over the two states of nature.

FHSa and FHSb provide a further discussion of these equilibrium concepts.

4. Experimental Results

There are two aspects to our reporting of results. The first is a comparison of the observed behaviour of each individual market with the theoretical predictions presented earlier. The second is a comparison of two or more markets that differ with respect to some 'treatment variable' of interest. These two aspects are related, since we are typically concerned with the effect of a treatment variable on market performance *relative* to some theoretical benchmark (e.g. does a market with event uncertainty converge more slowly to a perfect foresight equilibrium than a market without this feature?). Section 4.1 examines the observed behaviour of each market relative to our theoretical predictions, while in Section 4.2 some conclusions about the effects of even uncertainty and inside information on market performance are drawn.

4.1 Individual Market Behaviour

Figures 2.1 through 2.3 chart the time series of transacted prices in each market experiment. The various theoretical equilibria for each market are also identified, and summary statistics of observed prices presented. An 'X' refers to spot prices and 'O' to futures prices. Table 2.4 lists the observed allocations of spot and futures certificates at the end of each period in each experiment. Table 2.5 lists the ratios of (net) sold futures and 'non-bought' futures to spot holdings. These ratios may be viewed as a measure of the degree of hedging by those traders who sell futures and those traders who do not have bought futures positions, respectively.

In the next three subsections we provide a detailed market commentary for each experiment, relating the observed behaviour to our theoretical equilibrium predictions. It is convenient to refer to Periods A, B and C by the notation PA, PB and PC, respectively. Similarly, we refer to Years 1, 2,3, 4 and 5 as Y1, Y2, Y3, Y4 and Y5, respectively. All other abbreviations are as defined previously (viz. PI, EPI, URE and PF).

4.1.1 Experiment 1. *Period C (Futures)*: In Y1 futures prices are already above the private PC valuations of trader types I and II

Figure 2.1: Observed Price Behaviour — Experiment 1

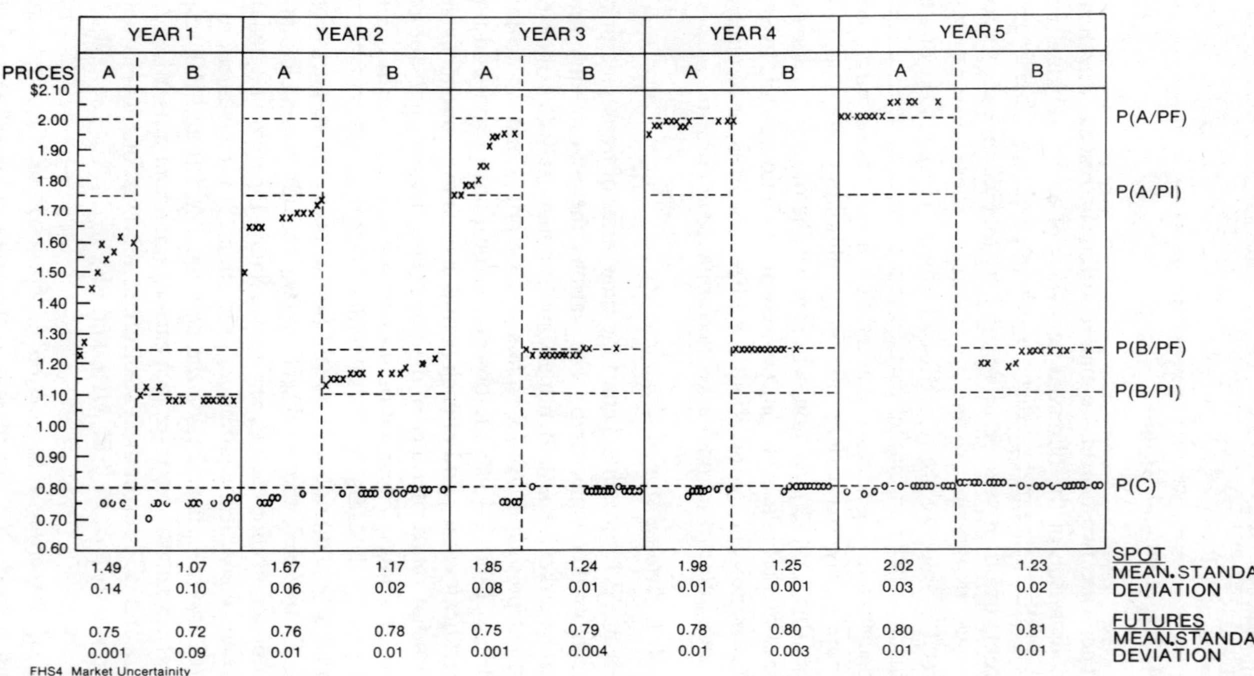

Figure 2.2: Observed Price Behaviour — Experiment 2

	YEAR 1 (X) A	YEAR 1 (X) B	YEAR 2 (Y) A	YEAR 2 (Y) B	YEAR 3 (Y) A	YEAR 3 (Y) B	YEAR 4 (X) A	YEAR 4 (X) B	YEAR 5 (X) A	YEAR 5 (X) B
SPOT MEAN	1.710	1.618	1.866	1.660	1.970	1.706	2.032	1.726	2.049	1.743
SPOT STANDARD DEVIATION	0.089	0.021	0.017	0.017	0.015	0.010	0.016	0.005	0.007	0.007
FUTURES MEAN	0.843	0.986	0.940	0.999	0.990	1.003	0.994	0.994		0.985
FUTURES STANDARD DEVIATION	0.019	0.013	0.001	0.003	0.008	0.005	0.005	0.013		0.005

PRICES: $2.30, 2.20, 2.10, 2.00, 1.90, 1.80, 1.70, 1.60, 1.50, 1.40, 1.30, 1.20, 1.10, 1.00, 0.90, 0.80

P(A/URE)
P(A/EPI)
P(B/PF)
P(B/PI)
P(C/URE) = P(C/PI) = P(C/PF)
P(C/EPI)

FHS6 Event Uncertainity
Experienced Subjects ;
Spot and Futures Trading

Figure 2.3: Observed Price Behaviour — Experiment 3

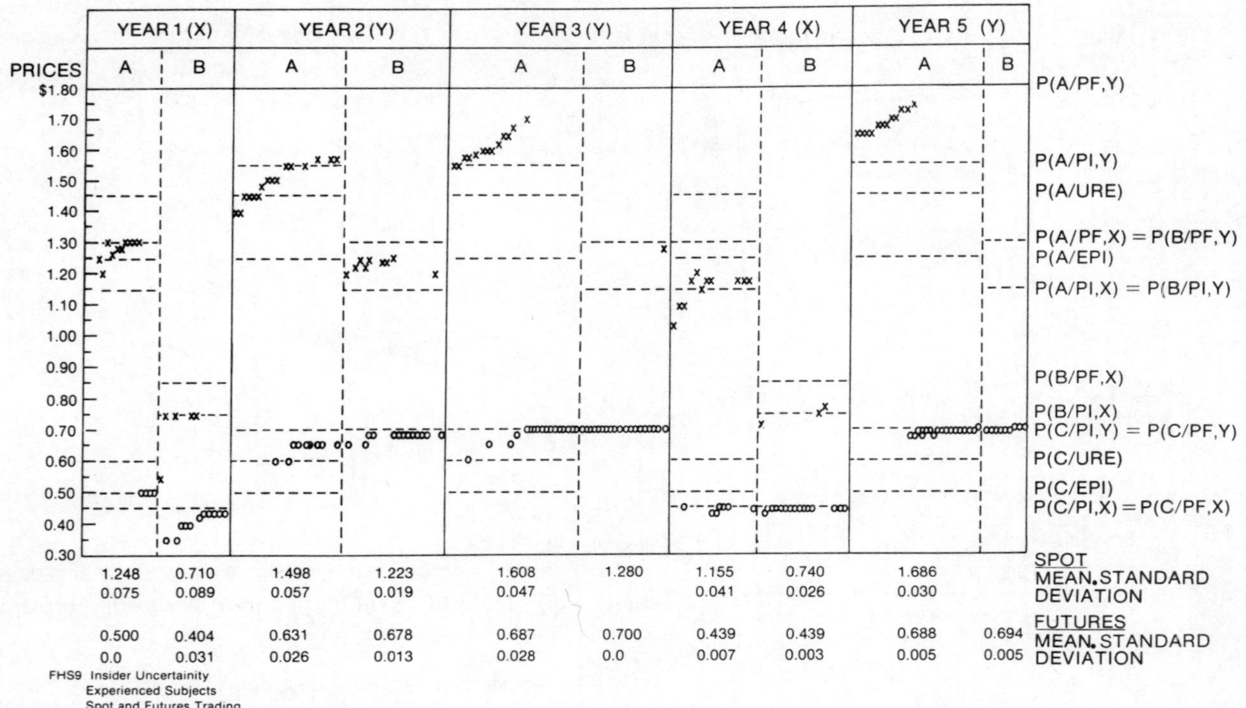

Table 2.4: Observed Spot and Futures Certificate Allocations

			Spot Certificates						Futures Certificate					
			Period A			Period B			Period A			Period B		
Experiment	Year	State	I	II	III	I	II	III	I	II	III	I	II	III
1	1	—	13	4	1	1	13	4	0	−3	3	−1	−13	14
	2	—	13	5	0	0	18	0	0	−5	5	0	−18	18
	3	—	13	5	0	0	18	0	0	−5	5	0	−18	18
	4	—	18	0	0	7	11	0	−7	0	7	−2	−11	13
	5	—	14	4	0	2	16	0	−9	−4	13	0	−15	15
2	1	X	6	5	7	3	13	2	−1	−5	6	−1	−12	13
	2	Y	11	5	2	5	12	1	0	2	−2	13	−12	−1
	3	Y	9	0	9	2	16	0	−1	3	−2	16	−16	0
	4	X	10	0	8	7	11	0	−7	4	3	−1	−10	11
	5	X	8	0	10	1	17	0	0	0	0	0	−17	17
3	1	X	6	5	7	7	8	3	−2	−2	4	−7	7	0
	2	Y	0	10	8	1	17	0	0	−6	6	−1	−15	16
	3	Y	0	18	0	0	18	0	0	−13	13	0	−16	16
	4	X	13	2	3	16	1	1	−5	3	2	−16	17	−1
	5	Y	0	18	0	0	18	0	3	−15	12	0	18	18

Notes: Positive futures certificate allocations imply a net bought position, and negative allocations a net sold position.

Table 2.5: Hedging Ratios

			Ratio of Sold Futures to Spot Holdings								Ratio of Non-Bought Futures to Spot Holdings							
			Period A				Period B				Period A				Period B			
Experiment	Year	State	I	II	III	Total	I	II	III	Total	I	II	III	Total	I	II	III	Total
1	1	—	—	0.75	—	0.75	1.00	1.00	—	1.00	0.0	0.75	—	0.18	1.00	1.00	—	1.00
	2	—	—	1.00	—	1.00	—	1.00	—	1.00	0.0	1.00	—	0.28	—	1.00	—	1.00
	3	—	—	1.00	—	1.00	—	1.00	—	1.00	0.0	1.00	—	0.28	—	1.00	—	1.00
	4	—	0.39	—	—	0.39	0.29	1.00	—	0.72	0.39	—	—	0.39	0.29	1.00	—	0.72
	5	—	0.64	1.00	—	0.72	—	0.94	—	0.94	0.64	1.00	—	0.72	0.0	0.94	—	0.83
2	1	X	0.17	1.00	—	0.55	0.33	0.92	—	0.81	0.17	1.00	—	0.55	0.33	0.92	—	0.81
	2	Y	—	—	1.00	1.00	—	1.00	1.00	1.00	0.0	—	1.00	0.15	—	1.00	1.00	1.00
	3	Y	0.11	—	0.22	0.17	—	1.00	—	1.00	0.11	—	0.22	0.17	—	1.00	—	1.00
	4	X	0.70	—	—	0.70	0.14	0.91	—	0.61	0.70	—	—	0.70	0.14	0.91	—	0.61
	5	X	—	—	—	—	—	1.00	—	1.00	0.0	—	0.0	0.0	0.0	1.00	—	0.94
3	1	X	0.33	0.40	—	0.36	1.00	—	—	1.00	0.33	0.40	—	0.36	1.00	—	0.0	0.70
	2	Y	—	0.60	—	0.60	1.00	0.88	—	0.89	—	0.60	—	0.60	1.00	0.88	—	0.89
	3	Y	—	0.72	—	0.72	—	0.89	—	0.89	—	0.72	—	0.72	—	0.89	—	0.89
	4	X	0.38	—	—	0.38	1.00	—	1.00	1.00	0.38	—	—	0.38	1.00	—	1.00	1.00
	5	Y	—	0.83	—	0.83	—	1.00	—	1.00	—	0.83	—	0.83	—	1.00	—	1.00

Notes: A dash indicates that the trader type did not have a net sold or net 'non-bought' futures position at the end of the period. Clearly that trader type may none the less have had a spot position; see Table 2.4 for a complete listing of spot and futures allocations.

($0.10 and $0.45 respectively). By the end of PB in Y2 they are near their equilibrium value, and from PB in Y3 on they provide a persistently clear signal.

Although *trades* in futures generally follow spot trading in each period in Y3 and Y4, there were numerous *unaccepted* bids and offers on futures at the time that spot contracts were being made. These bids and offers often contain useful information, despite not resulting in trades.

We shall discuss the allocation of futures contracts at the end of PA and PB when we discuss the spot certificate allocations below. It is useful, however, to examine the eventual PC holdings of *spot* certificates (these are just the *delivered* futures contracts pending at the end of PB). In Y1, Y2 and Y3 there were no misallocations in these holdings. In Y4 and Y5 some 13/18 and 15/18 were correctly allocated relative to both PI and PF concepts, which had identical predictions in this case. The misallocation in Y4 is discussed below.

Period B (Spot): Despite the futures prices observed in PA and during PB, in Y1 we see that PB spot prices are just below their PI equilibrium value. Significant learning apparently occurs in Y2, and PB prices are at their PF equilibrium value in Y3 and Y4.

In Y5 of this experiment we randomly reassigned agents to different dividend profiles without altering the aggregate market parameters. The issue here is the ability of agents to distinguish market signals from their private signal (viz. their own dividend profile) — the essence of our competing equilibrium notions. Despite a 'technical reaction' of sorts, especially in the PA spot market, the results essentially repeat the behaviour in Y4. The fact that we observe convergence to the PF equilibrium price in Y4 indeed tells us that agents had made the distinction between these two signals when forming their trading strategies; our results in Y5 confirm this conclusion.

The allocations of PB spot certificates in each year were 13/18, 18/18, 18/18, 11/18 and 16/18 relative to the PF prediction. All but one of the misallocations in Y1 are explained by the alternative PI prediction.

The misallocation in Y4 is attributable entirely to one type I agent (number 5). Her spot holdings at the end of PA in Y4 were seven certificates, and she had *mechanically* hedged by selling seven futures: impeccable PF behaviour so far. (In Y3 her only PA transaction was the purchase of one spot certificate, and she had sold all three spot certificates in PB as implied by PF behaviour.) From the sequence of unaccepted bids and offers it appears that she was determined to buy in her futures position in PB before selling off her spot holdings; recall that we did not allow net short positions at any stage of trading during any period, and that she had *fully* hedged in PA. There was a marked pattern in the sequence of trading in this experiment once prices were near to their PF values. The period would open with one or two errant (spot and futures) price signals away from the established equilibrium value, these bids or offers would go unaccepted (and were sometimes greeted with outward signs of amusement by other traders), and trading in spot *and then futures* would settle down at the previously established prices. Virtually all traders chose to establish their spot position and *then* enter the futures market.[11] Given this observed pattern in Y4, agent number 5 was 'locked in' to her spot position by an inability to buy in her futures position until the latter part of the period. She was able to buy five futures during PB, but was not able to sell any spot. However, she made no serious effort to extricate herself from her self-imposed corner by offering to buy futures for more than $0.80 and then offering to sell spot for less than $1.25 (the established PF prices).

From Table 2.5 we see that, with the notable exception of the episode in Y4 just described, virtually all of the 'non-bought' futures positions in PB represented *routine hedges*. This is not to say that all spot positions were hedged in this manner, or indeed that they were hedged at all (e.g. consider the holdings of type I in Y1, Y2 and Y3 shown in Table 2.4). However, Table 2.5 does indicate the extent of the hedge taken by those traders holding spot certificates who did not buy futures.

Period A (Spot): Given the futures prices available, PA spot prices as early as Y1 are well above their PI equilibrium value. Convergence to the PF value is nearly complete by the close of Y3 trading, and is complete by Y4. The 'technical reaction' in Y5, mentioned above, involved one trader aggressively bidding for spot certificates in PA at $2.05, some 5 cents higher than market signals would justify (given risk neutrality). Assessing her situation at the close of PA trading, the market 'allowed' her to lighten her spot holdings in PB at a discount (viz. some 5 cents below the PF price in PB). This is the same agent (number 5), incidentally, who tried to 'stonewall' the market in PB in Y4.

Allocations in each year were 13/18, 13/18, 13/18, 18/18 and 14/18 relative to the PF prediction. The alternative PI prediction accounts for 4/5, 5/5, 0/0 and 4/4 of the implied deviations in each year. The PA hedging ratio for non-bought futures certificates to spot holdings in Table 2.5 increases steadily throughout the experiment.[12]

4.1.2 Experiment 2. This is the first market with exogenous event uncertainty. Equilibrium prices in PB and PC were independent of the state of nature, but PA equilibrium prices were contingent. The futures certificate allocation predictions were contingent during PB trading, and PB spot allocation predictions were also contingent for the PI equilibrium concept. The random realizations of the state of nature provided a change of state in the first two years.

Period C (Futures): With uncertainty about the true state of nature in PA, futures prices in Y1 were at the EPI prediction. In Y2 there were several unaccepted bids at that value, and finally several trades closer to the URE prediction. From Y3 on, the PA futures prices were at the URE value. There were no futures trades in PA of Y5, but there was no *informational* need for any trades. That is, the non-acceptance of several bids just below the equilibrium value was a sufficient signal that the PC market valuation had not changed. After the first three trades in PB in Y1, virtually all PB futures prices in each year were at the predicted equilibrium level.

Spot allocations resulting in PC from PB futures positions were 15/18, 11/18 and 17/18 for the three X years (Y1, Y4 and Y5) relative to the equilibrium prediction, and 18/18 for each of the two Y years (Y2 and Y3). The misallocation in Y4 is discussed later.

Period B (Spot): There was a steady but slow movement of PB spot prices from the PI to the PF equilibrium prediction. This sluggish convergence occurred despite clear futures prices in PB as early as Y1 and the absence of any event uncertainty in PB.

Allocations showed a slow improvement to the PF prediction; they were 13/18, 11/18 and 17/18 in the X years, and 12/18 and 16/18 for the Y years. Virtually all of the misallocations in the Y years are explained by the alternative PI prediction. The severe misallocation in Y4 was due to one type I agent who failed to unload seven certificates, losing 60 cents on each one he failed to sell given prevailing prices (see below for further discussion). From Table 2.5 we note a clear tendency in PB towards the use of routine hedges.

Period A (Spot): Prices were below the EPI value in Y1, at the EPI value in Y2, and very slowly moving to the URE value in later years. The PC futures price signal was quite precise from Y3 on, although the PB spot signals were not as clear.

There were severe misallocations relative to the URE prediction, which was only correct in 6/18, 11/18, 9/18, 10/18 and 8/18 in each successive year. The alternative EPI prediction accounts for 5/12 and 5/7 of the misallocations in Y1 and Y2, respectively, but for *none* of the misallocations in the last three years. An explanation of these deviations as the result of event uncertainty is possible.

One implication of the presence of event uncertainty is the need to form some estimate of PC and PB prices *for each state* before forming reservation prices for PA trading. In the absence of event uncertainty such estimates could be *possible* as early as Y2 (even with a PC futures market in Y1, traders need to see PB spot prices for PA-valuation purposes). In the presence of event uncertainty, such estimates are only *possible* after traders had observed an X *and* a Y year, which could have been much later in the experiment if at all.[13] The necessarily greater amount of *initial* learning required to form URE reservation prices in PA (at least two years, compared to one year) in the presence of event uncertainty opened up numerous profitable disequilibrium trading strategies for certain traders that would be non-profitable at equilibrium prices. An excellent example of the availability of such *disequilibrium* strategies is provided in this experiment and accounts for the severe misallocations, relative to our *equilibrium* predictions, that were noted earlier.

The main culprit in the misallocations in Y3, Y4 and Y5 was a particular type III agent who went on a buying spree for PA spot (contrary to EPI and URE predictions). In Y1 and Y2 PB spot prices averaged \$1.618 and \$1.660, respectively; even if a trader had *not* realized that PB market valuations were state-independent, the expected PB price in Y3 would have been 0.5

(1.618) + 0.5 (1.660) = \$1.639. Given this estimate for PB prices and assuming risk neutrality on our type III agent's behalf, his reservation price in PA would have been composed of 0.5 (0.5) + 0.5 (0.3) = \$0.40 expected PA dividend *plus* a sale to market in PB for \$1.639, giving a total reservation price in PA of \$2.039. In fact he purchased at around \$1.97, sorrowfully learned that this was a Y year and collected his 30 cents dividend; he was then greeted with a PB spot market prepared to pay \$1.706 instead of the \$1.639 he had bargained for! Thus, despite Y3 being a 'bad year' for him, this trader was able to survive with a few cents profit.

The same strategy in Y4 and Y5, with some adjustment upwards in his PB estimate and hence his risk-neutral PA reservation price, earned him handsome profits (given that they were 'good years' for him in terms of PA dividends). Note that he was only able to profit from such a trading strategy because PA spot prices were so 'low'. Thus the misallocations in question were not at all due to this type III agent's irrationality or myopia, but market inefficiency in PA pricing. It was, in effect, the type I agents that were to 'blame', for not buying actively enough in PA.[14]

Relative to hedging behaviour in PB, we note from Table 2.5 a marked decline in the ratio of non-bought futures certificates to spot holdings in PA. In Y5, the third X year experienced, there was in fact no use of the futures market in PA for hedging purposes.

4.1.3 Experiment 3. This experiment introduces insiders into an event uncertainty environment. Parameters were chosen such that PA, PB *and* PC equilibrium *prices* were contingent. In Experiment 2 PB and PC equilibrium prices were not contingent, although the allocation predictions were.

Period C (Futures): Trading in PA of Y1 was at the EPI value. Surprisingly, however, it was the type III insider who bought in PA; his type is predicted to buy by the EPI rationale, but the insider knew that this was an X year. Perhaps realizing his error, he sold futures aggressively early in PB at low prices. The futures price eventually converged to the equilibrium value in PB.

A change in state occurred in Y2. In PA futures prices opened at the URE value, with the URE-predicted type III buying (only 2/6 to the insider) and type II selling (3/6 from the insider).

Futures prices then converged to the equilibrium PF and PI value for a Y year, possibly receiving a signal as to the true state of nature from PA *spot* prices (discussed further below). Type III bought (6/12 by the insider), as predicted by the PF and PI equilibria. Another Y realization occurred in Y3 and PA futures prices opened at the URE value. The type III outsider was buying from the type II insider at these prices. Consistent with leakage of insider information with these trades, futures prices in PA rapidly converged on their PF and PI equilibrium value for a Y year.

A fascinating thing happened in Y4: futures prices were at their PF and PI equilibrium value and a particular type I *outsider* began to mimic the trading stragegy of the type I *insider*. The insider sold two futures in PA, and the outsider sold three; the insider sold six futures in PB, and his 'shadow' sold five. This mimicry is also evident in the spot transactions of these two traders (discussed below).

In Y5 there was a return to state of nature Y. Following some intraperiod leakage of insider information in PA *spot* trading there was heavy futures trading at the PF and PI equilibrium prices. Futures prices in PB remained at this equilibrium.

Period B (Spot): Prices opened at a low level in Y1, generally at the PI value. *All* of the buyers were insiders and *all* of the sellers were outsiders. In PB spot prices were midway between the PI and PF equilibria; recall that initial PB futures price signals understated the true market value of a certificate in PC.

In Y3 an excellent futures price signal was available but there was only one spot trade in PB. This is easily explained: type II is predicted by PF equilibrium to hold spot certificates in PA *and* PB, and by the end of PA in Y3 indeed held all 18 spot certificates.[15] Thus there was simply no need for any spot trade in PB. The same result is observed in Y5, another Y year.

Y4 is an X year, with excellent futures price signals. Recall that a certain outsider had identified the insider of 'his' type; this accounts for their parallel spot purchases in PB. Despite this *partial leakage* of insider information to one outsider, PB spot prices were kept quite low at their PI equilibrium value.

Spot allocations in the Y years Y1, Y2 and Y3 were consistent with the PF prediction: 17/18, 18/18 and 18/18, respectively. The spot allocations in the X years Y1 and Y4 are severely misallocated relative to the PF prediction, with a mere 3/18 and 1/18 being correctly predicted. Moreover, only 8/15 and 1/17 of these deviations are explained by the alternative PI prediction. The explanation is the low PB spot prices (relative to the PF value) and the ability to lock-in profits with futures trades. Given the prevailing low PB spot prices *and the existence of a liquid futures contract,* the erstwhile type I 'culprits' did not lose on their spot purchases. This explanation accounts for 7/15 and 16/17 of the PF-deviations in Y1 and Y4. Given that type III agents were not buying in PB there was no opportunity cost to the type I agents pursuing their strategy. Note also that there was only a 5 cents difference in the PB dividends (per certificate) of types III and I.

Table 2.5 again indicates a strong tendency for hedging ratios to approach unity, indicating the adoption of routine hedges in PB.

Period A (Spot): In Y1 spot prices for PA certificates opened below the PI value, moved quickly to the EPI value, and settled around the PF value. The type I insider was an early bidder, and bought one unit at $1.10 and then another unit at $1.20; he thereby leaked this higher valuation to the market. The *selling* insiders generally held off until prices were above $1.25, reinforcing the leakage effect by refusing to supply at 'low' prices. Note also the tendency for spot prices to reach the PF value despite traders not having seen any PB spot valuations. This may have been due to two traders being able to sell PC futures at the 'overvalued' PC price (two of the four futures certificates were purchased by the type I insider), providing some justification for 'high' PA prices.

In Y2 there was a change in the state of nature. Spot prices opened below the URE value, passed throuh that value, and converged to the PI equilibrium. The final spot allocations hide heavy early buying by (non-PF-predicted) insiders at low prices for resale at higher prices later in the period. Spot prices in Y3, another Y year, opened where they had closed in Y2 (viz. at the PI value). There was then a sustained increase to the PF equilibrium value, accompanied by a parallel increase in futures prices from their URE value to their PF equilibrium. The type II insider was an early buyer at the lower prices.

Prices in Y4, the second X year, opened below the PI equilibrium for an X year and settled just above that value. Despite good futures price signals, the type I insider and his outsider 'shadow' were able to buy spot without any apparent leakage.

In Y5 spot prices picked up where they had closed in Y3, the most recent Y year. After opening midway between the PI and PF equilibria for a Y year, they increased steadily towards the PF equilibrium. The type II insider bought six of the first seven spot certificates traded, clearly revealing his inside information. The first five spot sales were by outsiders; again, the selling insiders held off before trading their endowments, in the knowledge that spot prices should be higher than was being initially offered.

Spot allocations in the X years Y1 and Y4 improve from 6/18 to 13/18 relative to the PF prediction, with the competing EPI prediction explaining 7/12 and 3/5 of the PF misallocations. Allocations in the Y years, Y2, Y3 and Y5, are consistent with the PF prediction: 10/18, 18/18 and 18/18, respectively, are correctly predicted. Corresponding to the relative performance of the PF spot predictions in X and Y years is the relative tendency towards routine hedges in Y years (see Table 2.5). The PA hedging ratios are much lower than those at the end of PB, a pattern also found in Experiment 2.

4.2 Comparative Market Behaviour

Tables 2.6 and 2.7 present descriptive statistics on the deviations of observed prices and allocations from predicted equilibrium values. Our measure of price convergence in Table 2.6 is the Root Mean Squared Deviation (RMSD) of transacted from predicted (equilibrium) price. Our measure of allocation convergence in Table 2.7 is the number of certificates misallocated relative to the prediction.[16] Our predictions about futures certificate allocations by the end of Period A are quite weak: the futures market opens again in Period B of each year, allowing traders further opportunity to establish their final positions. Moreover, we expect Period A futures positions to be taken by traders with no intent of holding that position at the end of Period B, as well as by traders who do have such an intent.

In Table 2.8 we examine the significance of the effects of event uncertainty (EU) and inside information (II) on market performance as measured by the forecast errors in Tables 2.6 and 2.7. The significance of these effects is given by the probability that the treatment variable indicated *increases* forecast error in prices or allocations. These probabilities are obtained from a (one-tail) non-parametric Mann-Whitney test for the 'slippage problem'; see Hoel (1971, pp. 310-18) or Conover (1980, pp. 215-23) for a

Table 2.6: Root Mean Squared Deviations from Equilibrium Price Predictions

			Spot Prices						Futures Prices				
				Period A			Period B			Period A			Period B
Experiment	Year	State	EPI	PI	URE	PF	PI	PF	EPI	PI	URE	PF	PI − PF
1	1	—	—	0.297	—	0.532	0.155	0.155	—	0.050	—	0.050	0.114
	2	—	—	0.104	—	0.342	0.087	0.087	—	0.044	—	0.044	0.018
	3	—	—	0.128	—	0.164	0.010	0.010	—	0.050	—	0.050	0.009
	4	—	—	0.232	—	0.022	0.001	0.001	—	0.019	—	0.019	0.003
	5	—	—	0.272	—	0.032	0.031	0.031	—	0.007	—	0.007	0.013
2	1	X	0.161	—	0.595	—	0.027	0.183	0.019	—	0.158	—	0.018
	2	Y	0.023	—	0.434	—	0.062	0.141	0.090	—	0.060	—	0.003
	3	Y	0.121	—	0.330	—	0.107	0.094	0.140	—	0.013	—	0.006
	4	X	0.182	—	0.269	—	0.126	0.074	0.144	—	0.008	—	0.014
	5	X	0.199	—	0.251	—	0.143	0.057	—	—	—	—	0.016
3	1	X	0.077	0.121	0.215	0.089	0.089	0.161	0.0	0.050	0.075	0.050	0.055
	2	Y	0.229	0.076	0.073	0.307	0.076	0.079	0.133	0.073	0.061	0.073	0.025
	3	Y	0.337	0.074	0.165	0.197	0.130	0.020	0.189	0.030	0.115	0.030	0.0
	4	X	0.127	0.040	0.289	0.151	0.024	0.112	0.062	0.013	0.137	0.013	0.011
	5	Y	0.412	0.139	0.238	0.118	—	—	0.188	0.013	0.113	0.013	0.007

Table 2.7: Number of Certificates Misallocated Relative to Equilibrium Predictions

				Spot Certificates					Futures Certificates		
				Period A			Period B		Period A		Period B
Experiment	Year	State	EPI	PI	URE	PF	PI	PF	EPI	PI—PF	PI—PF
1	1	—	—	5	—	5	5	5	—	15	4
	2	—	—	5	—	5	0	0	—	13	0
	3	—	—	5	—	5	0	0	—	13	0
	4	—	—	0	—	0	7	7	—	11	5
	5	—	—	4	—	4	2	2	—	5	3
2	1	X	13	—	12	—	16	5	12	12	5
	2	Y	13	—	7	—	13	6	20	18	5
	3	Y	18	—	9	—	16	2	20	19	2
	4	X	18	—	8	—	18	7	15	15	7
	5	X	18	—	10	—	18	1	18	18	1
3	1	X	12	12	12	12	10	15	14	20	11
	2	Y	10	10	18	8	18	1	12	12	2
	3	Y	18	18	18	0	18	0	5	5	2
	4	X	15	5	5	5	17	17	16	15	1
	5	Y	18	18	18	0	18	0	6	6	0

Note: Derived from Tables 2.3 and 2.4.

formal discussion.[17] The weaker-form (stronger-form) Period A equilibria used for this test in Experiments 1, 2 and 3 are, respectively, PI (PF), EPI (URE) and EPI (PF). The relevant equilibria in Period B are, of course, PI and PF in each experiment.

Consider the results in Table 2.8 for the *stronger-form* (SF) comparisons of *price RMSD.* There is some evidence that EU slightly decreases forecast error in PA prices, convincing evidence that II decreases forecast error, and a presumption that EU and II *jointly* have no effect on PA prices. The probability that EU increases SF forecast error in PB prices is very high, even when II is also present. The pooled results for PA and PB prices support the conclusion that EU and II have strong and offsetting individual effects on SF forecast errors, and that their joint effect is about equal (with perhaps a slight dominance of EU). The results for the *weaker-form* (WF) comparisons in PA prices are consistent with these conclusions.

Now consider the results for the *SF* comparisons of *certificate misallocations.* They strongly support the conclusion that EU increases misallocations, II decreases misallocations, and that they

Table 2.8: Effects of Event Uncertainty and Inside Information on Market Performance

			Spot Market						Futures Market				
			Period A		Period B		Period A and Period B		Period A		Period B	Period A and Period B	
Performance Measure	Experiments Compared	Treatment Variable	WF	SF	WF	SF	WF	SF	WF	SF	WF=SF	WF	SF
Prices	1 and 2	EU	0.155	0.345	0.845	0.925	0.485	0.962	0.944	0.722	0.421	0.610	0.302
	2 and 3	II	0.889	0.016	0.365	0.452	0.573	0.121	0.635	0.905	0.655	0.579	0.610
	1 and 3	EU and II	0.579	0.5	0.794	0.857	0.640	0.630	0.952	0.579	0.421	0.736	0.485
Allocations	1 and 2	EU	1.0	1.0	1.0	0.790	1.0	0.993	—	—	0.889	—	—
	2 and 3	II	0.232	0.111	0.726	0.345	0.367	0.218	—	—	0.210	—	—
	1 and 3	EU and II	0.995	0.655	1.0	0.655	0.999	0.685	—	—	0.5	—	—

Notes: EU — Event Uncertainty; II — Inside Information; WF — Weaker-form; SF — Stronger-form.
The values shown are the probability that the treatment variable *increases forecast error* in the particular performance measure.

have roughly offsetting effects when considered jointly (again, with a slight EU dominance). These conclusions hold for the PA and PB results, as well as in spot and futures markets.

Table 2.9 shows the significance of the effect of our treatment variables on the hedging ratios listed in Table 2.5. A Mann-Whitney test is also used, with the same general interpretation as in Table 2.8. The results support the conclusions drawn in Section 4.1: EU has the effect of discouraging Period A routine hedges (i.e. EU lowers the hedge ratio), and II has the opposite effect. These results are particularly significant when we use our preferred measure of the hedging ratio, with 'non-bought futures' in the numerator. Using this measure we also note that the II effect clearly dominates the EU effect when we consider the two measurements jointly.

5. Concluding Remarks

The three experimental markets studied support the following broad conclusions: (i) the presence of event uncertainty tends to retard the efficiency of asset markets, as measured by the extent to which prices and allocations reflect stronger-form equilibria; (ii) the presence of conclusive inside information encourages efficiency in an event uncertainty environment; (iii) the presence of event uncertainty *and* inside information have roughly offsetting effects on efficiency, although the effect of event uncertainty dominates slightly; (iv) event uncertainty is associated with a marked tendency to depart from routine hedging behaviour; and (v) the presence of conclusive inside information encourages the adoption of routine hedges, even when event uncertainty is a joint treatment variable.

It should be emphasized that our conclusions are drawn from a small sample of observations. A major methodological attraction of our experimental method, of course, is that our results may be confirmed or rejected by subsequent experiments designed to replicate ours. This feature is particularly important if our results are used in any adversarial context (e.g. the formation of policy concerning the treatment of 'insiders'); see Kirkwood (1981, pp. 616-21) for a discussion of the probative value of experiments in anti-trust cases. Moreover, although our conclusions have been drawn from a small sample we have relatively precise *prior* know-

Table 2.9: Effects of Event Uncertainty and Inside Information on Hedging Ratio

Experiments Compared	Treatment Variable	Ratio of Sold Futures to Spot Holdings		Ratio of Non-Bought Futures to Spot Holdings	
		Period A	Period B	Period A	Period B
1 and 2	EU	0.206	0.421	0.210	0.345
2 and 3	II	0.548	0.655	0.952	0.579
1 and 3	EU and II	0.075	0.5	0.925	0.421

Note: The values shown are the probability that the treatment variable *increases* the hedging ratio.

ledge concerning market structure and parameters. Thus the inferences we can draw from a given sample are relatively strong.

There are many directions in which one could extend our experimental design, several of which are the subject of continuing research. The effect of uncertain or incomplete inside information about the state of nature, such as implemented by Plott and Sunder (1982; Experiment 1) and Plott and Sunder (1983) respectively, could be compared to our examination of the effect of conclusive inside information. The effect of insider anonymity could be easily studied, as could the wider issue of the privacy of individual trader positions; computer mediation in experiments, such as introduced by Williams (1980), would greatly facilitate such extensions. Non-binding and binding price controls are a pervasive feature of many important agricultural spot markets which also feature heavily-traded futures markets; the price-control experiments of Isaac and Plott (1981) and Smith and Williams (1981) may be extended to asset markets with or without futures trading. A similar methodology could be used to study the effects of price limits and/ or price ranges on futures price movements. Finally, our experimental design could be extended to include deterministic or stochastic production activities and the effects of futures markets on them.

Notes

*University of Western Ontario, Canada. I am indebted to Daniel Friedman and Jon Salmon for helpful discussions, the Center for the Study of Futures

Markets (Columbia University) and the Social Sciences and Humanities Research Council of Canada for research support, and Len-Kuo Hu for research assistance. The usual disclaimer applies.

1. The material in the next few paragraphs is taken, with some slight modifications, from Friedman, Harrison and Salmon (1984, Section 1).

2. This result apparently conflicts with some conclusions drawn by Forsythe, Palfrey and Plott (1982b), hereafter FPPb. They extended their earlier study in two respects. They adopted a pay-out structure that was 'time-interdependent', in the sense that agents could not simply add their earnings from each trading period together to compute their earnings for the entire market experiment. Thus each agent's monetary returns from holding assets in a given-year were a non-additive (indeed, non-linear) function of the number of assets held in each period. The main implication of this unusual design feature is that an agent's return from holding assets in the final period of each market year depends on that agent's holdings at the end of the previous period of that year. The other extension was to study the informational role of futures markets in sequential asset markets more systematically than was done in FPPa. Nine experiments were conducted: five included a futures market and four did not. Note that FPPb are primarily concerned with the *joint* treatment variable of 'experience *and* the presence of a futures market'. Their control experiments (1, 3, 6 and 8) employed inexperienced subjects in a sequential spot market with a futures market. Their comparison experiments (2, 4, 7 and 9) employed experienced subjects in a sequential spot market without the presence of a futures market. FPPb intentionally designed their treatment variable in this manner in order to provide a strong test of the proposition that sequential spot markets converge more rapidly to an informationally efficient equilibrium when futures markets are present. FHSa was particularly concerned to isolate the separate roles of 'experience' and 'futures markets', thereby allowing an unambiguous conclusion with respect to the role of futures markets *alone* on spot price volatility.

3. The experiments listed as 1, 2 and 3 in the present study are listed as 2, 4 and 6 respectively, in FHSb. Further, our Experiment 1 has also been reported as Experiment 4 in FHSa. Note that although there is some overlap with these studies in our discussion of experimental design, the detailed results and market comparisons in Section 4 have not previously been reported. This type of overlap of experiments is common in the literature, as a market that contains a treatment variable in one study may be used as the control experiment in a subsequent study.

4. The material in this section is a modification of Friedman, Harrison and Salmon (1983, Section 2.2).

5. Any trader was free to accept the bid or offer currently before the market, but could not accept previous bids or offers. FPPa apparently allowed the latter procedure, since their raw data are recorded in order of tender and do not necessarily record acceptances in their real-time sequence. Our procedure has the advantages of allowing an 'ex post' check that all transactions satisfy budget and trading restrictions, and facilitating the type of analysis of real-time price formation processes presented in Friedman and Harrison (1984).

6. Plott and Sunder (1983) is the first study to allow short (spot) positions *within* a trading period. They employ a simple and apparently effective penalty on any trader short at the *end* of any period (viz. a fixed pecuniary penalty plus the requirement that the trader implicitly cover himself at the highest transaction price during the period).

7. A minor exception in Year 5 of Experiment 1 is noted in Table 2.1.

8. Plott and Sunder (1983) introduce the idea of actually announcing states of nature from a predetermined sequence. Although there is no evidence that this occurred in their experiments, we were concerned that traders not begin to 'second-guess' the sequence of events.

9. Inconclusive insider information (a series of 'clues' as to the true state) has been examined experimentally in Experiment 1 of PS. They find that convergence to the rational expectations equilibrium is much slower in this case compared to experiments with conclusive inside information. Plott and Sunder (1983) also implement inconclusive inside information (no trader knows the true state, but their pooled information set is conclusive).

10. FHSa define the PI equilibrium assuming that traders only know their *private* valuation of Period C certificates. This is a weaker concept than employed here. The present definition of PI equilibrium follows FHSb, and corresponds to the concept of 'Market Information' equilibrium in FHSa.

11. This is definitely *not* the observed pattern in earlier years in which the transition from PI to PF prices is incomplete. In these years there is a healthy mixture of concurrent spot and futures trading.

12. The behaviour of the type I traders in Y1, Y2 and Y3, holding 13/18 spot certificates and not selling *any* futures, illustrates the value of reporting the two different ratios in Table 2.5.

13. In fact it had occurred *prior* to Y3 in Experiments 2 and 3.

14. A simple explanation for their inactivity could of course be a severe aversion to risk. Thus we italicize the word 'blame'.

15. Note that type II is also predicted to hold spot certificates in PA by the EPI equilibrium concept.

16. The futures certificate predictions refer to the trader type predicted to be *long*. If that trader type is actually *short* in futures, the misallocation listed in Table 2.7 will exceed 18 certificates.

17. We state the test outcomes in terms of the probability of the hypothesis that slippage has occurred in favour of higher forecast errors in the second experiment listed. The alternative hypothesis is that both samples arise from the same population.

References

Conover, W.J. (1980) *Practical Non-Parametric Statistics*, New York: Wiley, 2nd edn.

Cox, C.C., (1976) 'Futures Trading and Market Information', *Journal of Political Economy*, vol. 84, 1215-37.

Forsythe, R., T.R. Palfrey and C.R. Plott [FPPa] (1982a) 'Asset Valuation in an Experimental Market', *Econometrica*, vol. 50, 537-67.

— [FPPb], (1982b) 'Futures Markets and Informational Efficiency: A Laboratory Examination', *GSIA Working Paper No. 11-81-83*, Carnegie-Mellon University.

Friedman, D. and G.W. Harrison (1984) 'Price Formation in Experimental Asset Markets: A Bayesian Approach', unpublished manuscript, Department of Economics, University of Western Ontario.

Friedman, D., G.W. Harrison and J.W. Salmon [FHSa] (1983) 'The Informational Role of Futures Markets: Some Experimental Evidence', in M.E. Streit (ed.), *Futures Markets — Modelling, Managing and Monitoring Futures Trading*, Oxford: Basil Blackwell.

— [FHSb] (1984) 'The Informational Efficiency of Experimental Asset Markets', *Journal of Political Economy*, vol. 92, 3, June.

Hoel, P.G. (1971) *Introduction to Mathematical Statistics*, New York: Wiley, 4th edn.

Isaac, R.M. and C.R. Plott (1981) 'Price Controls and the Behaviour of Auction

Markets: An Experimental Examination', *American Economic Review,* vol. 71, 448-59.
Kirkwood, J.B. (1981) 'Antitrust Implications of the Recent Experimental Literature on Collusion', in S.C. Salop (ed.), *Strategy, Predation and Antitrust Analysis,* Washington, D.C., US Federal Trade Commission.
Leamer, E.E. (1978) *Specification Searches: Ad Hoc Inference with Non-Experimental Data,* New York: Wiley.
— (1983) 'Let's Take the Con Out of Econometrics', *American Economic Review,* vol. 73, 31-43.
Plott, C.R. (1982) 'Industrial Organization Theory and Experimental Economics', *Journal of Economic Literature,* vol. 20, 1485-527.
Plott, C.R. and S. Sunder [PS] (1982) 'Efficiency of Experimental Security Markets with Insider Information: An Application of Rational-Expectations Models', *Journal of Political Economy,* vol. 90, 663-98.
— (1983) 'Rational Expectations and the Aggregation of Diverse Information in Laboratory Security Markets', *Social Science Working Paper No. 463,* Division of the Humanities and Social Sciences, California Institute of Technology.
Smith, V.L. (1982) 'Microeconomic Systems as an Experimental Science', *American Economic Review,* Vol. 72, 923-55.
Smith, V.L. and A.W. Williams (1981) 'On Nonbinding Price Controls in a Competitive Market', *American Economic Review,* vol. 71, 467-74.
Williams, A.W. (1980) 'Computerized Double-Auction Markets: Some Initial Experimental Results', *Journal of Business,* vol. 53, 235-58.

3 HEDGING, RISK AND PROFITS: NOTES ON MOTIVES FOR HEDGING ON FUTURES MARKETS

Basil Yamey*

1. Hedging and Price Risks

Once upon a time hedging by means of transactions in futures contracts was almost universally regarded as a practice intended by the hedger to avoid, reduce or eliminate the risk of price changes by shifting that risk on to others willing to bear it. Hedging was almost always defined, described or discussed in these terms, both in materials addressed to those engaged in business and also in academic publications. The analogy with insurance was commonly drawn. Here are some quotations from the work of the leading academic authors who had addressed themselves to the economics of futures trading before the Second World War.

For Alfred Marshall, the hedger 'does not speculate: he insures'. The short hedger 'by buying a future ... does *not* speculate; he throws on the shoulders of the general market the risks and the chances of gain that would have come to him through general movements external to his own business' (Marshall, 1919, p. 260). J.G. Smith wrote that the 'essence of the operation [of hedging]' is for the hedger to eliminate 'speculative risks for himself'. Hedging enables hedgers 'to insure against the risk of price fluctuations' (Smith, 1922, pp. 81, 95). Charles O. Hardy wrote that the hedger 'is securing protection against a definite risk in much the same way that one secures protection against unknown hazard through Lloyd's policy' (Hardy, 1923, p. 72).

As is well known, John Maynard Keynes discussed hedging in terms of risk avoidance and insurance (Keynes, 1930, vol. 2, pp. 142-4). John Hicks explained that the 'ordinary business man only enters into a forward contract if by so doing he can "hedge" — that is to say, if the forward transaction lessens the riskiness of his position' (Hicks, 1939, p. 137). And Kaldor pithily expressed the by then familiar notion that 'it is the speculators who assume the risks and the hedgers who get rid of them' (Kaldor, 1939-40, p. 197).

It follows from this line of thinking that any loss made by the hedger on the completed hedged transaction (i.e. in the case of short hedging, on the purchase and subsequent sale of the actuals, and on the sale and subsequent purchase of the futures) represents a sort of insurance premium paid to the risk-assuming speculator (e.g. Keynes, 1930, pp. 142-3); some authors added that the foregoing of the chance of making a profit on the unhedged actuals commitment is also an insurance premium paid for risk-avoidance (e.g. Smith, 1922, p. 86; Smith cautioned that the insurance analogy 'must not be pushed too far'). Some noted that in some market situations the premium might be too high, so that 'potential hedgers will prefer not to hedge' (Hicks, 1939, p. 139).

The most complete and elaborate discussion of hedging was that of G. Wright Hoffman. He also wrote about hedging in terms similar to those used by his contemporaries. 'The entire activity of future trading consists in either assuming risk as speculators or in shifting risk as hedgers' and: 'By hedging their purchases (or forward sales) [of actuals], they shift this price hazard to the shoulders of those assuming the opposite end of their hedges' (Hoffman, 1932, pp.4, 379-80). But his detailed study went well beyond the rather limited treatment to be found in the sparse theoretical literature, and in a number of directions drew attention to features which were to be given considerably more emphasis by others in some of the post-war contributions to the subject. For example, he carefully explained that for short hedging to be fully effective in eliminating risk it was undesirable that actuals and futures prices should move together in perfect parallelism; and he noted that skilful hedgers could make profits from their hedging if 'able to foresee ... relative changes in price'. He concluded that it was 'the business of hedgers ... to foresee accurately and take advantage of gains in basis and to avoid as far as possible basis losses' (Hoffman, 1932, pp. 409, 418).[1] All this is a far cry from the notion, most uncompromisingly expressed by Keynes, that hedgers regularly make 'losses' on their hedging, and do so willingly in exchange for the avoidance of the risk of larger losses on price movements.

Hoffman, however, did not lose sight of what he and his contemporaries considered to be the central element in hedging, namely the avoidance or reduction of the risk of loss from adverse price changes by transfer of the risk to others called speculators. Hedging and the avoidance or reduction of the risk of price changes went together, the former being motivated by the demand for the latter. In this respect some of the post-war developments in the specialist literature represent a significant break with tradition, as will be shown below. Some economists, in this new tradition, have taken great pains to avoid the risk of seeming to associate hedging in futures, or the operation of futures markets, with avoidance of the risk of price changes. The change in attitude cannot be accounted for as having been inspired by changes in the practice of hedging.[2]

2. Arbitrage Hedging in Perspective

It is self-evident that anyone hedging a commitment in actuals by the sale or purchase of futures contracts (whether or not equal in volume to the actuals commitment) places himself in a position which he regards as better than any other course of action open to him. A trader, processor or manufacturer hedges whenever he believes that hedging increases his income, pecuniary and non-pecuniary income taken together. It is evident that the total income from a hedged transaction is not necessarily the same as the direct *pecuniary income* derived from the change in the 'basis' over the life of the hedge — basis being the difference between the price of the futures contract used as the hedge and the price of the actuals or physicals (the commodity) involved.

Thus for a short-hedging trader the sources of income are as follows: (a) the direct pecuniary gain (loss), measured by the change in the basis; (b) indirect pecuniary gains, which are the counterpart of the convenience yield and stem from the trader's ability to satisfy promptly the unexpected requirements of preferred customers — a gain which in part may take the form of profits on further transactions with customers with whom the trader's goodwill is maintained or enhanced;[3] and (c) the non-pecuniary income enjoyed by a risk-averse trader as a result of his reduced exposure to price changes.[4] From this subdivision of gains from hedging it follows that a trader may carry a stock of the commodity and hedge it (fully or partially) even when he expects to incur a direct pecuniary loss as the result of a confidently expected unfavourable change in the basis.

In a series of papers beginning in 1948, Holbrook Working (whose contributions to the study of the economics of futures trading overshadow those of any of his predecessors, contemporaries or successors) placed heavy stress on hedging entered into by hedgers with the intention and expectation of making direct pecuniary profits. This type of hedging, which, following Working, may be termed carrying-charge or arbitrage hedging, is said to be motivated by the prospects, indeed sometimes the near certainty, of pecuniary profit resulting from changes in the basis relative to the cost of carrying inventory over time. Working has emphasized that this sort of hedging 'is not properly comparable with insurance'. It is not done 'from any special desire to minimise risks'.[5] In fact,

> the general concept of hedging as taking offsetting risks wholly, or even primarily, for the sake of reducing net risk, serves so badly as applied to most hedging on futures markets that we need another concept for that most common sort of hedging. To put it briefly, we may say that hedging in commodity futures involves the purchase or sale of futures in conjunction with another commitment, usually in the expectation of a favourable change in the relation between spot [actuals] and futures prices.[6]

The general impression left on the reader may well be that it is carrying-charge hedging that predominates in practice. And Anne Peck, writing in 1977, summarizes Working's views in these terms (Peck, 1977, p. 152):

> Working presents a completely revised view of hedger behavior. Hedgers are seen to be arbitragers, constantly evaluating the cash [actuals] price relative to the futures price, seeking to profit from differential moves in these prices. The continuing concern with the basis and its expected changes is at the center of each form of hedging Working delineates.

In fact, Working's position had become rather more complex than this.[7]

The richness of Working's treatment of hedging is apparent, for example, in an interesting shift in approach between two papers published respectively in 1953 and 1962. In the earlier paper Working writes:

> Incidentally, recognition of the fact that hedging may be done purely as a logical consequence of the reasoning on which the hedger acts (reasoning, for example, that the spot price is low relative to the future) rather than from any special desire to minimise risks, helps explain why many dealers and processors sometimes hedge and sometimes do not.

Here selectivity in hedging or the exercise of discretion in the decision whether to hedge or not depends upon expectations about changes in the basis. In the 1962 article, however, selective or discretionary hedging is not discussed in the section on carrying-charge hedging. Indeed, it is said that with carrying-charge hedging the potential hedger's decision 'is not primarily whether to hedge or not, but whether to store or not' (Working, 1962, p. 438).

Instead, a new type of hedging, 'selective hedging', is introduced and discussed separately. Here selectivity or discretion is exercized not according to the potential hedger's expectations about changes in *basis* but according to his expectations about changes in *price.* Now this sounds uncommonly like risk-avoidance or insurance-type hedging. However, Working wishes to avoid any such identification. He writes: 'Because the stocks are hedged when a price decline is expected, the purpose of [selective] hedging is not risk avoidance, in the strict sense, but avoidance of loss' (Working, 1962, p. 440). But there is no indication here or elsewhere how confident the hedger must be about his price expectation for his resulting hedging decision to be classed as one stemming from the desire to avoid loss rather than from the desire to avoid risk. In fact, Working clarifies his point of view when he equates 'pure risk-avoidance' hedging with routine hedging, which he says is 'unimportant or virtually non-existent in modern business practice' (Working, 1962, p. 442). This equation is made even more explicit in a paper published eight years later: 'if a business-man "hedges" regularly, making no effort to judge what price change is likely to occur, I shall call that "insurance-type" hedging' (Working, 1970, p. 33).

Now I doubt whether any applied economist who has described hedging as risk-avoiding has had in mind the routine and automatic covering of the hedger's entire actuals commitment practised by an entirely passive hedger[8] – one who hedges regardless of the 'premium' (if any) to be paid and the risk to be run unhedged. Working created a straw-man, and found him to have few counterparts in the real world. Oddly enough, it is Working who has provided examples of just such cases; the grain and cotton trades, he writes, are 'the principal ones in which routine hedging is accepted as a standard practice in most parts of the country' (Working, 1962, p. 440).

The view *à la* Working that arbitrage or carrying-charge hedging is preponderant in practice, that is to say the view that most hedging is done in the expectation of a direct pecuniary profit, has been expressed trenchantly by Roger Gray (1960, p. 77): 'Most hedgers are arbitragers trying to get ahead in the world', not 'a queer sort of conservative commercial idiot striving always and only to break even'. Nevertheless, as I have shown elsewhere (Yamey, 1968, pp. 360-1), both Working and Gray have referred in various writings to hedging which evidently is not carrying-charge hedging or speculation on basis changes, but is described in language which points directly to the notion of risk-avoidance hedging.

> Thus Working has referred to 'hedging pressure', a phenomenon which is incompatible with arbitrage hedging. He has also referred to the 'price at which hedged stocks will be carried', and to the rendering of a 'service for which hedgers are willing to pay'; and similarly, Gray has written: 'Coffee importers who require a short hedge have paid for it, as have short hedgers in Minneapolis wheat futures'. The inappropriateness for arbitrage hedging of such notions as paying a price for a service is obvious. Arbitrage hedging pertains to action based on the perception of a profitable opportunity. The arbitrage hedger is not under any constraint to act: he operates when he expects relative prices to move in his favour, and refrains when he does not. He does not need a 'service' which has a cost and for which he is prepared to pay. Yet, to take another example, both Working and Gray have written of hedging 'needs' or the 'need' for hedging — expressions which seem to apply more aptly to the practice of insurance hedging by those who want to hold stocks but to reduce the associated risk.

However, perhaps the most pronounced withdrawal from Working's position on the preponderance of carrying-charge hedging is to be seen in a different context from that just noted.

In a path-breaking paper published in 1967, Working examines the activities of floor traders or scalpers on futures exchanges. One of his conclusions is that 'to the extent that hedging orders affect the price, [short] hedgers tend to sell on price dips and to buy on price bulges'. They therefore 'tend to lose money on their transactions in futures'. Put differently, 'because the price dips and bulges occasioned by "market orders", and by bunches of such orders, are often fairly large, hedgers must incur a substantial cost [called the execution cost], in the form of price concessions, through their frequent use of market orders to insure prompt execution when they place their hedges, and again when they lift them'. The recognition of execution costs does not itself cast doubt on Working's earlier position on carrying-charge hedging; it simply means that the costs involved in hedging are higher than otherwise, regardless of the type of hedging involved. But Working goes much further. He asserts that 'the income flow from hedgers to speculators is much larger than has previously been estimated, and has been positive and substantial even in markets and during periods in which the seasonal trend of futures prices by itself has afforded no income, or has been a source of loss, to speculators as a group' (Working, 1967, pp. 5,44). Now this passage must mean that short hedgers tend to lose money on their completed hedged transactions (i.e. taking actuals and futures transactions together) in periods in which prices of the commodity have fallen or have been stable. Yet hedging is said to take place in these circumstances and to produce an 'income flow from hedgers to speculators'.[9]

Neither Working nor Gray (1967, p. 181) seems to be aware that this account of the importance of execution costs seriously undermines the notion of the preponderance of hedging of the arbitrage or carrying-charge type, which should tend to produce direct pecuniary profits for the hedgers, subject only to the risk of abnormal or unexpected basis changes. If it is true that hedgers tend to lose money on their completed hedged transactions in periods of price decline or stability, and should expect to do so in those conditions, they cannot then be arbitrage hedgers striving to 'get ahead in the world', not content merely to 'break even', let alone to lose money. In one respect this breed of hedgers are then close relatives of Keynes's variety of old-fashioned insurance-type hedgers made prominent in his theory of normal backwardation. Both are willing to 'lose money' to the accommodating speculators. The difference between them is that the former are willing to pay a price, the 'execution cost', in order to have the 'convenience' of prompt execution of their orders (Gray, 1967, p. 181; and 1972, p. 336), while the latter are willing to pay a price, the 'insurance premium', in order to be relieved of the risk of adverse price changes. What is clear is that both types are said to hedge even in market situations in which they would not expect to break even or make pecuniary profits (although, of course, as noted above, they would not hedge at all unless they considered hedging to improve their position).

In any event, the explanation that hedgers are willing to pay a price to speculators for the convenience of prompt execution of their orders begs the question why they should want to have hedging orders executed at all. The fact that hedging in futures flourishes only in respect of commodities and other assets subject to considerable price volatility suggests strongly that it is the avoidance or reduction of price risk that is involved, and that hedgers are prepared to pay something for its achievement.

3. Properties of Futures Markets

In three recent papers (one in collaboration with Harlow Higinbotham), Professor Lester Telser has argued that 'it is not the demand for price insurance that explains why there is an organized futures market' (Telser, 1980, p. 16). He is concerned to focus on what he calls 'the more fundamental properties of an organized exchange', and to criticize the erroneous convention adopted by 'most of the economists who have written on the subject', of 'focusing their attention on hedging and speculation' (Telser and Higinbotham, 1977, p. 972). His explanation of the existence of organized futures markets, 'briefly is this. An organized futures market facilitates trade among strangers' (Telser, 1981, p. 1). Moreover, it meets 'the demand for a fungible financial instrument traded in a liquid market' (Telser, 1980, p. 16).

The main point of attack on the traditional explanation, it seems, is that 'an organized futures market is not necessary in order to obtain the advantages of hedging' (Telser and Higinbotham, 1977, p. 970; also Telser, 1980, p. 14 and 1981, p. 5). Now this is certainly true of insurance-type hedging, the type to which Telser addresses his observations. Indeed, the same point that there are alternatives to hedging in futures is made in some of the earlier literature, beginning with Marshall.[10]

It is true that the earlier writings do not say much, if anything at all, about the impersonality of futures trading and the liquidity of active futures markets, characteristics on which Telser and Higinbotham properly lay considerable stress — perhaps the earlier authors took these things for granted.[11]

But whether or not earlier writers dealt with some of the points made by Telser, his objections to the conventional approach leave open the question why the 'fundamental properties' of futures trading arrangements are valued by those who use futures markets.[12] The fact, borne out most tellingly in the Telser-Higinbotham article[13], that these markets thrive only when there is considerable price volatility points to the conclusion that their hedger users are largely motivated by the desire to avoid or reduce the risk of adverse price changes. That hedgers usually prefer to use futures markets, where these are active, rather than to make other arrangements for 'hedging' their price risks, reflects no more than that for them futures contracts and futures markets have advantages of the kind emphasized by Telser.

Similar considerations apply to speculation. Speculators do not need organized futures markets to exercise their forecasting skills or to try their luck. But futures markets obviously facilitate speculation, just as they do hedging.

It does not follow that it is analytically or descriptively more relevant or correct to concentrate on the properties of an institution rather than on the uses to which the institution is put. Moreover, although Telser claims that his explanation of the existence of futures markets 'has more predictive power' than two rival views he identifies (Telser, 1981, p. 1), in fact the analytical model presented provides no way for discriminating between the existence of an organized market *without* futures trading and that of an organized market *with* futures trading.[14]

As regards the important question why there are futures markets for some commodities (and other assets) but not for others, the paper by Telser and Higinbotham, although it has few surprises, elaborates and refines the discussion inaugurated by Marshall in 1919. In particular their contribution is evident in their analysis of a feature which corresponds loosely to Marshall's condition that to be 'suitable to be handled in an organised market' a 'class of products' must be 'important enough to occupy large bodies of buyers and sellers' (Marshall, 1919, p. 256). Telser and

Higinbotham show that volume is important in reducing the unit costs of trading. Moreover, their proposition that the 'benefit of an organised market is an increasing function of the number of potential participants' and 'also an increasing function of the turnover of the potential participants in that market' (Telser and Higinbotham, 1977, p. 997) is interesting, although the proposition itself cannot be derived from the formal theory they present.

Telser and Higinbotham are critical of the hedging defence of futures markets on the grounds that the total of benefits flowing from such markets exceeds the benefit to hedgers alone, and, by implication, that the other components of benefit are more valuable than the benefit to hedgers. Working is mentioned as one 'who always put the emphasis on the functions of a futures market aside from its advantages to hedgers' (Telser and Higinbotham, 1977, p. 972). However, in so far as Working may have placed considerable emphasis on non-hedging benefits, he was anticipated by Hoffman, an author neglected by Telser and his co-author. Hoffman wrote (1932, p. 377):

> The feature stressed as being of greatest value has usually been the practice of hedging. This has been due partly to the fact that it is widely used and partly because the value of this function can be clearly demonstrated. The market-making function is also far-reaching in its effect but its economic value is much more difficult to demonstrate.

A further point is of interest. Hedging and speculation result in business from which those who constitute and operate the futures exchange benefit directly, for example, in the form of commissions. The wider economic benefits which flow from futures markets (e.g. improvements in price formation and reduction in the amplitude of price fluctuations) are of a public-goods character, and those who organize and operate the market are not requited for helping to make them possible. From the point of view of 'economic welfare' there may be too few futures markets for this reason alone. It may well be, however, that social benefits exceed appropriable private benefits in the case of all market institutions, and not only of those with futures trading.

4. Concluding Observations

As early as 1953 Working offered the following definition of hedging (Working, 1953b, p. 560): 'Hedging in futures consists of making a contract to buy or sell on standard terms, established and supervised by a commodity exchange, as a temporary substitute for an intended later contract to buy or sell on other terms.'

The comprehensiveness of the definition is evident. And this is perhaps the reason why it has attained increasing currency. Thus Anne Peck (1978, Introduction): 'Broadly speaking, a position in a futures market is a hedge position if it may be viewed as a substitute, albeit normally temporary, for an intended cash [actuals] transaction. The advantage of this definition is its generality.' But it is unfortunate that this definition gives no hint of the motives or reasons for hedging, and no indication that active futures markets and hedging in futures contracts are not to be found except where there is considerable volatility in prices. The demand for 'temporary substitute' contracts to stand in for intended eventual actuals contracts is non-existent or too limited to justify futures markets except where price changes are large and uncertain.

Price volatility and its role in the history of futures markets explain the traditional and still common association of hedging in futures with the avoidance or reduction of price risks. Perhaps the emphasis in the traditional definition of hedging on price risks captures more of the business reality of hedging than Working's all-embracing but bland definition or his earlier near-identification of hedging with carrying-charge hedging. At any rate there are no good grounds for de-emphasizing price risks in the discussion and analysis of hedging. This is so even though it is true that Working's earlier iconoclastic papers did much to attract more attention than before to other important aspects and features of hedging practices, and so have enriched the study of the economics of futures trading.

In recent years the application of portfolio theory to the activities of participants in futures trading once again sets risk in the centre of the hedging stage. But it is more explicit than before that risk has to share the stage with returns or profits. The risk that is usually emphasized concerns the variability of the expected returns. This approach, whether in the theory or in the related empirical studies, has so far added little to the understanding of the actual behaviour of hedgers. In particular, aside from routine hedging, it is unlikely that a hedger, when making his hedging and associated decisions in any particular situation, is influenced by the variability of returns on a succession of hedges in a past period or by the expected variability of returns on a succession of hedges in the impending period. It is on this type of risk measurement that empirical work examining prices in past periods has, perhaps perforce, been concentrated. Although these studies have their value in throwing light on the behaviour of price and basis in the markets and periods studied, in my view they add nothing of interest to the explanation of (non-routine) hedging practice.

These studies, and the theoretical approach they reflect, distract attention from the fact that the non-routine hedger tends to deal with each hedging decision in the light of the particular circumstances prevailing at the time, and not in the light of his expectations about the variability and size of returns from a sequence of (hypothetical?) transactions in the future (and which in turn can throw no light on the expected outcome of the particular hedge under consideration). Both traditional insurance-type hedging (allied, as it should be, with the notion of the exercise of discretion and judgement, as in Working's 'selective' hedging) and also Working's arbitrage hedging involve the hedger's assessment of each situation discretely and exclusively on its own merits. In this respect together they reflect the motivations of non-routine hedging. The portfolio-theory approach contributes only in that it may make more explicit the risk-return trade-off to be assessed by the hedger in each situation separately.

Perhaps the best description of non-routine hedging would run along these lines: hedging is the simultaneous making of offsetting, but not necessarily equal, transactions in related actuals and futures markets so as to reduce the risk of loss on adverse price changes, and sometimes with the intention of profiting from expected favourable basis changes. No doubt this description does not comprehend hedging practice in its variety and detail.[15] It does, however, highlight the two central features of the motivation of most hedging practice; and it also nicely blends the traditional view and a newer view associated with Holbrook Working's name.

Notes

*London School of Economics.

1. See also Hoffman's earlier exposition (1925) e.g. pp. 80-1; and Smith

(1922), ch. 7, *passim.*

2. Materials intended by exchanges or brokers for potential participants in futures business today still commonly describe the purpose of hedging in terms of the avoidance of price risks. A recent example is a pamphlet issued by the new International Petroleum Exchange of London: 'Hedging on futures markets is a form of price insurance against adverse price movements.'

3. For a fuller consideration of convenience yields, see Yamey (1971), pp. 418-19.

4. The trader may also be able to finance his stock more cheaply if banks consider hedgers to be more reliable borrowers because they are less exposed to price risks.

5. The following passage from Kaldor (1960, p. 25), shows clearly the distinction between risk-avoidance hedging and arbitrage hedging:

> The possibility of arbitrage, i.e. buying spot and selling futures simultaneously and holding the stock until the date of delivery, arises when the relationship between the futures price and the current price ensures a riskless profit. An arbitrage operation differs from an ordinary hedging operation only in that the ordinary hedger enters the futures market in order to reduce a risk arising out of a commitment which occurs independently of the existence of the forward market; whereas the arbitrageur assumes risk which he would not have assumed if the facilities of the forward market did not enable him to pass them on, on advantageous terms. Hence, any ordinary holder of stocks of a commodity becomes an 'arbitrageur' in so far as the existence of the futures market tempts him not only to hedge the stocks he would ordinarily hold, but to enlarge his stocks in relation to turnover owing to the advantageous terms on which they can be 'hedged'.

The reference to 'riskless profit' is a simplication, since there is always a risk, sometimes small, that the expected basis change may not materialize fully. Hence one encounters the fairly common statement that a hedger 'speculates' on basis change but not on price change (see, for example, Paul *et al.*, 1981, p. 27). Statements of this kind do not deny the (price) risk-avoidance aspect of hedging.

6. Quotations from Working (1953a).

7. In his 1953 paper Working noted that some hedging would take place even when a favourable change in basis was unlikely so that the completed hedged transaction would result in a direct pecuniary loss. The incurring of such losses was warranted in that commodity markets 'must try to keep adequate stocks ... to serve their customers'. In his 1962 paper, Working identifies and discusses several types of hedging in a manner which contradicts Peck's statement, viz. operational, selective, anticipatory and risk-avoidance hedging. Operational hedging, as explained by Working (p. 439), is such that 'expected changes in the spot-future price relation ... can be largely ignored; and it is this fact which chiefly distinguishes operational from carrying-charge hedging'. Basis and basis change are not mentioned in Working's discussion of the other three types of hedging. It may be noted that it is improbable that much long hedging falls within the arbitrage category: see Yamey (1971), especially p. 432. See also Working (1962), p. 441.

8. Thus Hoffman (1932, p. 407): 'While certain types of hedging are thus difficult for certain interests and in certain years, good hedging practice tends to avoid these types and to adopt a policy which will fit into the prevailing situation as far as possible. This is but another way of saying that hedging is something more than simply setting up counter future transactions and hoping for the best.' Tests of the effectiveness of hedging, the so-called stability-of-basis tests, make use of hypothetical programmes of routine hedging of a fixed actuals commitment. But these tests do not purport to be descriptions of actual hedging practice. Rather,

they should be seen as analyses of intermarket price relationships.

9. The passage in Working implies that the short-lived price dips and bulges are not reflected in available price series, so that the latter prices are not the transactions prices at which short hedgers place or lift hedges, and therefore those at which floor-trading speculators buy and sell futures. In a period in which prices tend to decline (or to remain stable), if one looked at available price series, speculators would seem to lose money (or break even) on their deals. However, according to Working the price dips and bulges are so large that the corresponding *transactions* prices enable speculators to tend to make profits despite the downward or stable price tendency in the market. By the same token, short hedgers tend to lose money on their futures transactions. Hence they would make money directly on their *completed* hedged transactions only if they make more money in the actuals market, i.e. only if actuals prices tend to rise by more than the futures prices tend to fall. However, it is quite implausible for the actuals prices to tend to rise in the postulated market conditions. Hence hedgers would tend to lose money on their hedging. In other words, according to Working, in the postulated market conditions the *effective* basis tends to widen over the life of the hedge (whatever the available price series might suggest), and hedgers would be aware of this tendency. Carrying-charge hedging requires the basis to narrow.

10. Marshall (1919), p. 266; Hardy (1923), pp. 72-3; Hoffman (1925), pp. 9, 18-20.

11. For some discussion of what Telser calls the 'fundamental properties' of futures exchanges, and of the choice between hedging in forward contracts in actuals and hedging in futures, see Goss and Yamey (1976), pp. 8-9, 18.

12. See also Bear (1980), p. 32.

13. 'There is more price variability for those goods that have an organised futures market than for the goods that lack such markets' (Telser and Higinbotham, 1977, p. 998).

14. 'The basic theory applies equally to any organised market', while the 'discussion centers on organised futures markets' (Telser and Higinbotham, 1977, p. 997).

15. Thus one may suppose that an insurance-type hedger would take account of the prevailing actuals-futures price relationships for each of the available contract maturities (i.e. for each of the various 'basis' values) and his expectations about changes in them when deciding whether and to what extent to hedge, in which futures maturity to hedge and, of course, how large a commitment in actuals to incur.

References

Bear, R.M. (1980) 'Commentary', in R.M. Leuthold and P. Dixon (eds.), *Livestock Futures Trading Symposium*, Chicago Board of Trade.

Goss, B.A. and B.S. Yamey (1976) 'Introduction', *The Economics of Futures Trading*, London and New York: Macmillan.

Gray, R.W. (1960) 'The Importance of Hedging in Futures Trading', in *Futures Trading Seminar*, vol. 1, 61-82, Madison: MIMIR.

— (1967) 'Prices Effects of a Lack of Speculation', *Food Research Institute Studies*, vol. 7, 177-94.

— (1972) 'The Futures Market for Maine Potatoes: An Appraisal', *Food Research Institute Studies*, vol. 11, 313-41.

Hardy, C.O. (1923) *Risk and Risk-Bearing*, Chicago.

Hicks. J.R. (1939) *Value and Capital*, London: Oxford University Press.

Hoffman, G.W. (1925) *Hedging by Dealing in Grain Futures*, Philadelphia.
— (1932) *Future Trading upon Organised Commodity Markets in the United States*, Philadelphia: University of Pennsylvania Press.
Kaldor, N. (1939-40) contribution in 'A Symposium on the Theory of the Forward Market', *Review of Economic Studies*, vol. 7, 1-27.
— (1960) *Essays on Economic Stability and Growth*, London: Duckworth.
Keynes, J.M. (1930) *A Treatise on Money*, vol. 2, London: Macmillan.
Marshall, A. (1919) *Industry and Trade*, London: Macmillan.
Paul, A.B., K.H. Kahl and W.G. Tomek (1981) *Performance of Futures Markets: The Case of Potatoes*, Washington DC.
Peck, A.E. (ed.) (1977) *Selected Writings on Futures Markets*, vol. 2, Chicago Board of Trade.
— (ed.) (1978) *Readings in Futures Markets: Views from the Trade*, Chicago Board of Trade.
Smith, J.G. (1922) *Organised Produce Markets*, London: Longmans, Green.
Telser, L.G. (1980) 'Reasons for Having an Organized Futures Market', in R.M. Leuthold and P. Dixon (eds.), *Livestock Futures Trading Symposium*, Chicago.
— (1981) 'Why there are Organized Futures Markets', *Journal of Law and Economics*, vol. 24, 1-22.
Telser, L.G. and H.N. Higinbotham (1977) 'Organized Futures Markets: Costs and Benefits', *Journal of Political Economy*, vol. 85, 969-1000.
Working, H. (1948) 'Theory of the Inverse Carrying Charge in Futures Markets', *Journal of Farm Economics*, vol. 30, 1-28.
— (1953a) 'Futures Trading and Hedging', *American Economic Review*, vol. 43, 314-43.
— (1953b) 'Hedging Reconsidered', *Journal of Farm Economics*, vol. 35, 544-61.
— (1962) 'New Concepts concerning Futures Markets', *American Economic Review*, vol. 52, 431-59.
— (1967) 'Tests of a Theory Concerning Floor Trading on Commodity Exchanges', *Food Research Institute Studies*, vol. 7, 5-48.
— (1970) 'Economic Functions of Futures Markets', in H.H. Bakken (ed.), *Futures Trading in Livestock*, Madison.
Yamey, B.S. (1968) 'Addendum', to 'An Investigation of Hedging on an Organized Produce Exchange', in P.T. Bauer and B.S. Yamey, *Markets, Market Control and Marketing Reform*, London: Macmillan.
— (1971), 'Short Hedging and Long Hedging in Futures Markets', *Journal of Law and Economics*, vol. 14, 413-34.

4 INTERTEMPORAL ALLOCATION IN THE AUSTRALIAN WOOL MARKET

Barry A. Goss and David E.A. Giles*

1. Simultaneous Equations Model of Price Determination and Storage

Several years ago Peston and Yamey (1960) published a paper which addresses the problem of the allocation of the available supply of a commodity between current consumption and storage, and the simultaneous determination of spot and futures prices. To the best of our knowledge that model has not been estimated. The model developed and estimated in this chapter is an extension of the Peston-Yamey model to Australian wool spot and futures markets.

The basic Peston-Yamey model distinguishes three markets — for present consumption, for storage and for futures contracts — and our model employs the same divisions. The market for present consumption is not identical with the spot market, the latter being a market where the commodity is currently priced for current delivery. An economic agent, however, may take current delivery for the purpose of (speculative) storage, and it will be seen that some traders in the storage market are responsive to the spot price. That part of available supply which is not currently consumed is allocated to storage, either in anticipation of future requirements, or in anticipation of a future gain from expected price changes. Traders holding such inventory may or may not hedge their price risks. Where traders do not hedge against the risk of a change in the spot price, the stock is classified as 'unhedged storage'. Where an economic agent simultaneously takes a position in inventory and an opposite position in futures, the inventory is classified as 'hedged storage'. In the futures market, traders may buy and sell futures contracts because they are hedging their commitments in the actual commodity against price risks, or because they anticipate a gain from an expected change in futures prices.

In the model presented here, six types of economic agent are distinguished: short hedgers, short speculators, long hedgers, long speculators, speculators in spot and consumers, although Peston-Yamey did not distinguish long hedgers and short speculators in futures.

Short hedgers are holders of stocks who match their position in spot with an equivalent sold position in futures. Their supply of hedged storage is an increasing function of the price spread (futures price minus spot price), because of either an increasing marginal net cost of storage (in the case of routine hedgers), or because of their expectations of the price spread (in the case of discretionary hedgers) in the sense of Working (1953). The latter determine the volume of their inventory and hedging according to their price spread expectations, although they are fully hedged (carrying-charge hedgers).[1] Interviews reported in an earlier study of the Sydney Wool Futures Exchange (Goss, 1972) indicated that only 1 in 25 floor member and associate member respondents hedged in a routine manner. Thus 'short hedgers' supply hedged storage and futures contracts. Short speculators sell futures contracts because of their expectations of a fall in the futures price.

Long hedgers are traders who have sold wool or wool products forward, and who hedge their price risk by a long (bought) position in futures. While their price risk is the opposite of that of short hedgers, their result from hedging is not the strict mirror image of that for short hedgers (Yamey, 1971). The Sydney wool futures market is unusual in that, for most of the months studied, the volume of long hedging exceeds that of short hedging; the theoretical literature has almost invariably assumed that hedgers are net short (see Hicks, 1939; Houthakker, 1968), and empirical studies dealing with open position data have found that hedgers are mostly net short (see, for example, Rockwell, 1967). Futures contracts are also demanded by long speculators who expect the futures price to rise.

Peston-Yamey assumed that the demand for futures by long speculators also constituted a demand for storage, on the ground that these traders planned to become momentary holders (only) of the commodity at the end of the period. This treatment seems to be simply a device to close off the model, perhaps because the activities of long hedgers are not explicitly included.[2] We shall assume that the demand for storage is provided by long hedgers, who, although they generally do not intend to take delivery under the futures contract, plan to acquire the physical commodity upon completion of the hedge: they are using the futures contract as a substitute for a merchandizing contract (Working, 1953). In periods in which the volume of long hedging exceeds that of short hedging, we shall assume that the supply of storage is provided by short hedgers and by short speculators to the extent that is necessary to balance the storage market. Similarly, in periods in which short hedging exceeds long hedging, we shall assume that the demand for storage is provided by long hedgers and by long speculators to the extent that is necessary to balance the storage market.

A further category of market operator is that of 'speculators in spot'. This group of traders holds unhedged inventory because they expect a rise in the spot price, and corresponds to the 'merchant' category in the Peston-Yamey model. Because there are no other economic agents dealing in unhedged storage, Peston-Yamey treat the holdings of this group as involving them in a reciprocal demand for and supply of unhedged storage, and we shall employ the same interpretation.

We also distinguish the category 'consumers', who demand the physical commodity for current usage, and are assumed to hold no inventories of wool. The supply of spot to consumers is in effect that part of available supply which is not allocated to storage. In addition to 'consumers', the original paper also distinguishes 'mixed traders', who are in effect discretionary hedgers, and 'mixed speculators', who are long in both spot and futures. We have treated these two categories of speculator separately.

Peston and Yamey (1960) have explained the simultaneous determination of static equilibrium values for spot and futures prices, and have shown that such an equilibrium is stable (pp. 359-60). The determination of equilibrium and the stability properties of the model are not affected by the addition of long hedging and short speculator categories of operator.

2. Specification of Functional Relationships

Demand for Unhedged Storage

Our initial experimentation with this relationship was based on an equation of the form:

$$U_t = a_1 + b_1A_t + c_1m_t + d_1A^*_{t+1} + e_1r_t + f_1i_t + v_{1t}$$

where: m_t = marginal net cost of storage. This is the marginal carrying charge (including interest) less marginal convenience yield, which is the subjective gain from holding inventory and being 'open to sell' (see Kaldor, 1939, 1961; Yamey, 1971);

i_t = foreign rate of interest;

r_t = marginal risk premium;

A^*_{t+1} = expected spot price, for period t + 1, formed in period t.

This basic demand equation is based on the demand function for speculative storage in Brennan (1958), and Kaldor (1939, 1961). Holders of unhedged inventories expect to gain from a rise in the spot price in excess of their marginal net cost of storage and marginal risk premium. In effect, their demand price is $A^*_{t+1} - (m_t + r_t)$: such traders will adjust their holdings of spot[3] until $A^*_{t+1} = A_t + m_t + r_t$. Hence, the coefficients b_1, c_1 and e_1 are expected to be negative, while d_1 is expected to be positive in sign, *a priori*. The foreign interest rate variable is included because of the dominance of unhedged storage by the Australian Wool Corporation (AWC) from 1975 onwards. The coefficient f_1 is expected to be positive, *a priori*, because such interest rates vary inversely with foreign inventory, and the latter varies inversely with AWC inventory. Although positive estimates of f_1 were obtained, the inclusion of this interest rate variable (variously defined) adversely affected other estimates of parameters in the model. The variables m and r failed to perform, and so all three were subsequently deleted from the equation. In this and all other equations, except for (4) below, seasonal dummy variables were found to be (jointly) insignificant.

In preliminary estimation the adaptive expectations hypothesis performed better than Mills (1962) implicit expectations hypothesis, and was finally adopted in the unhedged storage demand equation. Beginning with the simplified relationship:

$$U_t = a_1 + b_1A_t + d_1A^*_t + v_{1t},$$

with

$$(A^*_{t+1} - A^*_t) = \alpha_1 (A_t - A^*_t) \; ; 0 < \alpha_1 < 1$$

we obtain:

$$U_t = (1 - \alpha_1)U_{t-1} + (b_1 + \alpha_1 d_1)A_t + b_1(\alpha_1 - 1)A_{t-1}$$
$$+ a_1\alpha_1 + (v_{1t} + (\alpha_1 - 1)v_{1t-1})$$

or

$$U_t = \theta_1 U_{t-1} + \theta_2 A_t + \theta_3 A_{t-1} + \theta_4 + u_{1t} \qquad (1)$$

The anticipated signs on α_1, b_1 and d_1 noted already imply $0 < \theta_1 < 1$, $\theta_3 > 0$, and either $\theta_2 > 0$ or, if it is negative, then $|\theta_2| < (\theta_3/\theta_1)$.

The traders whose behaviour is represented by equation (1) may be seen as maximizers of expected net revenue in the sense of Brennan (1958).

Demand for Futures by Long Speculators

Our initial specification of this equation was:

$$FLS_t = a_2 + b_2 P_t + c_2 P^*_{t+1} + d_2 r_t + u_{2t}$$

where: P^*_{t+1} = expected futures price for period t + 1, formed in period t.

The interpretation of this equation is similar to that of the basic unhedged storage equation above, except that these speculators are holders of futures rather than actuals. In this case our attempts to represent P^*_{t+1} by an adaptive expectations hypothesis were unsuccessful, and shifts in expectations were represented by a series of dummy variables linked to major events in the international wool diary during the sample period. Of these, the dummies representing anticipation of a recession (D_2, D_4) failed to survive preliminary estimations, as did the risk premium variable. Hence the final version of this relationship is:

$$FLS_t = \theta_5 P_t + \theta_6 D_{1t} + \theta_7 D_{3t} + \theta_8 + u_{2t} \qquad (2)$$

where the expected parameter signs are $\theta_5 < 0$, θ_6, $\theta_7 > 0$, and

$D_{1t} = 1$: January 1972 – March 1974; to represent worldwide commodity boom; = 0 elsewhere.

$D_{2t} = 1$: July 1974 – February 1976; to represent generalized recession; = 0 elsewhere.

$D_{3t} = 1$: March 1976 – December 1976; to represent textile consumption revival; = 0 elsewhere.

$D_{4t} = 1$: January 1977 – December 1977; to represent lack of confidence about textile consumption; = 0 elsewhere.

Supply of Hedged Storage

Short hedging is undertaken by growers (with respect to growing crops of wool) and by brokers and merchants (with respect to inventories). Such traders may take routine hedges, or they may pursue an uncertain gain subject to the constraint of risk reduction (see Johnson, 1960).

The volume of short hedging is likely to be an increasing function of the forward premium for at least two reasons. First, traders are likely to believe that the larger the current forward premium, the more likely it is to decline in the future (it must disappear at maturity), and a forward premium which declines gives a gain to short hedgers. Second, if inventory holders are a competitive group independently seeking to maximize profits, they may be assumed to equate the marginal net cost of storage with the forward premium (which is the return per unit on a hedge held to maturity). If marginal net storage costs increase with inventories, as is usually assumed, then inventories will increase with the forward premium. A spot premium which narrows over time results in losses to short hedgers. The holding of stocks at such times is explicable in terms of the convenience yield, which can make net storage costs negative at the margin. Two possible indicators of the volume of wool eligible for hedging are the monthly output of greasy wool, and non-AWC inventories. We have chosen the latter because of its better performance in experimental work.

Our relationship for the supply of hedged storage is:

$$H_t = \theta_9 (P_t - A_t) + \theta_{10} NK_t + \theta_{11} + u_{3t} \qquad (3)$$

where NK_t is the non-AWC stock of wool, and both θ_9 and θ_{10} are expected to be positive in sign.

Consumption of Wool

In specifying this relationship we have partly followed the lead of the Bureau of Agricultural Economics (BAE) (1967) in their estimation of the derived demand for raw wool in the United Kingdom. In their log-linear equation, consumption was a function of the price of raw wool; parameters of the demand curve for wool products (including population, personal disposable income and the demand for stocks of wool tops); and parameters of the supply curve of 'other factors' (including the quantity of synthetics competing with wool in production).

The main differences between the BAE model and the demand for wool by consumers in the model presented here are first that consumers in our model are assumed to carry no stocks (as consumers), that function being undertaken by holders of unhedged storage or by short hedgers. The second major difference is that our period of study in the 1970s was assumed to be one where synthetic production did not set the limit to market penetration by synthetics, as it apparently did in the 1960s. Accordingly, substitution between wool and synthetics, in both consumption and production, was assumed to be sensitive to relative prices.

Our attempts to include personal disposable income as an explanatory variable were unsuccessful as a result of the strong collinearity with other variables in the system. An index of textile production (M_t) was used as a proxy for the influence of changes in consumers' tastes, and also to capture population effects. Only in this equation were seasonal dummy variables found to be significant, and the specification is:

$$\ln C_t = \theta_{12}\ln(A_t/S_t) + \theta_{13}\ln M_t + \sum_{j=14}^{24} \theta_j SEAS_{(j-13)t} + \theta_{25} + u_{4t} \qquad (4)$$

where: S_t = price of synthetic fibres.
$SEAS_{it}$ = seasonal dummy variable for the ith month of the calendar year.

Demand for Futures by Long Hedgers

The specification of this equation is:

$$FLH_t = \theta_{26}(P_t - A_t) + \theta_{27}D_{5t} + \theta_{28} + u_{5t}, \tag{5}$$

where: D_{5t} = dummy variable to reflect the absence of excess stocks in Japan during 1973-4.
(D_{5t} = 1, January 1973 to December 1974;
= 0, elsewhere.)

Demand for futures by long hedgers is undertaken by traders who have made forward sales of wool or wool products. The price at which such forward contracts are written is not necessarily the spot price of wool, because spot and forward actuals transactions refer to different delivery dates. However, the forward actuals price is unknown, and so it is proposed to use the current spot price as a proxy for this, although we acknowledge that the forward actuals price will also reflect some influences bearing upon the similarly dated futures price (Yamey, 1971). Hence, the difference between the current spot and futures prices is likely to overstate the difference between the forward actuals price and the current futures price. Subject to this qualification, the position of the long hedger is the negative of the position of the short hedger. That is, the volume of long hedging is a decreasing function of the spread between the futures price and the forward actuals price, and so θ_{26} is expected to be negative, *a priori.*

The dummy variable D_5 was introduced partly to represent the impact of changes in Japanese textile inventories upon Japanese textile production and Japanese wool purchases in Australia, as emphasized in market reports. Another reason for including D_5 was the lack of success with estimates obtained when planned textile production was included in the equation. (We believed that planned production in approximately four months' time would be appropriate, because interviews with floor members indicated that such hedges are held for an average of 18 weeks. Actual textile production with a lead of four months was employed as a proxy for these plans, which were in effect assumed to be realized.) The coefficient of D_5 in (4) is expected to be positive.

Supply of Futures by Short Speculators

Speculators who expect the futures price to fall will sell futures contracts, and will close their positions by buying futures at the anticipated lower price, expecting a profit in return for their risk-taking. Their supply of futures contracts is assumed to vary directly with the current futures price, given their expectations, and to vary inversely with their expected price, given the current futures price. Short speculators in futures may not be active until the current futures price exceeds their expected price by an amount which is at least equal to a required marginal risk premium.

The representation of short speculators' price expectations by the adaptive expectations hypothesis failed to perform satisfactorily in preliminary estimates, as did the marginal risk premium variable. Accordingly, shifts in expectations are represented by two dummy variables, each of which represents anticipation of a slump in futures prices:

D_{6t} = 1 ; March 1974-March 1975
= 0 ; elsewhere.

D_{7t} = 1 ; May 1976-April 1977
= 0 ; elsewhere.

The resulting specification is:

$$SS_t = \theta_{29}D_{6t} + \theta_{30}D_{7t} + \theta_{31} + \theta_{32}P_t + u_{6t} \quad (6)$$

where θ_{29}, θ_{30} and θ_{32} are expected to be positive in sign.

Identities

In the accounting identity:

$$K_t + C_t \equiv K_{t-1} + Z_t - X_t \quad (7a)$$

where: Z_t = current production;
X_t = current exports;
K_t = closing stock in period t.

we define the left side of (7a) as the disposal of available domestic supply of wool, and the right side to be the domestic availability of wool (assuming imports of raw wool to be zero).[4] Assuming that demand for and supply of hedged storage are equal at the equilibrium futures price, then equilibrium in the consumption and storage markets requires:

$$C_t + H_t + U_t = C_t + FLH_t + U_t \tag{7b}$$

In periods in which FLH_t exceeds H_t at the equilibrium futures price, we would have to include on the left side of (7b) sufficient (Y_t) of SS_t to balance the hedged storage market. Similarly, in periods in which H_t exceeds FLH_t at the equilibrium futures price, we would have to include on the right side of (7b) sufficient (W_t) of FLS_t to balance the market for hedged storage. This yields:

$$C_t + H_t + U_t + Y_t = C_t + FLH_t + U_t + W_t \tag{7c}$$

where:

$$\begin{aligned} W_t &= 0, \text{ when } FLH_t \geqslant H_t \\ &= (H_t - FLH_t), \text{ when } H_t > FLH_t \end{aligned}$$

and

$$\begin{aligned} Y_t &= 0, \text{ when } H_t \geqslant FLH_t \\ &= (FLH_t - H_t), \text{ when } FLH_t > H_t. \end{aligned}$$

The left side of (7c) represents quantities supplied, while the right side represents quantities demanded. Subtracting C_t from both sides gives the equilibrium condition in the storage market, and in equilibrium each side after this deduction is also equal to K_t, the quantity of stock in existence. As we assume that the storage market achieves equilibrium every trading period, so that only equilibrium values are observed, then either side may be employed to derive the identity (7) below.

We have chosen the right side giving:

$$K_t \equiv U_t + FLH_t + W_t \tag{7d}$$

The expression in (7) is not an accounting identity in the sense that it holds even at times of disequilibrium; it is an identity of observed values which holds in every trading period.

We can also write:

$$H_t + SS_t \equiv FLS_t + FLH_t \tag{8}$$

which is the equilibrium condition in the futures market. Because it is assumed that equilibrium is achieved in the futures market every period, (8) may be interpreted as an identity of observed values.

Hence, we have eight endogenous variables: U_t, C_t, H_t, SS_t, FLH_t, FLS_t, P_t and A_t, together with six behavioural equations and the two identities (7) and (8). The variables NK_t, M_t, S_t, K_t and the dummy variables are treated as exogenous.

3. Data

This section discusses the definition, the collection and generation, and the interpretation of data employed in estimating the model presented in Section 1. The data are discussed under the headings 'Spot and Futures Prices', which are the endogenous prices in the model, 'Other Endogenous Variables' and 'Other Variables'.

Spot and Futures Prices

The spot price of wool (A_t) is the monthly average of weekly auction quotations for 'average 64s' (21 micron in 1976, 22 micron in 1977) provided by the Australian Wool Corporation in *Wool Market News.* It is quoted in cents per kilogram, clean basis.[5]

The futures price (P_t) is the monthly average of daily prices for a futures contract approximately six months from maturity, quoted in cents per kilogram, clean basis, and provided in the weekly *Statistical Report* of the Sydney Futures Exchange Ltd. There are only five delivery months for wool on the Exchange (March, May, July, October and December), so that it was necessary to employ an arbitrary definition of a 'six months' future', which is given below.[6] Such a definition is necessary to obtain a continuous series of futures prices, because the maximum period for which any contract is quoted on the exchange is 18 months. Moreover, interviews for the study reported in Goss (1972) indicated that typically hedges are of 18 weeks' duration in a future approximately six months from maturity. Futures price quotations refer to 'standard wool' in the futures contract which is 64 type 78 (22 micron type 78 from 1976).

Other Endogenous Variables

Australian commodity futures markets, unlike most of their United States counterparts, do not publish or make available data on turnover or commitments, classified according to type of transaction such as hedging, speculative, etc., nor do the data exist in the records of the Exchange or the Clearing House. Hence, the procedure adopted in the present project was first to obtain monthly turnover summaries for all floor members of the Exchange, and for other members of the Clearing House. Information was then obtained as to which floor members each of the other clearing members directed their business. Finally, all floor members of the Exchange who traded during the sample period were interviewed (whether they were still trading or not), and asked the percentage composition of their business in the categories 'short hedging', 'long hedging' and 'speculation' during the sample period, taking into account any sub-periods which they wished to distinguish.

This proportionate breakdown of business for each floor member was applied to that member's turnover for each month studied, and aggregation across members generated monthly turnover data classified into 'short hedging', 'long hedging' and 'speculation'. The speculation category was then divided between the long and short sides so as to balance the futures market. Turnover in the categories of short and long speculation (SS_t and FLS_t) refers to purely speculative transactions, while turnover in the categories of short and long hedging (H_t and FLH_t) refers to routine and discretionary hedging transactions.[7]

Data for U_t were obtained as follows. In periods where the volume of long hedging exceeded that of short hedging, the values of FLH_t, being the total demand for hedged storage, were subtracted from values of total stock, K_t, which is treated as exogenous. Hence, the equilibrium quantities of unhedged storage (U_t) were generated as a residual. Similarly, in periods when short hedging predominated, values of H_t, being the total supply of hedged storage, were subtracted from values of K_t, the equilibrium values of U_t again being generated as a residual.

Monthly values of AWC inventory were available and these were added to the NK_t data, obtained as described below, to form K_t. All variables in identities (7) and (8) are expressed in terms of contracts ('lots') traded on the Exchange, where a contract refers to a quantity of greasy wool equal to 1,500 kilograms clean.

Quarterly data on Australian consumption of raw wool from Australian Bureau of Statistics sources were made available by the AWC and were interpolated, using the program TRANSF (Wymer, 1977c), to provide monthly data for C_t, expressed in million kilograms, clean basis. These data were then converted to contracts traded.

Other Variables

Non-AWC stock (NK_t), which appears in equation (3), was obtained by interpolating the available annual data, using the TRANSF program. NK_t is measured in million kilograms, clean basis.

The index of manufacturing activity (M_t) which appears in equation (5) is the index of manufacturing activity in Australian wool textiles, as reported in the ANZ Bank's *Quarterly Survey.*

The synthetic price variable (S_t) which appears in equation (5) is the average price of acrylic tow in the USA, Japan and the EEC, weighted according to production, and expressed in UK pence per kilogram. The data are made available in the International Wool Secretariat report, *Competition From Synthetic Fibres.*

4. Estimation and Results

Estimation of the Model

The eight-equation simultaneous model described in Section 1 has been estimated using monthly time-series data covering the period January 1973 to December 1977. The model is linear in the 32 parameters, but non-linear in the endogenous variable A_t. The latter variable appears in level form in parts of the model, but in logarithmic form in equation (4). Although $\ell n(C_t)$ also appears in this equation, C_t itself does not appear elsewhere in the system, so the model may be treated as being linear in the logarithm of this variable. Equation (4) was linearized with respect to A_t by means of a first-order Taylor approximation about sample mean values, and the resulting (linear) restrictions on the intercept term were retained in the subsequent estimation. Each of the six stochastic equations in the model is overidentified.

The computer package SIMUL (Wymer, 1977b) was used to obtain Full Information Maximum Likelihood (FIML) estimates of the structural parameters. Both Ordinary Least Squares (OLS) and Three Stage Least Squares (3SLS) estimates were used as starting values for the Newton-Raphson algorithm in SIMUL, and the same (local) maximum of the associated likelihood function was reached in each case. This result is most encouraging, given the substantial differences between the OLS and 3SLS estimates of some of the parameters in the system. The convergence tolerance for the FIML algorithm was set to 0.1 per cent in all cases.

The principal weakness of these FIML results was the apparent lack of independence among the residuals of the structural equations (1), (2), (3) and (4). Temporal independence for lags up to twelve periods was tested by means of the non-parametric Sign Reversal Test (e.g. Griliches *et al.*, 1962). This test has been used in a simultaneous equations context by Giles (1977). Although there was evidence of higher-order temporal dependence, first-order auto-correlation appeared to be the dominant phenomenon.

To take account of this, the model was re-estimated, allowance being made for separate first-order auto-regressive processes in the structural errors of those equations noted above. For example, equation (3) becomes:

$$H_t = \theta_9 (P_t - A_t) + \theta_{10}NK_t + \theta_{11} + u_{3t},$$

$$u_{3t} = \rho_3 u_{3t-1} + e_{3t}$$

$$H_t = \rho_3 H_{t-1} + \theta_9(P_t - A_t) - \rho_3\theta_9(P_{t-1} - A_{t-1}) + \theta_{10}NK_t - \rho_3\theta_{10}NK_{t-1} + \theta_{11}(1-\rho_3) + e_{3t},$$

where ρ_3 is an auto-correlation parameter to be estimated, and e_{3t} is a 'well-behaved' disturbance term. The other affected equations are transformed in a corresponding way, so that each version of the model is now non-linear in the parameters. Constrained FIML estimates were obtained with the package RESIMUL (Wymer, 1977a). Certain other error structures could be allowed for in a similar way, although we have not pursued this possibility further. Finally, inequality restrictions were placed on three of the parameters to ensure that $\hat{\theta}_1 > 0$ and $\hat{\theta}_3 > 0$, and to constrain the price elasticity implied by $\hat{\theta}_9$ to a magnitude consistent with the available prior information. The latter point is discussed in connection with Table 4.3 below.

Results

In this section we shall first discuss the results for the model as a whole, and we shall then consider the estimates for each individual equation. The FIML estimates of the structural parameters of the model are presented in Table 4.1, together with the FIML

Table 4.1: FIML Parameter Estimates

Parameter	Equation Dependent Variable	Variable	Estimate	Asymptotic Standard Error
θ_1	(1)	U_{t-1}	0.763	0.181
θ_2	U_t	A_t	−1.527	0.924
θ_3		A_{t-1}	1.342	0.871
θ_4		constant	82.773	50.376
θ_5	(2)	P_t	−0.005	0.002
θ_6	FLS_t	D_{1t}	1.005	0.222
θ_7		D_{3t}	0.075	0.184
θ_8		constant	2.225	0.597
θ_9	(3)	$(P_t - A_t)$	0.067	0.023
θ_{10}	H_t	NK_t	0.887	0.375
θ_{11}		constant	− 9.713	5.613
θ_{12}	(4)	$\ell n(A_t/S_t)$	−0.662	0.185
θ_{13}	ℓnC_t	ℓnM_t	0.039	0.060
θ_{14}		$SEAS_{1t}$	-0.386×10^{-3}	0.234×10^{-3}
θ_{15}		$SEAS_{2t}$	-0.285×10^{-4}	0.595×10^{-3}
θ_{16}		$SEAS_{3t}$	0.196×10^{-3}	0.773×10^{-3}
θ_{17}		$SEAS_{4t}$	0.114×10	0.908×10^{-3}
θ_{18}		$SEAS_{5t}$	0.193×10^{-2}	0.109×10^{-2}
θ_{19}		$SEAS_{6t}$	0.248×10^{-2}	0.124×10^{-2}
θ_{20}		$SEAS_{7t}$	0.310×10^{-2}	0.140×10^{-2}
θ_{21}		$SEAS_{8t}$	0.343×10^{-2}	0.152×10^{-2}
θ_{22}		$SEAS_{9t}$	0.354×10^{-2}	0.164×10^{-2}
θ_{23}		$SEAS_{10t}$	0.317×10^{-2}	0.179×10^{-2}
θ_{24}		$SEAS_{11t}$	0.304×10^{-2}	0.190×10^{-2}
θ_{25}		constant	8.061	0.594
θ_{26}	(5)	$(P_t - A_t)$	−0.025	0.005
θ_{27}	FLH_t	D_{5t}	1.409	0.328
θ_{28}		constant	3.452	0.199
θ_{29}	(6)	D_{6t}	1.473	0.134
θ_{30}	SS_t	D_{7t}	0.025	0.110
θ_{31}		constant	0.393	0.378
θ_{32}		P_t	0.203×10^{-2}	0.110×10^{-2}
ρ_1	(1)		−0.082	0.075
ρ_2	(2)		0.296	0.109
ρ_3	(3)		0.850	0.051
ρ_4	(4)		0.939	0.026

estimates of the auto-regression parameters associated with the equations for which the structural errors are assumed to follow a first-order auto-regressive process. These results are based on the non-linear (in the parameters) model arising when this allowance for auto-correlation is made. The usual likelihood ratio test for the validity of the over-identifying restrictions yields a χ^2 value of 613.0 (degrees of freedom = 186). The corresponding 5 per cent critical value is 703.4, so the over-identifying restrictions cannot be rejected on the basis of this asymptotic test.

All of the estimated parameters in Table 4.1 have the anticipated signs. As the standard errors reported in these tables are based on the asymptotic covariance matrix, and assuming that the quantity $(\hat{\theta}_i - \theta_i)/\text{a.s.e.}(\theta_i)$ is approximately standard normal in distribution (at least asymptotically), by far the majority of these estimates are also significant at the 5 per cent level.

Table 4.2 reports the Sign Reversal Test values calculated from the structural residuals associated with the estimates in Table 4.1, after allowance for auto-correlation. These statistics are based on residual sign changes between periods t and $(t - \mu)$ in the sample, and are asymptotically $\chi^2(1)$ in distribution. There is little evidence of remaining auto-correlation, except in equation (1). The latter exception might be explained by the fact that u_{1t} follows a moving average (rather than autoregressive) process if v_{1t} is 'well-behaved'. Unfortunately, we are unable to allow for this particular possibility in our estimation procedure.

Table 4.2: Sign Reversal Test Statistics

	Equation					
τ	(1)	(2)	(3)	(4)	(5)	(6)
1	8.31*	0.11	1.11	13.34*	1.38	1.36
2	0.33	1.84	0.01	2.58	3.42	0.07
3	0.02	4.89	0.73	0.18	1.38	0.43
4	0.00	0.56	0.21	0.09	1.24	0.26
5	0.16	0.20	0.35	0.51	0.01	0.54
6	1.10	0.05	0.04	0.47	0.73	2.87
7	7.22*	0.53	0.00	2.81	2.27	0.01
8	0.29	0.12	1.08	0.40	0.32	1.26
9	0.23	0.60	0.25	3.54	2.37	0.16
10	0.87	0.06	0.59	4.73	0.08	1.21
11	0.18	1.17	0.06	1.74	2.46	1.54
12	1.62	0.01	0.90	0.01	0.34	2.29

* Significant at the 1 per cent level of significance.

Table 4.3 contains the estimated price elasticities for each of the equations. Except in equation (4), these are calculated at the sample mean values for the variables concerned, and asymptotic standard errors are reported in parentheses. These estimated elasticities are generally plausible, although those for equation (5) are a little smaller in absolute value than anticipated: discussions with some major floor members indicated that they would have expected long and short hedgers each to adjust their market positions by at least 200 contracts in response to a price change of three cents, during the period studied.

The within-sample predictive performance of the model is summarized in Table 4.4 in terms of percentage root mean squared (forecast) error. These predictions are based on the restricted reduced form. The complete within-sample prediction paths are compared with the corresponding actual paths for a selection of the endogenous variables in Figures 4.1 to 4.4.

We shall now consider the results for each equation in turn. In

Table 4.3: Estimated Price Elasticities

	Equation							
	(1)	(2)	(3)		(4)	(5)		(6)
Price	A	P	P	A	(A/S)	P	A	P
	−5.08	−2.30	5.99	−6.04	−0.57	−1.86	1.87	0.32
	(2.14)	(0.79)	(4.44)	(4.48)	(0.18)	(0.40)	(0.40)	(0.25)

Table 4.4: Within-sample % RMSE from Restricted Reduced Form

Endogenous Variable	% RMSE
A	8.25
P	6.71
U	5.92
H	48.70
FLH	50.29
FLS	111.07
SS	90.05
C	4.69

Figure 4.1: Wool Spot [Cash] Price

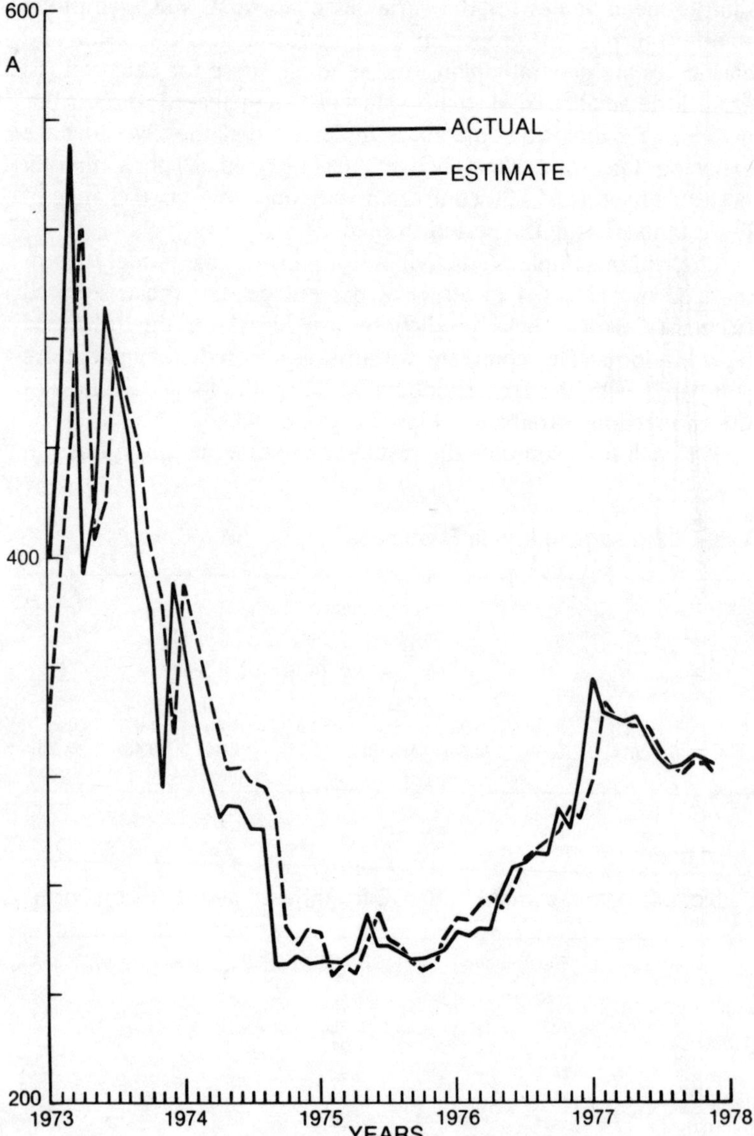

Figure 4.2: Wool Futures Price

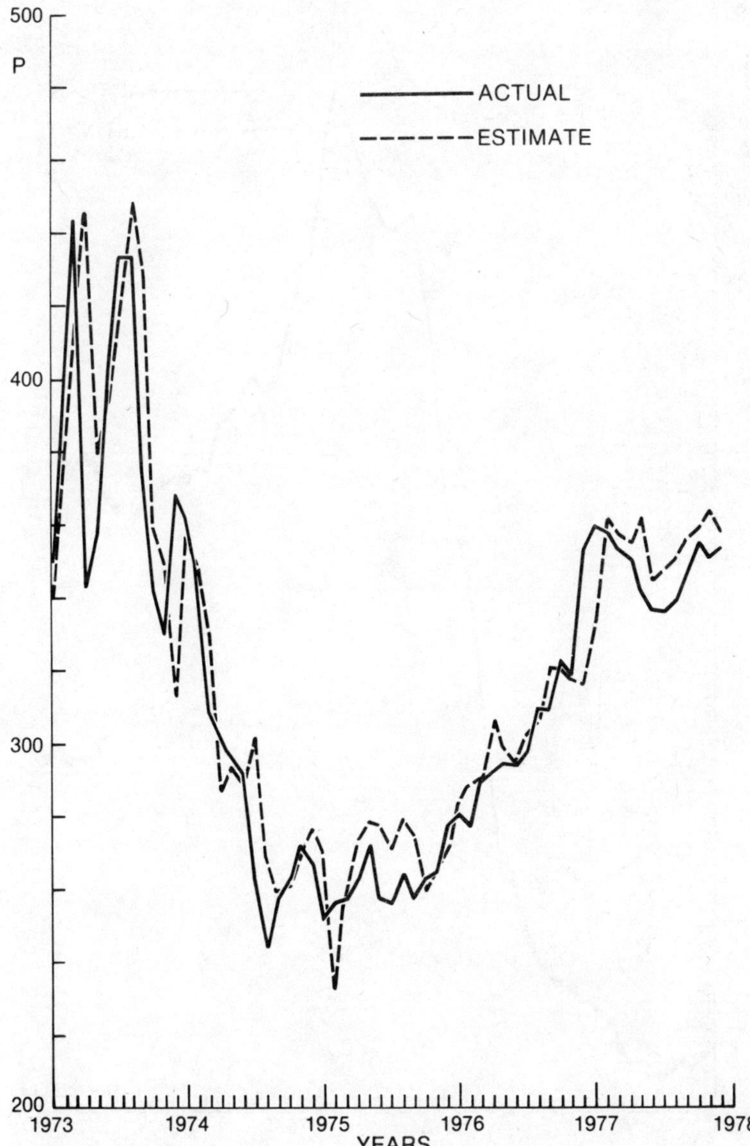

Figure 4.3: Wool Unhedged Storage

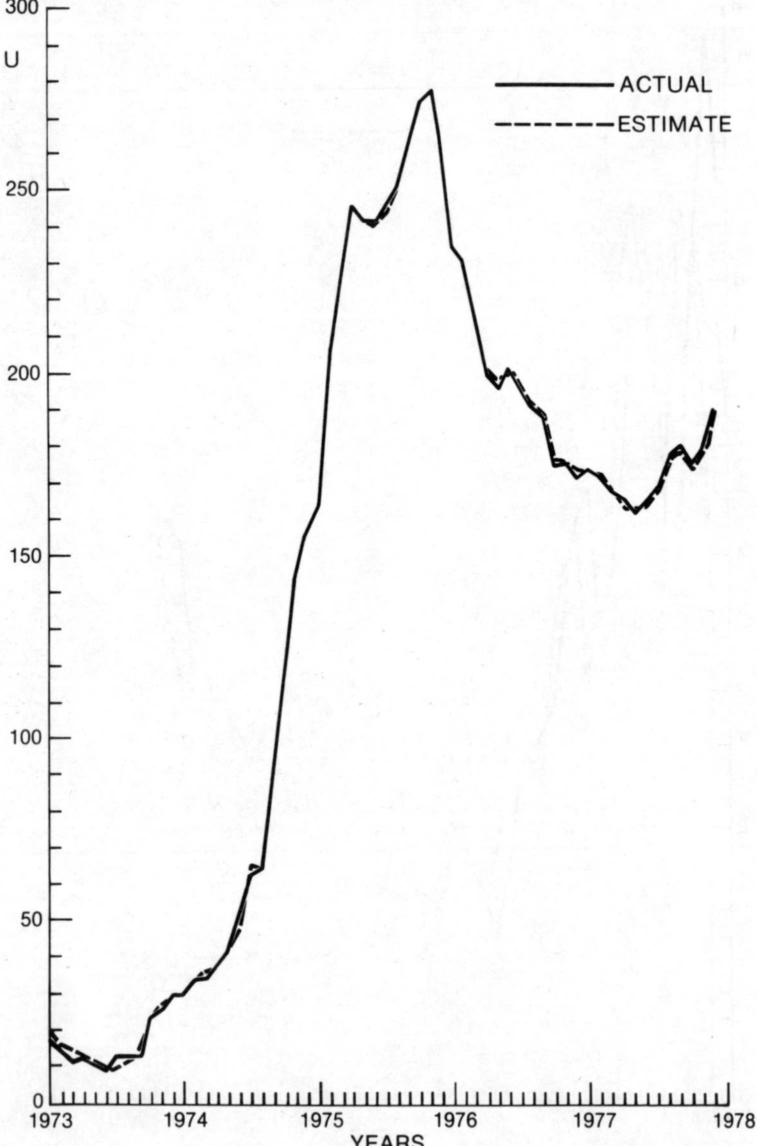

Figure 4.4: Wool Hedged Storage

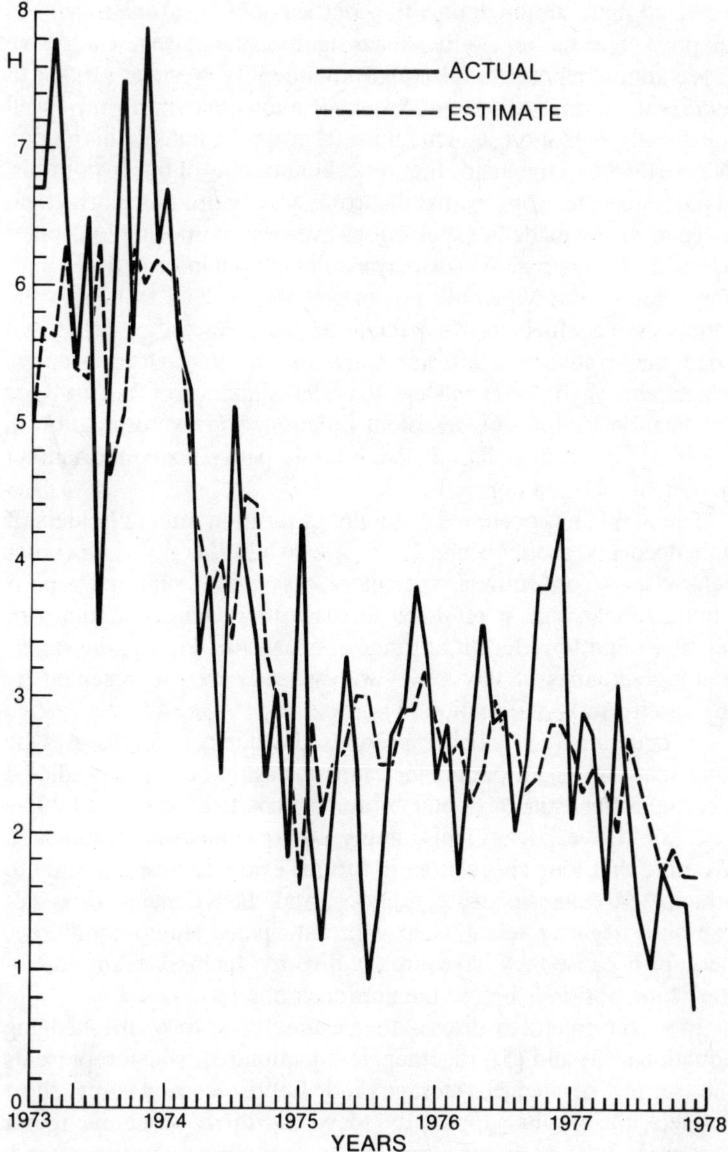

equation (1), which represents the holding of unhedged inventories of wool, the coefficients of all price variables have the expected signs, although only the coefficient of U_{t-1} (one minus the adaptive expectations coefficient) is significant. Hence, the adaptive expectations hypothesis, although intended by Nerlove (1958) to represent 'normal' or long-term expectations, has performed well statistically in its short- and medium-term applications in this model. We are aware of the major theoretical limitations of this hypothesis, in particular the property that if current expectations are correct, no revision will be made to expectations even if new information comes to hand. However, if, as is usually assumed, such information comes about randomly, we would not expect this to lead to bias in the estimates of coefficients of expectational variables, although it would affect their statistical significance. In addition, although the adaptive expectations hypothesis will lead to underestimation of the true price expectation in times of persistent inflation, and overestimation in times of persistent deflation, our sample period exhibited neither persistent inflation nor deflation.

The AWC has occupied a dominant position among holders of unhedged inventories since 1975, and while the AWC does not behave as a conventional speculator, its market support responsibilities mean that it tends to increase its inventory at times of recession and to reduce it at times of expansion. Hence, the stockholding activities of the AWC are evidently well represented by the specification of equation (1).

In equation (2), which represents the demand for futures by long speculators, all parameter estimates again have the predicted signs, and the estimates obtained for the coefficients of the futures price and the expectational dummy D_1 are statistically significant. We note that long speculators in futures evidently respond only to anticipated expansionary conditions, and their demand does not exhibit a negative relationship with anticipated slump conditions, perhaps because they have already divested themselves of most of their long positions before the approach of a recession.

It is convenient to discuss the results for both of the hedging equations, (3) and (5), together. In equation (3), which represents the supply of hedged storage and futures contracts by short hedgers, the results support the view that these economic agents determine their positions according to changes in the price spread, either for reasons for marginal net cost of storage or expected basis change, as discussed above in Section 2. The parameter estimates for both non-AWC inventories and the price spread have the predicted signs and both are statistically significant.

Equation (5) represents the demand for hedged storage and futures contracts by long hedgers. Although economic theory is less informative about the behaviour of long hedgers than about that of short hedgers, we would have expected the positions of long hedgers to vary inversely with the price spread, as explained in Section 2. The results obtained support this view, and the estimated coefficients of the price spread and the dummy variable D_5, representing the impact of the Japanese textile industry on the Australian wool market, have the predicted signs, and both are statistically significant. Persuasive evidence of the behaviour of long hedgers is scarce, perhaps because of the belief — which economic theory has tended to reflect — that in practice hedgers are generally net short. In any case the results reported here for equation (5) may be one of the first empirical analyses of long-hedger behaviour.

Equation (4), the consumption relationship, performs well with a significant estimate of the relative price elasticity and a production elasticity of the predicted sign. In this equation the seasonal dummy variables also play an active role. As explained in Section 2, the textile production index is used as a proxy for the influences of consumers' tastes and population changes, so the interpretation of the estimated elasticity of 0.026 is not straightforward.

In equation (6), which represents the supply of futures contracts by short speculators, all parameter estimates have the predicted signs, although only one, the coefficient of the expectational dummy D_6, is significant. We observe that short speculators in futures evidently respond only to an anticipated slump in futures prices and not to an anticipated boom, possibly for the same reason suggested above for the lack of response of long speculators to anticipated slump conditions.

5. Conclusions

This chapter presents a simultaneous equations model of commodity market behaviour, based on Peston and Yamey (1960) and modified for estimation purposes and to accommodate the characteristics of the Australian wool market. We believe that this is for the first application of the Peston-Yamey model, which, in its reformulated version, has shown itself to be a potentially complete and sensitive formulation of commodity market phenomena. Further experimentation with expectations hypotheses will be made in subsequent work on other markets with this model by the authors.

The market studied is a useful vehicle for investigating the properties of the Peston-Yamey model: it is the world's largest wool futures market, and is a moderately large futures market by world standards. Moreover, it is a well-informed market in which traders participate in an efficient price formation process (see Praetz, 1975). A special feature of this market is that, for most of the sample period, hedgers were net long, a feature not encountered in previous theoretical and empirical work.

An important aspect of our data-processing is the generation of data on the supply of and demand for futures by long hedgers, short hedgers and speculators, which has hitherto been unavailable for the Australian wool futures market. This has been achieved by the utilization of floor member interview data and Clearing House turnover records.

The model presented in this chapter contains functional relationships for long and short hedgers and for long and short speculators in futures, as well as holders of unhedged inventories and consumers. The best performing relationships, with respect to intrasample prediction, are those for consumers and for holders of unhedged inventories, the latter being especially encouraging because most inventories of Australian wool are held unhedged. The hedging relationships, in which both groups of hedgers are found to respond *inter alia* to changes in the price spread, perform moderately well. The least well-performing functions are the speculative futures relationships, an outcome which may be due to our unsophisticated representation of those agents' expectations. Nevertheless, both spot and futures prices are well predicted by the model within the sample period.

Finally, our conclusion is that these results are sufficiently encouraging to warrant further research on specification of the functional relationships, especially the representation of expectations, and an extension to other commodities.

Notes

*Monash University, Australia. Earlier versions of this chapter were presented at Eighth Conference of Economists, La Trobe University, Melbourne, in August 1979, and to a Monash workshop. The research on which this chapter is based is part of a continuing project supported by the Australian Research Grants Committee. Thanks are due to the Sydney Futures Exchange and Floor Members of the Exchange, International Commodities Clearing House, and the Australian Wool Corporation for the provision of data. We also wish to thank Louis Phlips for his helpful advice and Jenny Lau for her painstaking research assistance. Any remaining errors are the responsibility of the authors.

1. Hedgers' actuals commitments are represented in the long- or short-hedging categories only to the extent that they are fully hedged. Unhedged actuals positions or futures positions not matched by actuals commitments are assumed to be included in the appropriate speculation category.

2. In law, the purchase of a futures contract does not give a title to any particular unit of the physical commodity, and in reality most such positions are closed out by reversal (selling futures) rather than by taking delivery.

3. The models of Kaldor and Brennan assume identical expectations, so that A^{*}_{t+1} is the mean expectation for all individuals, and the market expectation. If heterogeneous expectations are assumed, then the market expectation A^{*}_{t+1} may be interpreted as a weighted average of individuals' mean expected prices.

4. Peston and Yamey (1960) do not precisely define the term 'available supply'. On page 355 it is referred to as a 'given supply' to be allocated, while on page 358 it is stated that 'the total stock ... must be allocated'. An alternative interpretation to that adopted in this paper is to re-write the left side of (7a) as $\Delta K_t + C_t$ and to define $Z_t - X_t$ as the 'available domestic supply' of wool, and $\Delta K_t + C_t$ as the disposal of that supply. In some months of the period studied, however, ΔK_t is negative and the Peston-Yamey model is not defined for negative changes in stocks, although conceivably it could be reformulated to admit such cases.

5. The price clean varies inversely with the yield, for a given greasy price. Prior to 1973, AWC spot price quotations were thought to be inflated because subjective appraisal of yield was employed for wools sold at auction, and subjective appraisal evidently understates the yield compared with objective (core-testing) appraisal (see Douglas and McIntyre, 1970, where the reported estimates of the subjective appraisal are on average 3.61 per cent below those of the objective appraisals). Spot prices during our sample period are to some extent affected by this factor because core-testing techniques have been introduced progressively for wools sold at auction from 1973 onwards, the proportion of auction wool so tested ranging from 17 per cent in 1973-4 to 75 per cent by the end of our sample period. Nevertheless, when spot prices were adjusted for the presence of subjective appraisal the results, especially for equations (1) and (4) were less satisfactory, and the adjustment was deleted. (Deliverable wools on the Sydney Futures Exchange are core tested.)

6. The definition of the six months future is as follows: when the month is January, February, the future is July; when the month is March, April, the future is October; when the month is May, June, July, the future is December; when the month is August, September, the future is March; when the month is October, November, the future is May; when the month is December, the future is July.

7. To the extent that farmers' hedging of growing wool is included in H_t, this variable overstates the volume of inventory of raw wool.

References

Brennan, M.J. (1958) 'The Supply of Storage', *American Economic Review*, 48, 50-72.

Bureau of Agricultural Economics (1967) *The Price Elasticity of Demand for Wool in the United Kingdom*, Wool Economic Research Report no. 11, Canberra.

Douglas, S.A.S. and G.A. McIntyre (1970) *Subjective and Objective Appraisal of Wool*, Wool Economic Research Report no. 20, Bureau of Agricultural Economics, Canberra.

Giles, D.E.A. (1977) 'Statistical Inference and the RBA76 Project', in W.E. Norton (ed.), *Conference in Applied Economic Research*, Sydney: Reserve Bank of Australia.

Goss, B.A. (1972) 'Trading on the Sydney Wool Futures Market: a Test of a Theory of Speculation at the Level of the Individual', *Australian Economic Papers*, 11, 187-202.

Griliches, Z., G.S. Maddala, R. Lucas and N. Wallace (1962) 'Notes on Estimated Aggregate Quarterly Consumption Functions', *Econometrica*, 30, 491-500.

Hicks, J.R. (1939) *Value and Capital*, London: Oxford University Press.

Houthakker, H.S. (1968) 'Normal Backwardation', in J.N. Wolfe (ed.), *Value, Capital and Growth: Papers in Honour of Sir John Hicks*, Edinburgh: Edinburgh University Press.

Johnson, L.L. (1960) 'The Theory of Hedging and Speculation in Commodity Futures', *Review of Economic Studies*, 27, 139-51.

Kaldor, N. (1939, 1961) 'Speculation and Economic Stability', *Review of Economic Studies*, 7, 1-27. Reprinted in N. Kaldor (ed.), *Essays on Economic Stability and Growth*, London: Duckworth.

Mills, E.S. (1962) *Price, Output and Inventory Policy*, New York: Wiley.

Nerlove, M. (1958) 'Adaptive Expectations and Cobweb Phenomena', *Quarterly Journal of Economics*, 72, 227-40.

Peston, M.H. and B.S. Yamey (1960) 'Intertemporal Price Relationships With Forward Markets: A Method of Analysis', *Economica*, 27, 355-67.

Praetz, P.D. (1975) 'Testing the Efficient Markets Theory on the Sydney Wool Futures Exchange', *Australian Economic Papers*, 14, 240-9.

Rockwell, C.S. (1967) 'Normal Backwardation, Forecasting, and the Returns to Commodity Futures Traders', *Food Research Institute Studies*, 7, Supplement, 107-30.

Working, H. (1953) 'Futures Trading and Hedging', *American Economic Review*, 43, 314-43.

Wymer, C.R. (1977a) 'Computer Programs: RESIMUL Manual', International Monetary Fund, Washington, D.C., mimeo.

— (1977b) 'Computer Programs: SIMUL Manual', International Monetary Fund, Washington, D.C., mimeo.

— (1977c) 'Computer Programs: TRANSF Manual', International Monetary Fund, Washington D.C., mimeo.

Yamey, B.S. (1971) 'Short Hedging and Long Hedging in Futures Markets: Symmetry and Asymmetry', *The Journal of Law and Economics*, 14, 413-34.

5 AN ANALYSIS OF INVESTMENT HORIZON AND ALTERNATIVE RISK-RETURN MEASURES FOR COMMODITY FUTURES MARKETS

Cheng-Few Lee and Raymond M. Leuthold*

1. Introduction

The nature of risk and returns, and how to measure them in investment markets, has been discussed for many years. Regarding commodity futures markets, Keynes (1930) first proposed that speculators earned a risk premium as their reward for absorbing hedgers' risks. Gray (1961) could not find the suggested price biases required to support Keynes's underlying hypothesis. Rockwell (1967) measured rates of return for groups of traders in commodity futures markets with semi-monthly data, but did not examine risks. Futures contracts have long been recognized for their ability to transfer risk from hedgers to speculators, but little is known about the risk and return relationship and how it changes over investment horizons.

Considerable methodological advancement has been made in the last 15 years with respect to identifying, measuring and determining risk and returns. Best known for its development and empirical use are the Sharpe (1963) single index model (market model) and the capital asset pricing model (CAPM) developed by Sharpe (1964) and Lintner (1965). These models will determine to what extent variations in individual rates of return are systematically related to variations in market rates of return, and the market model can be used to decompose total risk into systematic and unsystematic risk components. These models have been applied to such securities as stocks, bonds, options and mutual funds, but to date the only known applications to commodity futures markets are Dusak (1973) and Bodie and Rosansky (1980).

Dusak estimated systematic risk for a sample of semi-monthly prices of wheat, corn and soybean futures contracts, 1952-67, and found it to be close to zero in all cases. Average realized returns were also close to zero. These results may be non-representative, however, because many traders in commodity futures markets have very short-run investment horizons. Semi-monthly data may not capture the true nature of the risk and return relationship that these traders face. Bodie and Rosansky (1980) also found systematic risk near zero for 23 commodities over a 27-year period, but holding period returns were strongly positive. Their results, however, are based on quarterly data, or three-month holding periods, which far exceed average investment horizons. When examining commission house records, Ross (1975) found that 52 per cent of the trades were held less than seven days. Only 30 per cent were held 15 or more days. Since these data did not include floor traders who usually have investment horizons shorter than one day, the average length a contract is held is undoubtedly shorter than that reported by Ross. Trade experts sometimes talk of an average holding period of three days.

Recently, several analysts have examined the relationship between investment horizon and measures of risk and returns. Cheng and Deets (1971) discussed the statistical biases associated with security rates of return estimates. Levhari and Levy (1977) point out the disparities which arise when arbitrarily selected data are used for a period which is different from the 'true' horizon. Blume (1974) derived some unbiased estimators of long-run expected rates of return. These authors all demonstrate the importance of the impact of investment horizon on the estimate of expected rates of return and related risk proxies. Empirical investigations of this for common stock have been done by Cheng and Deets (1973), Levhari and Levy (1977), Lee and Morimune (1978), Lee (1976) and others.

In addition, skewness or kurtosis in the distribution of returns may vary with investment horizon. The shape of the return distribution could be used as a criterion for determining the appropriateness of an investment horizon. For example, Hagerman (1978) has shown that the distribution of stock market rates of return is not independent of changes in time horizon, while Folger and Radcliffe (1974) have found the degree of skewness for stock market rates of return is not independent of investment horizon. Such relationships in commodity futures markets are not known.

The purpose of this chapter is to estimate the betas from the market model for 42 selected commodity futures contracts from 1972-7 in order to test the relationship between investment horizon and alternative risk-return measures, to describe the probability distribution of price changes in futures over different interval lengths, and to explore the sensitivity of the results to alternative measures of wealth. We do this by using daily futures prices, varying investment horizons from 1 to 22 days, and using both a stock price index and a commodity price index as proxies for the return on wealth. Since a proxy for daily risk-free rates of return is difficult to obtain, the market model instead of the CAPM is used in this empirical study.

The data used in this study are described in the second section. The third section explores the relationship between horizon and each of the first four moments of the rates of return. In the fourth section, rates of return for the commodity futures contracts are regressed against each of the two indices as risk is decomposed in each contract. The fifth section tests the risk-return trade-offs, and the results of the chapter are summarized in the final section with possible future research indicated.

2. The Data

The stock index used in this paper is the Standard and Poor (S&P) Composite Index of 500 industrial common stocks collected daily. The daily commodity futures index (CFI) is based on 27 commodities and is constructed by the Commodity Research Bureau, Inc. The 42 individual contracts analysed are the December corn, wheat, hogs and cattle contracts, and the November soybean contract, all for 1972-7. Since there is no corresponding year-ending contract for pork bellies, the following February contract was selected for analysis. Thus, in the tables presented below, the results for pork bellies under any given calendar year refer to the February contract maturing the following year (for example, under 1973 will be results for the February 1974 pork belly contract). Also analysed are the December gold (International Monetary Market), silver (Chicago Board of Trade) and Treasury Bill (International Monetary Market) contracts for 1976-7. Since the contracts for differing maturities of one commodity usually fluctuate fairly close together, using one contract per commodity within a year is sufficient for analysis. The above commodities also represent the most actively traded commodity futures contracts and provide an ample cross-section of alternative investment possibilities.

Most contracts trade for about one year, although the exact dates for trading vary among commodities. Table 5.1 lists the number of observations for each of the 42 contracts analysed.

Commodity futures contracts are highly leveraged. Typically, an investor needs to post only about 10 per cent of the value of the contract. As is becoming commonly accepted, and argued by Dusak (1973), from a general equilibrium point of view the spot commodity is the relevant asset. Spot price data, however, are not readily accessible, and in some cases involve estimating and discounting for storage costs. Also, the degree of leverage cannot be measured on an individual basis. Thus, for computational convenience we utilize futures prices, and measure returns as percentage changes in unleveraged contract values. Leveraged returns would exceed those reported here by about a factor of 10. Both logarithmic and arithmetic rates of return are calculated and analysed. The average logarithmic rates of return will be slightly smaller than the average arithmetic rates of return, although the results are so similar that we present only the arithmetic results.

Many professional traders do not hold positions overnight. Those data are not available to us, but the techniques developed here could be applied to transaction-by-transaction data. We chose a 22-day horizon as the maximum, since that is approximately the number of trading days in one calendar month. Due to limited computer funds and similarity of results over horizons, we report individual commodity results only for horizons of 1-10, 15, 16, 21 and 22 days.

Table 5.1: Number of Observations in Each Contract Analysed

	Year					
Commodity	1972	1973	1974	1975	1976	1977
Wheat	242	240	243	301	244	304
Corn	244	306	323	312	303	304
Soybeans	224	285	302	289	285	276
Hogs	239	282	303	287	279	329
Cattle	240	258	243	246	209	290
Pork bellies	282	236	364	316	236	301
Gold					358	366
Silver					349	373
Treasury Bills					244	373

3. Statistical Distributions of 42 Individual Futures Contracts and their Time-Moment Relationships

Rates of return, both discrete and continuous, were computed for each of the 42 futures contracts for each of the above 14 horizons. For the ith horizon, returns are computed for the formulation $(P_{t+i} - P_t)/P_t$. The returns are computed for non-overlapping horizons. For example, with 242 observations for the 1972 wheat contract, there are 241 one-day horizons and 24 ten-day horizons. These returns are for the 'long' side of the market, that is, for those who buy and hold futures contracts. Since for every buyer there must also be a seller of a futures contract, an investor maintaining a 'short' position in the futures market would have the negative of the return calculated for the 'long' position. Commissions and other trading costs are ignored in this analysis.

For each of the 588 combinations of contract and investment horizon, the average rate of return, the standard deviation, coefficient of variation, skewness and kurtosis were estimated. Individual results will not be presented. Rather, the relationship of each moment with respect to time will be discussed. This will give some understanding of the nature of the distribution.

First, tests were conducted on the skewness and kurtosis coefficients to determine whether rates of return are normally distributed. The formulas are: skewness = moment 3/(cubed standard deviation), and kurtosis = moment 4/(squared variance). The standard errors used to test the relativeness of the coefficients are (Snedecor and Cochran, 1967, pp. 86-8):

$$S_1 = [6n(n-1)/(n-2)(n+1)(n+3)]^{1/2} \quad (1)$$

$$S_2 = [24n(n-1)^2/(n-3)(n-2)(n+3)(n+5)]^{1/2} \quad (2)$$

where S_1 is the standard error for skewness, S_2 is the standard error for kurtosis and n is sample size. There is no apparent pattern to the percentage of skewness and kurtosis coefficients by commodity and horizon which are sufficiently different from zero, except that rates of return are more likely to be normally distributed at the longer horizons. Overall, 16 per cent of the skewness coefficients and 18 per cent of the kurtosis coefficients are significantly different from zero. Thus, the vast majority of commodity rates of return over alternative horizons are normally distributed, indicating standard statistical tests can be conducted.

To investigate time-moment relationships, the first four moments and the coefficient of variation for each of the 42 futures contracts were regressed against the horizon length. Each contract was regressed individually, using the moments from each horizon. Both linear and non-linear relationships were tested, but the coefficients for the non-linear variables were for the most part not significantly different from zero. Among these contracts, linear relationships were by far the most prevalent. In any event, these tests are designed to summarize results, and not meant to test linearity *per se.*

The slope coefficients for the average rate of return are presented in Table 5.2. All of the mean rate of return slope coefficients, as well as all of the standard deviation slope coefficients and all but five of the coefficient of variation slope coefficients,

Table 5.2: Slope Coefficient from Time-Moment Relationship — Mean Rate of Return ($\bar{R}_T = a + bT$)

	Year**					
Commodity	1972	1973	1974	1975	1976	1977
Wheat	.231*	.416*	.030*	−.123*	−.122*	−.054*
	(.006)[a]	(.007)	(.008)	(.003)	(.004)	(.003)
Corn	.080*	.254*	.200*	−.068*	−.048*	−.058*
	(.013)	(.008)	(.002)	(.003)	(.002)	(.002)
Soybeans	.090*	.240*	.128*	−.160*	.072*	−.011*
	(.005)	(.006)	(.006)	(.002)	(.008)	(.004)
Hogs	.089*	.254*	.039*	.069*	−.053*	.051*
	(.005)	(.008)	(.004)	(.007)	(.009)	(.005)
Cattle	.059*	.048*	−.087*	.073*	−.018*	−.026*
	(.008)	(.009)	(.004)	(.002)	(.004)	(.004)
Pork bellies	.117*	.127*	.063*	.066*	−.064*	.026*
	(.005)	(.006)	(.003)	(.002)	(.004)	(.004)
Gold					−.077*	.069*
					(.002)	(.004)
Silver					−.085*	−.030*
					(.001)	(.002)
Treasury Bills					.008*	.007*
					(.000)	(.000)

Notes: [a] The standard error is in parenthesis.

* Significantly different from zero at the 95 per cent level of confidence.

** All estimates in this table have been multiplied by 10^2.

were significantly different from zero. This means that the change in these descriptive statistics is significantly related to the change in investment horizon.

Table 5.2 indicates that of the 42 contracts, 26 mean rates of return slopes were positively related to the change in horizon, while 16 contracts were negatively related. A positive (negative) relationship implies that the average rate of return increases (decreases) with respect to an increase in investment horizon. The sign reflects the trend of that particular contract from the 'long' side and demonstrates the importance of prior forecast analysis. All of the slopes for 1972 and 1973 and all but cattle for 1974 had positive relationships. The signs of the slopes were mixed for 1975-7. The results of positive investment returns conform in general to those given by Bodie and Rosansky (1980), where quarterly data were examined. The reader is reminded that our rates of return are for unlevered contracts.

All the slope coefficients for the standard deviations regressed against time are positive, meaning standard deviation increases with increased investment horizon. The signs for the significant coefficient of variation slopes are the opposite of those in Table 5.2 for the average rates of return. Of the five slopes which are insignificant, individual mean returns are near zero, sometimes alternating sign over horizon, thereby influencing the magnitude of the coefficient of variation.

Further investigation of these results showed that mean returns always increase (in absolute value) faster than the standard deviation as horizon increases. Thus, an increase in the holding period can improve investment performance providing one is on the 'right' side of the market, i.e. long as prices rise and short when prices fall.

Finally, 13 of the 42 futures contracts have skewness significantly related to investment horizon, while kurtosis and investment horizon are significantly related in 21 cases. For the most part, if skewness of a contract is related to horizon, kurtosis of the contract is not related and vice versa. Thus, as opposed to the first two moments, the third and fourth moments are largely independent of each other. The results indicate that the shape of the distribution of commodity future rates of return are not independent of alternative horizons used. However, no distinct pattern emerges.

4. Systematic Risk and Non-Systematic Risk Decomposition for 42 Individual Futures Contracts

Based upon the theory and concepts of the market model developed by Sharpe (1963) and Fama (1973), the rates of return of the 42 individual commodity futures contracts are regressed on the stock market index and the commodity futures index. The regression models are defined as:[1]

$$R_{jt} = \alpha + \beta_s R_{mt} + E_{jt} \tag{3}$$

$$R_{jt} = \alpha' + \beta_c R_{ct} + E'_{jt} \tag{4}$$

where R_{jt} = rates of return for jth futures contracts in period t,

R_{mt} = stock market (S&P) rates of return in period t,

R_{ct} = futures market (CFI) rates of return in period t,

E_{jt}, E'_{jt} = error terms.

Since there are 588 contract-horizon combinations, only summaries will be presented. Table 5.3 indicates the number of β_c coefficients significantly different from zero, while Table 5.4 indicates the number of β_s coefficients significantly different from zero (in each case out of 14). These results show that rates of return of individual futures contracts are strongly related to the rates of

Table 5.3: Number of β_c Coefficients Significant (.05 Level) over 14 Alternative Horizons (1, 2, . . ., 10, 15, 16, 21, 22)

	Year					
Commodity	1972	1973	1974	1975	1976	1977
Wheat	13	10	14	14	14	13
Corn	14	14	14	14	14	14
Soybeans	10	14	14	14	14	14
Hogs	7	14	14	10	14	14
Cattle	9	14	14	11	6	14
Pork bellies	4	11	13	10	13	9
Gold					4	8
Silver					12	14
Treasury Bills					0	0

Table 5.4: Number of β_s Coefficients Significant (.05 Level) over 14 Alternative Horizons (1, 2, ..., 10, 15, 16, 21, 22)

	Year					
Commodity	1972	1973	1974	1975	1976	1977
Wheat	1	0	0	0	0	0
Corn	1	0	0	0	0	0
Soybeans	10	1	2	0	0	0
Hogs	3	0	0	1	1	0
Cattle	1	0	0	0	4	0
Pork bellies	0	0	1	0	0	0
Gold					0	0
Silver					0	1
Treasury Bills					0	4

return of the CFI; however, the rates of return of individual futures contracts are generally not significantly related to rates of return of S&P.

Table 5.3 indicates that β_c for corn is always significantly different from zero, regardless of horizon. However, gold has less than half of the β_c coefficients significant, and none is significant for Treasury Bills. These latter results probably reflect the 'agricultural' bias to the CFI, and that these commodities are countercyclical to agricultural prices. It is interesting, however, that most of the silver β_c coefficients are significant. Finally, 1972 stands out as a year of relatively less significant β_c coefficients in Table 5.3, although the reason is not clear.

Table 5.4 shows that most of the β_s coefficients are not significantly different from zero for both agricultural and non-agricultural commodities. The only unusual result is for soybeans, 1972, where 10 of the 14 horizons are significant.

As a means of further evaluation, equations (3) and (4) were combined into a multiple regression equation where the rate of return was regressed on both indexes at the same time. The results were virtually identical to those in Tables 5.3 and 5.4. Over 80 per cent of the β_c coefficients were significant and substantially less than 10 per cent of the β_s coefficients were significant. There was also a distinct trend for the R^2 to increase as horizon increased for any given contract. Because of its relative simplicity, the single-index model seems appropriate for our study.

These results show that commodity futures contracts have a high degree of systematic risk relative to the CFI, but mostly unsystematic risk with respect to S&P. So for a portfolio consisting of common stocks, commodity futures contracts would provide diversification and would be attractive to the investor. On the other hand, an investor with a portfolio of commodity futures contracts would probably not want to add more non-diversifiable futures contracts to the portfolio, except for gold and Treasury Bills.

These latter results support in part those of Dusak (1973), who found little to no systematic risk between commodity futures contracts and the stock index using semi-monthly data. Most of the β coefficients in Bodie and Rosansky (1980) based on quarterly data were also insignificant. They confirm Holthausen and Hughes' (1978) findings that the β coefficients are very sensitive to the market index selected. Unfortunately, an overall wealth index does not exist.

To show whether the CFI is related to the S&P index, the CFI is regressed on the S&P index to test for the existence of systematic risk in the CFI, using the equation:

$$R_{ct}^{T} = \alpha + \beta R_{mt}^{T} + \varepsilon_t \tag{5}$$

where R_{ct} = rates of return for CFI

R_{mt} = rates of return to S&P

T = 1, . . ., 22.

(The regression results for each of 22 horizons are not reproduced here for reasons of space, but are available upon request.)

The β coefficient is significantly different from zero only for the twelve-day horizon, where the coefficient is negative. That is, there is little to no relationship, or systematic risk, between the two indexes.[2] These results imply that commodities in the CFI can be included in an equity portfolio to reduce risk and improve performance of the portfolio. Futures contracts as a whole have no systematic risk relative to stocks, and would serve to provide diversification within a portfolio composed of stocks. The orthogonal relationship between R_{ct} and R_{mt} can also empirically be used to demonstrate why the empirical results of a single-index model are almost indentical to those of a multi-index model.

In order to see the relative magnitudes of the various β coefficients, Tables 5.5 and 5.6 present the average β_c and β_s over

Table 5.5: Average β_c over Horizon

Commodity	1972	1973	1974	1975	1976	1977
			Year			
Wheat	1.666 (.257)[a]	1.165 (.262)	1.344 (.133)	1.542 (.074)	1.465 (.135)	.926 (.111)
Corn	1.573 (.286)	1.522 (.155)	1.417 (.078)	1.259 (.071)	.900 (.127)	1.110 (.093)
Soybeans	.767 (.418)	1.888 (.237)	1.686 (.309)	1.554 (.113)	1.988 (.169)	1.889 (2.15)
Hogs	.610 (.174)	1.007 (.223)	1.507 (.322)	.781 (.171)	1.097 (.164)	.952 (.151)
Cattle	.758 (.203)	.689 (.289)	1.100 (.290)	.648 (.121)	.590 (.138)	.631 (.089)
Pork bellies	.542 (.289)	.867 (.224)	1.286 (.180)	.954 (.163)	1.474 (.183)	.878 (.246)
Gold					.289 (.137)	.635 (.129)
Silver					.973 (.212)	.652 (.077)
Treasury Bills					−.008 (.018)	−.001 (.023)

Note: [a] The standard deviation is in parenthesis.

horizons for each of the 42 contracts, respectively, while Table 5.7 shows both coefficients averaged across commodity contracts for each horizon.

In Table 5.5 almost all of the β_c coefficients for the grains (wheat, corn and soybeans) are greater than 1.0, meaning those commodities have been more volatile than the futures market as a whole. Conversely, most of the meat product (cattle, hogs and pork bellies) β_c coefficients are less than 1.0, but greater than zero. These commodities have been less volatile than the market as a whole. The gold and silver coefficients are between zero and 1.0, but the Treasury Bill coefficients are very small and negative.

Table 5.6 shows that most of the β_s coefficients are small in value, especially relative to their standard errors, with a high proportion of them negative. This again shows that there is little relationship between changes in the stock index and changes in the value of individual commodity futures contracts.

Table 5.7 shows the β_s coefficients when measured across commodities to be very small for all horizons, and all negative beyond

Table 5.6: Average β_s over Horizons

Commodity	Year					
	1972	1973	1974	1975	1976	1977
Wheat	.487	−.199	.080	−.279	.267	.207
	(.334)[a]	(.348)	(.158)	(.142)	(.180)	(.156)
Corn	.085	−.080	−.145	−.150	.106	.064
	(.223)	(.259)	(.133)	(.270)	(.131)	(.184)
Soybeans	.474	.171	−.027	−.305	−.101	.148
	(.180)	(.811)	(.244)	(.338)	(.123)	(.362)
Hogs	−.521	.049	−.000	−.294	.138	−.158
	(.199)	(.235)	(.160)	(.288)	(.376)	(.236)
Cattle	−.423	.173	−.150	−.302	−.681	−.092
	(.405)	(.295)	(.179)	(.226)	(.438)	(.078)
Pork bellies	−.472	−.138	.032	−.310	−.297	−.260
	(.279)	(.441)	(.208)	(.336)	(.675)	(.252)
Gold					−.016	−.102
					(.162)	(.415)
Silver					.061	.060
					(.350)	(.239)
Treasury Bills					.019	.037
					(.017)	(.026)

Note: [a] The standard deviation is in parenthesis.

the four-day horizon. The β_c coefficients are all slightly larger than 1.0 and very similar in magnitude regardless of the horizon. Thus, the β_c coefficients show no sensitivity to horizon, while the β_s coefficients, all small in magnitude, show decreasing, but probably not significantly changing, systematic risk with respect to S&P over horizon.[3]

5. Risk-Return Trade-Off Test

In Section 1, the importance of testing the existence of a risk premium (in a total risk sense) for the commodity futures contracts was explored. Alternative cross-sectional models used to test this are:

$$\bar{R}_j = a_1 + b_1\sigma_j \tag{8}$$

$$\bar{R}_j = a_2 + b_2\beta_s \tag{9}$$

Table 5.7: Average β across Commodities for each Horizon

Horizon (Days)	β for Stocks	β for Commodities
1	.041	1.028
	(.132)[a]	(.476)
2	.012	1.018
	(.151)	(.454)
3	.013	1.060
	(.186)	(.474)
4	.017	1.051
	(.240)	(.449)
5	−.033	1.067
	(.203)	(.445)
6	−.046	1.048
	(.267)	(.468)
7	−.037	1.055
	(.306)	(.486)
8	−.067	1.057
	(.362)	(.526)
9	−.124	1.041
	(.307)	(.551)
10	−.137	1.057
	(.312)	(.516)
15	−.152	1.095
	(.514)	(.539)
16	−.157	1.077
	(.590)	(.557)
21	−.101	1.071
	(.604)	(.591)
22	−.260	1.133
	(.619)	(.641)

Note: [a] The standard deviation is in parenthesis.

$$\bar{R}_j = a_3 + b_3\beta_c \tag{10}$$

where $\bar{R}_j$ = average rate of return for the jth contract

σ_j = standard deviation for the jth contract

β_s, β_c = as previously defined.

The empirical results for equations (8-10) using 42 contracts for observations are presented for 14 alternative horizons in Table 5.8. No relationship exists between average rates of return and the esti-

Table 5.8: Results of Regressing Mean Rate of Return on Selected Variables in Analysing Risk-Return Trade-offs

	Independent Variable					
Horizon (Days)	σ_j	R^2	β_s	R^2	β_c	R^2
1	.0494 (.0294)[a]	.07	.0000 (.0014)	.00	.0003 (.0004)	.01
2	.0964* (.0380)	.14	.0002 (.0024)	.00	.0008 (.0008)	.03
3	.1040* (.0461)	.11	.0005 (.0029)	.00	.0011 (.0011)	.02
4	.1004 (.0547)	.08	.0023 (.0029)	.02	.0009 (.0016)	.01
5	.1317* (.0578)	.11	−.0005 (.0044)	.00	.0018 (.0020)	.02
6	.1342* (.0604)	.11	−.0012 (.0040)	.00	.0014 (.0023)	.01
7	.1242 (.0651)	.08	.0024 (.0041)	.01	.0008 (.0026)	.00
8	.1814* (.0645)	.17	−.0007 (.0040)	.00	.0025 (.0027)	.02
9	.1844* (.0661)	.16	−.0007 (.0053)	.00	.0026 (.0030)	.02
10	.2088* (.0662)	.20	−.0026 (.0058)	.01	.0046 (.0035)	.04
15	.2824* (.0780)	.25	.0006 (.0054)	.00	.0013 (.0051)	.00
16	.2597* (.0737)	.24	.0076 (.0049)	.06	.0079 (.0052)	.06
21	.2292* (.0909)	.14	.0085 (.0061)	.05	.0046 (.0063)	.01
22	.3218* (.0736)	.32	−.0154* (.0063)	.13	.0096 (.0064)	.05

Note: [a] The standard error is in parenthesis.

* Significantly different from zero at the 95 per cent level of confidence.

mated β_s and β_c except for β_s at the 22-day horizon. There is, however, a significant positive relationship between $\bar{R}_j$ and σ_j for all horizons except one-, four- and seven-day horizons. These results imply that there may exist a risk premium for commodity futures contracts if the total risk instead of the systematic risk measure is used. Nevertheless, this analysis does not shed any light on the normal backwardation hypothesis, since we did not adjust futures prices for the rise in cash prices (Gray, 1961). Also, this analysis identifies only ex-post risk-return trade-offs.

Most recently, Levy (1978) has shown that the CAPM is not necessarily an applicable tool for decomposing the total risk into systematic and non-systematic risk unless some strong assumptions are held. One of these assumptions is that the security should be widely held by investors. If the security is held by only a small group of investors, then the market rates of return obtained from an overall index (e.g. S&P) will be subject to measurement error and the estimated beta will be downward biased. As futures contracts are not widely held, the market rates of return calculated from the S&P index will probably be inappropriate. Nevertheless, results in this section have shed light on the usefulness of the market model, or CAPM, and the importance of investment horizon in determining the risk-return relationship of commodity futures contracts.

6. Implications and Conclusions

Futures markets are widely recognized as a means for transferring risks through hedging. This chapter reports the investigation of the statistical distribution and the time-moment relationships among 42 futures contracts and the impact of investment horizon on the estimated beta coefficient. Daily data on contracts from 1972-7 are used in the analysis. The use of daily data is important because most contracts are held for only a few days.

The mean rates of return depend upon the direction of the price moves during the life of the contract, and they were positive for all but one contract during 1972-4. Results for 1975-7 were mixed with regard to sign. However, all rates of return (in absolute value) and standard deviations became larger as horizon increased, showing returns were not independent of horizon. Thus, investment performance improved as horizon increased, as long as one was on the 'right' side of the market. The shape of distributions of rates of return is also not independent of alternative horizons used. Few contracts, however, had significant third or fourth moments, indicating rates of return are normally distributed.

The rates of return for the 42 contracts show strong systematic (non-diversifiable) risk with respect to the commodity futures index, but in general only non-systematic (diversifiable) risk with respect to the stock index. These latter results apply to agricultural and non-agricultural commodities alike. Hence, commodity futures permit reduction of risk through diversification for a stockholder. For the commodities investor, such risk diversification can come only through investing in gold or Treasury Bill futures. In general, individual stock investors seeking risk reduction would have found the addition of commodity futures to their portfolio attractive. This set of results would be magnified if futures positions had been leveraged in the analysis. However, whether the investor should be on the short or long side of the market is a matter of forecast analysis and beyond the scope of this chapter. These results are quite consistent across contracts as well as horizon. Unsystematic risk and horizon are basically independent of each other.

Further work needs to be done analysing why the divergent results exist between the two indexes. The security market index does not appear to be a good proxy for a capital market index, especially in the study of commodities. A composite wealth index is needed. It may also be that industry rather than general market factors influence the pattern of inter-relationships among commodity futures market returns. Industry factors may be highly correlated with returns ex post. It remains to be explored how futures relate to general equilibrium pricing conditions.

To investigate the appropriateness of the CAPM in studying returns, we regressed cross-sectional mean returns against the individual betas for each horizon. Expecting positive relationships between mean returns and non-diversifiable risks, we found only 1 of 28 relationships significant. There was, however, a significant relationship between the mean returns and standard deviation in 11 out of 14 cases. Thus, there may be a slight risk premium in a total market sense, but not necessarily from normal backwardation. Further work is needed on the use of CAPM in commodity futures, especially investigating alternative horizon and index combinations.

Finally, the fact that commodity futures contracts have limits in their daily price moves suggests that truncated distribution techniques of analysis may be appropriate and sensitive. Another important area of research would be the impact of inflation on the futures contracts and risk-return relationships over alternative horizons and against alternative indexes. The existence of a risk premium in commodity futures contracts needs more careful analysis to distinguish between different measures of risk. Besides the standard deviations and beta coefficient, semi-variance and mean absolute deviation can also be used as risk proxies (Stone, 1973). Further investigation is also needed on the impact of autocorrelation on the moments of the distribution and risk (premium) estimates. Nevertheless, the empirical work here has provided additional information concerning commodity futures contracts within the realm of asset price determination and portfolio management.

Notes

*Department of Finance and Department of Agricultural Economics, respectively, University of Illinois at Urbana-Champaign. This research was partly funded by the Chicago Mercantile Exchange.

1. The derivation of this equation in essence comes from the concept of portfolio theory. A portfolio consists of several individual assets, and to regress the returns of an individual security on the returns of the portfolio (or market returns) measures the sensitivity or responsiveness of the security to that of the market. This market model can be used either for forecasting or risk decomposition. Our concern is for the latter. The total risk for the jth futures contract, Var R_{jt}, can be decomposed as follows:

$$\text{Var } R_{jt} = \beta_j^2 \text{ Var } R_{mt} + \text{Var } E_{jt}$$

where β_j^2 Var R_{mt} is systematic (non-diversifiable) risk, and Var E_{jt} is non-systematic (diversifiable) risk. Since Var R_{mt} is common to every futures contract, β_j can be used as a relative measure of systematic fluctuation between the jth contract and all other contracts in the market which are represented by a market index.

2. An update of this analysis through 1981 shows no change in the lack of relationship between the two indexes (see Lee, Leuthold and Cordier, 1985).

3. To investigate the time-variance relationships for β_c and β_s, 42 regressions were run in accordance with the following two equations:

$$\beta_{cT} = a_1 + b_1T \tag{6}$$

$$\beta_{sT} = a_2 + b_2T. \tag{7}$$

The results demonstrate that there exists some relationship between the magnitude of β_c and β_s and investment horizon, although less than half of the coefficients are significant and the significant ones are scattered across commodities and years. As expected from the previous set of tables, most of the slope coefficients for the β_{sT} regression (equation (7)) are negative. Thus, there is not a strong relationship between the size of the β coefficient, indicating systematic risk, and investment horizon.

References

Blume, M.E. (1974) 'Unbiased Estimators of Long-run Expected Rates of Return', *Journal of the American Statistical Association*, 69, 634-8.

Bodie, Z. and V. Rosansky (1980) 'Risk and Return in Commodity Futures', *Financial Analyst Journal*, 36 (May-June), 27-39.

Cheng, P.L. and M.K. Deets (1971) 'Statistical Biases and Security Rates of Return', *Journal of Financial and Quantitative Analysis*, 6, 977-94.

— (1973) 'Systematic Risk and the Horizon Problem', *Journal of Financial and Quantitative Analysis*, 8, 299-316.

Dusak, K. (1973) 'Futures Trading and Investors' Returns: An Investigation of Commodity Market Risk Premiums', *Journal of Political Economy*, 81, 1387-406.

Fama, E.F. (1973) 'A Note on the Market Model and the Two-Parameter Model', *Journal of Finance*, 28, 1181-5,

Fogler, H.K. and R.C. Radcliffe (1974) 'A Note on Measurement of Skewness', *Journal of Financial and Quantitative Analysis*, 9, 485-9.

Gray, R.W. (1961) 'Search for a Risk Premium', *Journal of Political Economy*, 69, 250-60.

Hagerman, R.L. (1978) 'More Evidence on the Distribution of Security Returns', *Journal of Finance*, 33, 1213-21.

Holthausen, D.M. and J.S. Hughes (1978) 'Commodity Returns and Capital Asset Pricing', *Financial Management* (Summer), 37-44.

Keynes, J.M. (1930) *A Treatise on Money, II*, London: Macmillan, 142-7.

Lee, C.F. (1976) 'Investment Horizon and the Functional Form of the Capital Asset Pricing Model', *Review of Economics and Statistics*, 58, 356-63.

Lee, C.F., R.M. Leuthold and J.E. Cordier (1985) 'The Stock Market and the Commodity Futures Market: Diversification and Arbitrage Potential', *Financial Analyst Journal*, 91, (July-August), 53-60.

Lee, C.F. and K. Morimune (1978) 'Time Aggregation, Coefficient of Determination and Systematic Risk of the Market Model', *The Financial Review*, 36-47.

Levhari, D. and H. Levy (1977) 'The Capital Asset Pricing Model and the Investment Horizon', *Review of Economics and Statistics*, 59, 92-104.

Levy, H. (1978) 'Equilibrium in an Imperfect Market: A Constraint on the Number of Securities in a Portfolio', *American Economic Review*, 68, 643-58.

Lintner, J. (1965) 'Security Prices, Risk and Maximal Gains from Diversification', *Journal of Finance*, 20, 587-615.

Rockwell, C.S. (1967) 'Normal Backwardation, Forecasting, and the Returns to Commodity Futures Traders', *Food Research Institute Studies*, 8 (Supplement), 107-30.

Ross, R.L. (1975) 'Financial Consequences of Trading Commodity Futures Contracts', *Illinois Agricultural Economics*, 15 (July), 27-32.

Sharpe, W. (1963) 'A Simplified Model for Portfolio Analysis', *Management Science*, 277-93.

— (1964) 'Capital Asset Prices: A Theory of Market Equilibrium Under Conditions of Risk', *Journal of Finance*, 19, 524-42.

Snedecor, G.W. and W.G. Cochran (1967) *Statistical Methods*, 6th edn, Ames: Iowa State University Press.

Stone, B. (1973) 'A General Class of Three Parameter Risk Measures', *Journal of Finance*, 28, 675-85.

6 TRADING VOLUME AND PRICE VARIABILITY: NEW EVIDENCE ON THE PRICE EFFECTS OF SPECULATION

David J.S. Rutledge*

I had always looked on 'futures' as the creatures of wild speculation and eminently uncertain, and I could not avoid a feeling of wonder that such operations could be reduced within the dominion of scientific investigation, which alone is a great step in advance. (Remarks of Sir Francis S. Powell, MP, Chairman at a Meeting of the Royal Statistical Society, London, 24 April 1906)

1. Introduction

This chapter is concerned with the relationship between the volume of trading and the extent of price variability on commodity futures markets. The existence of such a relationship has been documented in several places (Kent, 1973; Powers, 1970), although there is less than unanimous agreement as to the underlying mechanism by which it is generated. A comparable relationship has been found on security markets (Crouch, 1970; Epps, 1974; Epps and Epps, 1976; Osborne, 1967), and theoretical models have been proposed there to explain it. However, these models do not appear to be readily adaptable to commodity markets as they do not incorporate any explicit discussion of the behaviour of floor traders.

The topic has received remarkably little attention in the context of commodity markets, usually arising incidentally in studies of the statistical distribution of price changes. However, as we shall attempt to show here, it deserves study in its own right since it bears directly on the question of the price effects of speculation and, hence, on certain aspects of market regulation.

As a point of departure, we may first note that in discussing day-to-day variations in trading volume we are in fact considering day-to-day variations in *speculation.* This is because transactions involving hedgers on either side comprise only a small proportion of daily trading volume. Current statistics to support this claim are not available, but a review of the fragmentary historical data, summarized in Table 6.1, provides an indication of the orders of magnitude involved. For the purpose of this chapter, the relevant figures are those relating to trading on the Chicago Board of Trade, since the empirical analysis to be reported below is concerned only with 'central' markets. On the smaller exchanges, a very high proportion of non-hedged trading involves spreading to the Chicago Board of Trade with the result that trading volume on these markets shows a considerably higher component of hedging activity (Gray, 1961, 1967). The time periods covered in Table 6.1 are somewhat atypical, being periods of unusually wide price movement. Even if the figures in the table considerably underestimate the usual volume of hedging transactions, however, it

Table 6.1: Percentage of Trading Volume Involving Hedgers

Period	Exchanges	Commodity	Hedging Transactions as Percentage of Total Volume
2 January 1925 – 18 April 1925[a]	Chicago Board of Trade	Wheat Corn	3
3 January 1927 – 31 October 1927[b]	Chicago Board of Trade	Wheat	5
	Chicago Board of Trade	Corn	4
	Minneapolis Grain Exchange	Wheat	23
	Kansas City Board of Trade	Wheat	26
	Duluth Grain Exchange	Wheat	45
	Kansas City Board of Trade	Corn	15
18 September 1947[c]	Chicago Board of Trade	Wheat	15

Notes: [a] See US 69th Congress (1926), p. 29. These figures refer to trading in the May future only.
[b] See US 71st Congress (1930), p. 15.
[c] See Withrow (1960, p. 182).

remains clear that movements in daily trading volume primarily reflect movements in speculative activity.

In the subsequent sections of this chapter, we shall discuss alternative interpretations of the price effects of speculation, paying special attention to the possible effects of speculation on price variability. We shall then describe a methodology for testing for the direction of causality between two variables and apply this methodology to the relationship between trading volume (speculation) and price variability. Finally, we shall consider the implications of the results for market regulation.

2. Price Effects of Futures Trading

Widespread agreement can be found among even the most casual students of futures markets that these markets facilitate speculation. There is considerable disagreement, however, as to the effects of such speculation.

One school of thought holds that speculation performs a welfare-increasing function which is effected in a variety of interdependent ways. First, speculation is required for a futures market to grow to sufficient maturity to facilitate hedging operations. Thus, in so far as futures trading itself produces benefits, these may, at least in part, be attributed to speculation. Benefits of this kind include generation of increased traders' information about supply and demand influences (Crouch, 1970), facilitation of transactions among strangers (Telser and Higinbotham, 1977) and facilitation of risk-management by handlers of commodities (Working, 1970).

A further strand of the argument is that speculation promotes price stability. By providing an intertemporal array of price information, a futures market (and, hence, speculation) enables stockholding, production, consumption and processing activities to be allocated over time in an efficient fashion, thereby reducing the amplitude of seasonal fluctuations in *cash prices.* At the same time, according to this view, speculation has the effect of mitigating short-run fluctuations in futures prices. The notion is that speculators buy futures when prices drift 'too low' and sell when they go 'too high'. In each case, the extent of futures price variability is reduced. This latter view, stated in the form that profitable speculation necessarily exerts a stabilizing influence on price, has been associated with Friedman (1953), although it can be traced back at least as far as Irving Fisher (1930, p. 218). As we shall see below, it has given rise to a protracted theoretical debate among economists.

On the other hand is the view, sometimes expressed before congressional hearings, that speculation has a *destabilizing* influence on price and, in particular, that 'waves' of speculative activity motivated by factors unrelated to fundamental market influences may distort prices and cause them to fluctuate to an unwarranted degree. This view prevailed in 1958 when trading in onion futures was prohibited in the United States, and it lay behind at least some of the criticism of futures trading which led to extensive amendments to the Commodity Exchange Act in 1974.

The gist of this view was expressed clearly enough by Congressman Conte:[1]

> Both producers and consumers have suffered as a result of huge price fluctuation. I am convinced that someone, somewhere is profiting from all of this. And I suspect that in some cases at least, the people *responsible* for the price fluctuations are among those benefitting from them. [emphasis added] (US 93rd Congress, 1973)

Furthermore, the view that speculation may exacerbate futures price movements has been accepted by some close observers of the market place. The then administrator of the Commodity Exchange Authority, R.R. Kauffman, commented in 1957 on speculation in the onion market as follows:

> Wide and rapid price swings attract speculation which at times further widens the swings, thus attracting more speculation. This speculative fever continues until the individual speculators have either lost their money or made enough to satisfy them for the time being. (US 85th Congress, 1957)

Congress has seen some merit in this argument as the Commodity Futures Trading Commission Act of 1974 states, in part:

> Excessive speculation in any commodity under contracts of sale of such commodity for future delivery made on or subject to the rule of contract markets causing sudden or unreasonable fluctu-

> ations or unwarranted changes in the price of such commodity, is an undue or unnecessary burden on interstate commerce in such commodity. For the purpose of diminishing, eliminating, or preventing such burden, the Commission shall, from time to time, after due notice and opportunity for hearing, by order, proclaim and fix such limits on the amount of trading which may be done on positions which may be held by any person under contracts of sale of such commodity for future delivery on or subject to the rules of any contract market as the Commission finds are necessary to diminish, eliminate or prevent such burden. (US 93rd Congress, 1974, pp. 54-5)

At present, speculative position limits and daily trading limits have been fixed by the Commission for cotton, rye, soybeans, eggs, potatoes, corn and wheat.

As noted above, it is possible to construct theoretical models of speculative behaviour in which speculation tends to diminish the magnitude of price fluctuations. Why then has the contrary view received widespread support and legislative approval? The answer lies not only in populist prejudice against speculation and the 'middleman', but also in the fact that economic theory provides no unequivocal conclusion as to the price effects of speculation.

Baumol (1957), Stein (1961) and Kemp (1973) have shown that it is possible to construct models in which speculation is profitable yet destabilizing. Baumol's illustrations of this proposition have been criticized by Telser (1959) as being unrealistic, while Stein's example rests on institutional characteristics of the foreign exchange market which may not be relevant for the present case. Nevertheless, more recent work by Farrell (1966) and Schimmler (1973) suggest that the formal conditions under which the proposition that 'profitable speculation is price stabilizing' is valid are quite restrictive. It is difficult not to agree with Baumol that 'the effect of ... speculation on stability is in part an empirical question and that attempts to settle it by *a priori* comments must somewhere resort to fallacy' (Baumol, 1959, p. 302).

Empirical resolution of this question is no easy matter, however. The course of action usually adopted is to examine the variability of cash prices of a given commodity for two time periods, one in which an active futures market for the commodity existed and one in which there was no such market. In order to attribute any observed differences in price variability to the influence of futures trading or speculation, one must resort to a *post hoc ergo propter hoc* argument and consequently the results of such studies must be interpreted with caution. Analysis along these lines has been undertaken for wheat (Hooker, 1901; Tomek, 1971), onions (Gray, 1963; Johnson, 1973; Working, 1960), cotton (Chapman and Knoop, 1906; Emery, 1896), pork bellies and live cattle (Powers, 1970; Taylor and Leuthold, 1974). These studies generally show a reduction in price variability concomitant with futures trading.

The present chapter examines the question from a somewhat different viewpoint. The correlation, noted at the start of the chapter, between trading volume and price variability might be construed as evidence in support of the hypothesis that speculation destabilizes price. On the other hand, it is not difficult to envisage models of speculative behaviour in which an increase in the volume of trading can be considered as a *response* to, rather than a *cause* of, increased price variability. This view is consistent with the activities of scalpers and day traders as described by Working (1977, 1967).

Consider, for example, the activities of scalpers who can be characterized as 'always standing ready to either buy at 1/8 cents below the last price or sell at 1/8 cents above the last price'.[2] If prices are regarded as promptly and appropriately reflecting new information which flows to the market place at an uneven rate, then the trading activities of scalpers will clearly be greater on days when prices fluctuate more. The same conclusion can be seen to apply to 'day traders', whose activities have been described in more detail by Working (1977, pp. 188-90). Another important class of speculative trading is 'price-level trading'.[3] Here again the greater the degree of price fluctation the more likely it is that potentially profitable short-run trends may emerge, giving rise to increased trading activity.

Some ideas have been expressed in another way by an officer of a large trading firm:

> the average speculator is interested in trading in a commodity that moves. If oats are fluctuating within a range of 1/4 to 1/2 cent and soybeans have a range of 2 to 3 cents a day, the speculator is going to be attracted to the soybean market. (Withrow, 1960, p. 168)

Much importance, therefore, attaches to the *direction of causality* underlying the correlation between trading volume and price variability. Evidence that causality runs from trading volume to price variability would strongly support the critics of futures markets and would provide a more satisfactory base on which regulation of speculative positions and daily trading activity could be based. Evidence in the other direction, when combined with that described above on cash price variability, would provide empirical support for those who argue for some modification of these regulations.

It should be remembered in the following sections that when we speak of trading volume 'causing' price instability, or price variability 'causing' trading volume we are in fact glossing over a very complex mechanism. In fact, of course, the observed relationship between these variables is a reflection of the extent to which traders react differently to perceived new information. The truly 'causal' variables cannot be observed and hence our portrayal of the relationship between trading volume and price variability as a causal one is a very crude characterization of the microstructure of futures markets.

3. Testing for Causality: Methodology

That correlation implies nothing about cause and effect is a proposition firmly impressed upon all students of statistics. There are many examples of 'nonsense correlations'; even when a correlation is symptomatic of a causal mechanism, it is generally accepted that there are no empirical means of identifying the direction of causality.[4]

In part the difficulty is one of actually defining what the term *causality* means, a question which has fascinated philosophers at least since the time of Hume (1888). More recently, attempts have been made to develop more explicit (and, hence, more restrictive) definitions of causality which may, in some instances, allow us to identify the direction of causality between two variables. The concept of causality to be employed here is essentially that defined by Suppes:

> one event is the cause of another if the appearance of the first event is followed with a high probability by the appearance of

> the second, and there is no third event we can use to factor out the probability relationship between the first and second events. (Suppes, 1970, p. 10)

This definition rests on two intuitive notions. First, that the future cannot cause the past and, second, that causality must essentially be a probabilistic concept (Granger and Newbold, 1977, pp. 224-5). These ideas have been more rigorously developed by Granger (1969) and Sims (1972), and operational procedures which permit testing for the direction of causality have been devised by Sims (1972).

To illustrate, suppose that we want to test for causality between two time series $\{Y_t\}$ and $\{X_t\}$.[5] Employing the idea that the future cannot cause the past, we estimate an equation in the form:

$$Y_t = \alpha + \sum_{i=1}^{m} \beta_i X_{t+i} + \sum_{i=0}^{n} \gamma_i X_{t-i} + u_t \tag{1}$$

If we reject the joint hypothesis $\{\beta_i = 0; i = 1, \ldots m\}$ it follows that future values of X help us to 'predict' the current value of Y, and we conclude that X *cannot* cause Y. Suppose, for purposes of illustration, that this indeed occurs. The next step is to reverse the roles of X and Y, and estimate an equation of the form:

$$X_t = \alpha + \sum_{i=1}^{m} \beta_i Y_{t+i} + \sum_{i=0}^{n} \gamma_i Y_{t-i} + u_t \tag{2}$$

Suppose, in equation (2) the joint hypothesis $\{\beta_i = 0; i = 1, 2, \ldots m\}$ is not rejected. The possibility that Y causes X thus remains open. Finally we estimate an equation of the form:

$$X_t = \alpha + \sum_{i=0}^{n} \gamma_i Y_{t-i} + u_t \tag{3}$$

If the hypothesis $\{\gamma_i = 0; i = 0, 1, 2, \ldots n\}$ is not rejected, and if the estimated coefficients $\{\gamma_i\}$ are plausible, we conclude that the data support the hypothesis that Y causes X rather than the converse.

When this procedure is applied to data on two variables, Y and

X, between which a significant correlation has been observed, there are several possible outcomes.

(a) We may conclude that Y causes X.
(b) We may conclude that X causes Y.
(c) The procedure may prove to be inconclusive. This could occur because we do not reject the hypothesis $\{\beta_i = 0, i = 1, \ldots m\}$ in either equation (2) or equation (3). Alternatively, it may occur because $\beta_i = 0, i = 1, 2, \ldots n$ is rejected in equation (1) but $\{\gamma_i = 0; 1, 2, \ldots m\}$ is not rejected in equation (3).
(d) We may conclude that there is no causality between X and Y. This may occur if the hypothesis $\{\beta_i = 0; i = 1, 2, \ldots n\}$ is rejected in both equations (2) and (3).

It should be emphasized that this procedure cannot *prove* that causality runs in a particular direction. Furthermore, the possibility remains that causality may spuriously be identified as flowing from one variable to another. This may occur because we can examine variables only in a pairwise fashion. However, Sims has argued (1972, pp. 541-3) that, with this qualification, the test will fail only in a few specific circumstances unlikely to apply in the present study.

The Granger-Sims procedure outlined above clearly relies on the existence of time lags in the causal mechanism which are at least as long as the period between observations. The importance of this for the present study will be further discussed below.

4. Results

In this section, we describe the results of applying the procedure outlined above to daily data on trading volume and price variability for a number of commodity futures contracts. In the results reported here, the measure of price variability to be employed is the absolute value of the percentage change in daily closing price. This is not the only available measure of price variability and it may not be the most appropriate — daily range suggests itself as a promising alternative. Preliminary analysis indicates that the conclusions of the study would not be significantly altered if range were used and, as most previous studies of the relationship between trading volume and price variability have used measures based on daily closing prices, this has been regarded as a convenient point of departure. It is intended that this question be pursued further in extensions of this study.

The data base initially constructed consisted of daily closing prices and daily trading volume for 15 commodities. For each commodity, three time periods of approximately four months' length were selected. These sample periods were selected to enable comparisons to be made between several delivery months. Data for two of the commodities originally selected (live hogs and frozen pork bellies) were not fully analysed because of the very high proportion of limit price movements in the sample periods. Limit price movements do not necessarily present a problem for the type of analysis conducted here, but if, as sometimes occurs, there are several successive days of limit movements, the underlying relationship between trading volume and price variability is distorted. On some days, limit movements are accompanied by very low trading volume and on others by very high trading volume. The number of observations in each sample period (generally about 80) is large enough to facilitate statistical analysis but not so great as to give rise to concern over instability in the underlying model. Full details as to the commodities, contracts and time periods used can be found in the Appendix to this chapter. For the time being, however, it is worth noting that the range of commodities and time periods selected for study represents a very great diversity of price behaviour, trading activity and commodity characteristics.

In each estimated equation, a time trend has been included to allow for any long-run influences not directly accounted for in the relationship between trading volume and price variability, and all equations have been estimated, using the Cochrane-Orcutt iterative procedure to take account of first-order serial dependence in the errors. The values of m and n (the lead and lag lengths) were set at three and five respectively in equations (1) and (2). These values were selected arbitrarily but seemed sufficiently generous on *a priori* grounds.

A further matter for consideration is the specification of the trading volume variable. It may well be preferable to express volume as a proportion of the open interest rather than to work with volume itself. This is likely to be especially so in analysing data from very long sample periods, but is less likely to be a problem in the present case. Furthermore, inclusion of the time-trend variable, at least in equations with trading volume as the dependent variable, appears to do a satisfactory job of accounting for the effects of open interest movements. Nevertheless, extensions of the study will include explicit incorporation of open interest data.

Several additional technical points must be mentioned. Tests of the joint hypothesis $\beta_i = 0; i = 1, 2, \ldots m$ and $\gamma_i = 0; i=0, 1, 2, \ldots n$ were carried out using the usual F-tests for sets of linear restrictions. In all cases, 5 per cent levels of significance were used. Because the dependent variable is always constrained to be non-negative, the error term in equations (1), (2) and (3) cannot be normally distributed. Although extensive testing has not yet been undertaken, preliminary indications using the Shapiro-Wilk test on the Cochrane-Orcutt residuals (Huang and Bolch, 1974) suggest that non-normality is not a serious problem in the present case.

In all, 136 contracts in 13 commodities were retained for analysis. Table 6.2 summarizes the results of applying the Granger-Sims procedure to these contracts.[6] Illustrative results for three contracts are shown in Tables 6.3, 6.4 and 6.5. As can be seen, the results provide remarkably strong support for the hypothesis that movements in trading volume represents a response to, rather than a cause of, movements in price variability.

Of the 136 contracts examined, 23 exhibit so weak a relationship between trading volume and price variability that the question of causality does not arise. Sixteen of these (in the soybean complex, silver and IMM contracts) are commodities where spreading activities are particularly important and where, as a consequence, one would expect a simple relationship between trading volume and price variability to be less prevalent. Most of the other contracts falling into this category are in commodities where futures trading is a relatively recent phenomenon.

In 80 of the remaining 113 cases, the procedure was unable to identify the direction of causality between trading volume and price variability. This is almost certainly a reflection, not of the lack of a causal relationship, but rather of the period between observations being too great relative to the time lags involved. A very great proportion of variation in trading volume is a reflection of the activities of day traders who hold zero positions overnight. Even if the trading of this group is significantly influenced by price variability, as has been suggested in Section 2, we should not expect to find many lagged responses greater than one day in length. However, as we have seen in the previous section, the

Table 6.2: Summary of Results

Commodity	Year	Number of Contracts	Number of Cases in which Significant Relationship Exists: Vol-Var[a]	Var-Vol[b]	Can't Say	Number of Cases in which no Significant Relationship Exists
Wheat	1973/74	4	0	4	0	0
	1974/75	4	0	3	1	0
	1975/76	4	0	0	4	0
Corn	1974	4	0	3	1	0
	1975	4	0	0	4	0
	1976	4	0	3	1	0
Oats	1973/74	3	0	0	3	0
	1974/75	3	0	2	1	0
	1975/76	3	0	0	3	0
Live cattle	1973/74	4	0	1	2	1
	1974/75	4	0	1	1	0
	1975/76	4	0	1	3	0
Iced broilers	1974	4	2	2	0	0
	1975	3	0	0	2	1
	1976	4	0	0	3	1
Plywood	1974	4	0	0	1	3
	1975	4	0	1	3	0
	1976	4	0	0	3	1
Soybeans	1974	5	0	1	2	2
	1975	5	0	0	4	1
	1976	5	0	0	5	0
Soybean oil	1974	4	0	2	2	0
	1975	5	0	0	1	4
	1976	4	0	0	4	0
Soybean meal	1974	4	0	1	3	0
	1975	4	0	0	4	0
	1976	4	0	1	3	0
Silver	1974	4	0	0	2	2
	1975	4	0	1	3	0
	1976	4	0	0	4	0
Gold	1975	4	0	2	0	0
	1976	4	0	0	3	1

DM	1974	2	0	0	0	2
	1975	2	0	0	0	2
	1976	2	0	0	2	0
Yen	1975	2	0	0	0	2
Total		136	2	31	80	23

Notes: [a] Indicates number of cases in which causality is identified as running from trading volume to price variability.
[b] Indicates number of cases in which causality is identified as running from price variability to trading volume.

Table 6.3: Wheat, May 1975 Contract

Dependent Variable Estimated Coefficient	Var_t $\times 10^6$	Var_t $\times 10^6$	Vol_t	Vol_t
β_3	−0.7567 (0.4673)		39487.6 (29073.4)	
β_2	0.9500 (0.4898)		−21017.3 (29798.8)	
β_1	1.1986 (0.4990)		15185.8 (29487.6)	
γ_0	0.2678 (0.4979)	0.8204 (0.5015)	40602.5 (29054.1)	40606.6 (28631.5)
γ_1	−0.04779 (0.4989)	0.07252 (0.5173)	79024.1 (28820.0)	77236.8 (28682.7)
γ_2	−0.2782 (0.5040)	−0.4566 (0.5325)	66873.9 (29005.4)	63528.8 (28618.3)
γ_3	0.6937 (0.4998)	0.8112 (0.5319)	−24083.3 (28890.0)	−24061.8 (28534.5)
γ_4	−0.3347 (0.4945)	−0.3158 (0.5263)	22769.9 (28790.4)	24088.0 (28491.6)
γ_5	0.3521 (0.4921)	0.8365 (0.5167)	−2500.72 (28493.1)	−3044.35 (28380.1)
F_β	3.77*		0.97	
F_γ		0.87		2.29*

Notes: * Denotes statistically significant at 5 per cent level.
F_β Denotes value of F-statistics for testing $\beta_1 = \beta_2 = \beta_3 = 0$.
F_γ Denotes value of F-statistics for testing $\gamma_0 = \gamma_1 = \ldots \gamma_5 = 0$.

Table 6.4: Gold, March 1977 Contract

Dependent Variable Estimated Coefficient	Var_t $\times 10^4$	Var_t $\times 10^4$	Vol_t	Vol_t
β_3	0.6897 (0.1652)		−83.6890 (1001.30)	
β_2	−0.01842 (0.1803)		−128.411 (993.513)	
β_1	0.3655 (0.1787)		44.6761 (1052.87)	
γ_0	0.2506 (0.1774)	0.2832 (0.1848)	1638.77 (1043.99)	1601.91 (978.823)
γ_1	−0.03023 (0.1769)	−0.09688 (0.1900)	1384.61 (1064.68)	140.96 (980.055)
γ_2	0.2123 (0.1775)	0.1329 (0.1919)	680.007 (1048.25)	697.260 (996.805)
γ_3	0.02801 (0.1788)	−0.08402 (0.1918)	3270.66 (1055.21)	3252.72 (998.856)
γ_4	0.1003 (0.1769)	0.09573 (0.1904)	1294.90 (1053.79)	1306.65 (1001.90)
γ_5	−0.6667 (0.1564)	−0.004908 (0.1846)	−1647.20 (1077.74)	−1602.74 (1003.01)
F_β	8.03**		0.01	
F_γ		0.47		3.15*

*See notes to Table 6.3

presence of longer lags is required for the test procedure to be able to identify the direction of causality.

Most importantly, of the 33 cases in which the procedure does identify the direction of causality, only two show causality running from trading volume to price variability. In all other cases, the evidence supports the hypothesis that trading volume responds to price variability rather than causes it.

The two exceptions are of some interest also. They both occur in ‘distant’ iced broiler contracts in 1974[7] in which trading activity was particularly thin. In this connection, it is worth noting that the thinness of the iced broiler contract at the Chicago Board of Trade has recently attracted both trade and academic comment (Emery, 1896, p. 41; Schrader, 1978).

Table 6.5: Iced Broilers, August 1974 Contract

Dependent Variable Estimated Coefficient	Var_t $\times 10^5$	Var_t $\times 10^5$	Vol_t	Vol_t
β_3	−0.8161 (3.012)		295.681 (336.133)	
β_2	−3.778 (3.307)		735.477 (338.059)	
β_1	0.2037 (3.415)		770.979 (336.360)	
γ_0	16.59 (3.343)	15.60 (3.004)	2037.02 (337.656)	1890.48 (351.660)
γ_1	0.7089 (3.376)	0.6886 (3.315)	526.545 (342.707)	518.702 (357.878)
γ_2	1.121 (3.426)	1.025 (3.366)	34.9577 (343.921)	133.968 (360.656)
γ_3	0.4499 (3.542)	0.6472 (3.448)	−113.348 (345.827)	78.4356 (360.172)
γ_4	−0.2991 (3.515)	−0.9272 (3.411)	35.7533 (348.739)	98.3929 (362.995)
γ_5	−0.2680 (3.241)	−0.5734 (3.149)	1.30372 (347.531)	−78.0271 (360.355)
F_β	0.74		4.65*	
F_γ		3.04*		6.00*

*See notes to Table 6.3.

5. Conclusions

In July 1976, the Commodity Futures Trading Commission Advisory Committee on the Economic Role of Contract Markets reported in the following terms:

> The Advisory Committee is in general agreement that the current daily trading limits for speculators should be changed to daily limits on net position change. The present flat fixed limit on the number of contracts a speculator can trade during the day may actually cut back participation of speculators at the very time when they are most needed. On active trading days some speculators are forced out of the pit during the later hours of daily trading — reducing liquidity. The Committee feels these daily trading limits are probably more binding on market per-

formance than the speculative position limits. (Commodity Futures Trading Commission, 1976, p. 22)

The empirical evidence reported in the present chapter must be regarded as providing considerable support for the Advisory Committee's recommendations. While it does not provide direct evidence that speculative activity stabilizes prices in the short run, it clearly forms the basis for rejecting the alternative view that speculative activity destabilizes price.

Finally, it is to be emphasized that a good deal of further work along the lines of this chapter remains to be done. In addition to the more technical extensions mentioned in Section 4, analysis of additional time periods and commodities would strengthen the analysis. Nevertheless, the results as presented do represent a contribution to our knowledge about the role of speculation in commodity markets.

Appendix: Details of Sample Periods and Contracts Used in Empirical Analysis

Exchange	Commodity	Sample Period	Contracts Used
Chicago Board of Trade	Wheat	1/11/73-2/28/74	March 1974, May 1974, July 1974, Sept. 1974
		1/11/74-2/28/75	March 1975, May 1975, July 1975, Sept. 1975
		1/11/75-2/29/75	March 1976, May 1976, July 1976, Sept. 1976
	Corn	1/1/74-4/30/74	May 1974, July 1974, Sept. 1974, Dec. 1974
		1/1/75-4/30/75	May 1975, July 1975, Sept. 1975, Dec. 1975
		1/1/76-4/30/76	May 1976, July 1976, Sept. 1976, Dec. 1976
	Oats	1/11/73-2/28/74	March 1974, May 1974, July 1974
		1/11/74-2/28/75	March 1975, May 1975, July 1975
		1/11/75-2/29/76	March 1976, May 1976, July 1976
	Soybeans	1/1/74-4/30/74	May 1974, July 1974, Sept. 1974, Nov. 1974, Jan. 1975
		1/1/75-4/30/75	May 1975, July 1975, Sept. 1975, Nov. 1975, Jan. 1976
		1/1/76-4/30/76	May 1976, July 1976, Sept. 1976, Nov. 1976, Jan. 1977

	Soybean oil	1/1/74-4/30/74	May 1974, July 1974, Oct. 1974, Dec. 1974
		1/1/75-4/30/75	May 1975, July 1975, Oct. 1975, Dec. 1975, Jan. 1976
		1/1/76-4/30/76	May 1976, July 1976, Oct. 1976, Dec. 1976
	Soybean meal	1/1/74-4/30/74	May 1974, July 1974, Oct. 1974, Dec. 1974
		1/1/75-4/30/75	May 1975, July 1975, Oct. 1975, Dec. 1975
		1/1/76-4/30/76	May 1976, July 1976, Oct. 1976, Dec. 1976
	Silver	2/1/74-5/31/74	June 1974, Aug. 1974, Dec. 1974, Feb. 1975
		2/1/75-5/31/75	June 1975, Aug. 1975, Dec. 1975, Feb. 1976
		2/1/76-5/31/76	June 1976, Aug. 1976, Dec. 1976, Feb. 1977
	Iced broilers	1/2/74-4/30/74	May 1974, June 1974, July 1974, Aug. 1974
		1/2/75-4/30/75	May 1975, June 1975, July 1975
		1/2/76-4/30/76	May 1976, June 1976, July 1976, Aug. 1976
	Plywood	1/2/74-4/30/74	May 1974, July 1974, Sept. 1974, Nov. 1974
		1/2/75-4/30/75	May 1975, July 1975, Sept. 1975, Nov. 1975
		1/2/76-4/30/76	May 1976, July 1976, Sept. 1976, Nov. 1976
Chicago Mercantile Exchange	Live cattle	10/1/73-1/30/74	Feb. 1974, April 1974, June 1974, Aug. 1974
		10/1/74-1/30/75	Feb. 1975, April 1975, June 1975, Aug. 1975
		10/1/75-1/30/76	Feb. 1976, April 1976, June 1976, Aug. 1976
International Monetary Market	Gold	2/27/75-5/31/75	June 1975, Sept. 1975, Dec. 1975, March 1976
		2/1/76-5/31/76	June 1976, Sept. 1976, Dec. 1976, March 1977
	Deutsche Mark	2/1/74-5/31/74	June 1974, Sept. 1974
		2/1/75-5/31/75	June 1975, Sept. 1975
		2/1/76-5/31/76	June 1976, Sept. 1976
	Japanese Yen	2/1/75-5/31/75	June 1975, Sept. 1975

Notes

*Sydney Futures Exchange. This chapter was prepared while the author was Visiting Associate Professor, Food Research Institute, Stanford University.

1. For evidence of a different kind to be presented in this chapter, which suggests that this view is false, see US General Accounting Office (1975).

2. This definition refers to 'unit scalping' in the grain markets. However it applies *mutatis mutandis* to other commodities.

3. The term is Working's, who notes that in trade practice this is frequently designated 'position trading' (Working, 1967, p. 201).

4. For an interesting illustration of this argument in the context of the price effects of futures trading, see Hieronymus (1960), Shepherd (1960).

5. The following discussion is necessarily a somewhat loose summary of a rather sophisticated literature. The interested reader is referred to the papers of Granger and Sims for a more rigorous presentation.

6. As noted above, 5 per cent significance levels have been used. Use of more generous levels of significance (say, 10 per cent) does not greatly reduce the number of 'can't say' cases and does not alter the balance between columns 2 and 3 in Table 6.2.

7. The two iced broiler contracts involved are for July 1974 and August 1974 delivery.

References

Baumol, W.J. (1957) 'Speculation, Profitability and Stability', *The Review of Economics and Statistics*, XXXIX(3) (August), 263-71.

— (1959) 'Reply', *The Review of Economics and Statistics*, 3 (August) 301-2.

Chapman, S.J. and D. Knoop (1906) 'Dealings in Futures on the Cotton Market', *Journal of the Royal Statistical Society*, 69(2) (June), 321-73.

Commodity Futures Trading Commission (1976) *Report of the Advisory Committee on the Economic Role of Contract Markets*, Washington D.C., 17 July.

Cox, C.C. (1976) 'Futures Trading and Market Information', *Journal of Political Economy*, 84(6) (December), 1215-37.

Crouch, R.L. (1970) 'The Volume of Transactions and Price Changes of the New York Stock Exchange', *Financial Analysts Journal*, 26(4) (July-August), 104-9.

Donnelly, R.A. (1977) 'Commodities Corner', *Barron's*, 12 December, pp. 40-1.

Emery, H.C. (1896) *Speculation on the Stock and Produce Exchange of the United States*, New York: Columbia University Press.

Epps, T.W. (1974) 'Security Price Changes and Transaction Volumes: Theory and Evidence', *American Economic Review*, LXV(4) (September), 586-97.

Epps, T.W. and M.L. Epps (1976) 'The Stochastic Dependence of Security Price Changes and Transaction Volumes: Implications for the Mixture-of-Distributions Hypothesis', *Econometrica*, 44(2) (March), 305-21.

Farrell, M.J. (1966) 'Profitable Speculation', *Economica*, N.S. XXXIII(130) (May), 183-93.

Fisher, I. (1930) *The Stock Market Crash and After*, New York: Macmillan.

Friedman, M. (1953) *Essays in Positive Economics*, Chicago: University of Chicago Press.

Granger, C.W.J. (1969) 'Investigating Causal Relations by Econometric Models and Cross-Spectral Methods', *Econometrica*, 37(3) (July), 424-38.

Granger, C.W.J. and P. Newbold (1977) *Forecasting Economic Time Series*, New York: Academic Press.

Gray, R.W. (1960) 'The Importance of Hedging in Futures Trading; and the Effectiveness of Futures Trading for Hedging', in *Futures Trading Seminar, I*, Madison: Mimir Publishers, pp. 61-82.

— (1961) 'The Relationship Among Three Futures Markets', *Food Research Institute Studies*, II(1) (February), 21-32.

— (1963) 'Onions Revisited', *Journal of Farm Economics* (May), 273-6.

— (1967) 'Price Effects of a Lack of Speculation', *Food Research Institute Studies*, VII, Supplement, 17-94.

Hieronymus, T.A. (1960) 'Effects of Futures Trading on Prices', *Futures Trading Seminar, I*, Madison: Mimir Publishers, pp. 121-62.

Hooker, R.H. (1901) 'The Suspension of the Berlin Produce Exchange and Its Effects upon Corn Prices', *Journal of the Royal Statistical Society*, 64 (December), 574-604.

Huang, C.J. and B.W. Bolch (1974) 'On the Testing of Regression Disturbances for Normality', *Journal of the American Statistical Association*, 69(346) (June), 330-7.

Hume, D. (1888) *A Treatise on Human Nature*, ed. L.A. Selby-Bigge, Oxford: Clarendon Press.

Johnson, A.C. (1973) *Effects of Futures Trading on Price Performance in the Cash Onion Market, 1930-68*, USDA, E.R.S. Technical Bulletin 1470, February.

Kemp, M.C. (1973) 'Speculation, Profitability and Price Stability', *The Review of Economics and Statistics*, XLV(2) (May) 185-9.

Kent, P.K. (1973) 'A Subordinated Stochastic Process with Finite Variance for Speculative Prices', *Econometrica*, 41(1) (January), 135-55.

Osborne, M.F.M. (1967) 'Some Quantitative Tests for Stock Price Generating Models and Trading Folklore', *Journal of the American Statistical Association*, 62 (June), 321-40.

Powers, M.J. (1970) 'Does Futures Trading Reduce Price Fluctuations in Cash Markets?', *American Economic Review*, LX(3) (June), 460-4.

Rocca, L.H. (1969) 'Time Series Analysis of Commodity Futures Prices', unpublished PhD dissertation, University of California, Berkeley.

Schimmler, J. (1973) 'Speculation, Profitability and Price Stability: A Formal Approach', *The Review of Economics and Statistics*, LV(1) (February), 110-14.

Schrader, L.F. (1978) 'Pricing Problems in the Food Industry: Broiler Chickens and Eggs', paper presented at Symposium on Pricing Problems in the Food Industry, Washington D.C., 2-3 March.

Shepherd, G. (1960) 'Effects of Futures Trading on Prices: Discussion', *Futures Trading Seminar, I*, Madison: Mimir Publishers, pp. 181-91.

Sims, C.A. (1972) 'Money, Income and Causality', *American Economic Review*, LXII(4) (September), 540-52.

Stein, J.L. (1961) 'Destabilizing Speculative Activity Can Be Profitable', *The Review of Economics and Statistics*, XLIII(3) (August),301-2.

Suppes, P. (1970) *A Probabilistic Theory of Causality*, Amsterdam: North-Holland.

Taylor, G.S. and R.M. Leuthold (1974) 'The Influence of Futures Trading on Cash Cattle Price Variations', *Food Research Institute*, XIII(1), 29-36.

Telser, L.G. (1959) 'A Theory of Speculation Relating Profitability and Stability', *The Review of Economics and Statistics*, XLI(3) (August), 295-301.

Telser, L.G. and H.N. Higinbotham (1977) 'Organized Futures Markets: Costs and Benefits', *Journal of Political Economy*, 85(5) (October), 969-1000.

Tomek, W.G. (1971) 'A Note on Historical Wheat Prices and Futures Trading', *Food Research Institute Studies*, X(1), 109-13.

US 69th Congress (1926) 1st Session, Senate, *Fluctuations in Wheat Futures*, Senate Document No. 135, 28 June.

US 71st Congress (1930) 2nd Session, Senate, *Reports by Members of Grain Futures Exchanges*, Senate Document No. 123, 6 January.

US 85th Congress (1957) Senate, *Hearings Before a Subcommittee of the Committee on Agriculture and Forestry*, 12 August.

US 93rd Congress (1973) 1st Session, House, *Hearings Before the Subcommittee on Special Small Business Problems of the House Permanent Select Committee on Small Business*, 25 July.

US 93rd Congress (1974) 2nd Session, Senate, Committee on Agriculture and Forestry, *The Commodity Futures Trading Act of 1974*, 15 November.

US General Accounting Office (1975) *Improvements Needed in Regulation of Commodity Futures Trading*, Washington DC, 24 June.

Withrow, R.M. (1960) 'Effects of Futures Trading on Prices: Discussion', *Futures Trading Seminar, I*, Madison: Mimir Publishers, pp. 163-72.

Working, H. (1977) 'Price Effects of Scalping and Day Trading', in *Selected Writings of Holbrook Working*, Chicago: Chicago Board of Trade, pp. 181-94.

— (1960) 'Price Effects of Futures Trading', *Food Research Institute Studies*, I(1), 1-31.

— (1967) 'Tests of a Theory Concerning Floor Trading on Commodity Exchanges', *Food Research Institute Studies*, VII, Supplement, 5-48.

— (1970) 'Economic Functions of Futures Markets', in *Futures Trading in Livestock – Origins and Concepts*, ed. H. Bakken, Chicago: Chicago Mercantile Exchange.

7 THE FORWARD PRICING FUNCTION OF THE LONDON METAL EXCHANGE

Barry A. Goss*

Futures prices are rationally formed current prices relating to later delivery dates; they are not forecasts of subsequent spot prices. Yet, if all available information, including economic agents' expectations, is fully taken into account in the price formation process, then both current spot and futures prices may be regarded as market anticipations of subsequent spot prices. This chapter explores the hypothesis that futures prices (and spot) are predictors of subsequent spot prices in this sense. It assesses the predictive performance of futures prices for four non-ferrous metals traded on the London Metal Exchange using a simple linear model, the parameters of which are estimated by ordinary least squares or instrumental variables in the case of serial correlation (because of the presence of a lagged endogenous regressor). The results suggest that the unbiasedness hypothesis should not be rejected for copper, tin or lead, but marginally may be rejected for zinc. The chapter begins with a discussion of the functions of futures markets, including a review of the literature on the forward pricing function.

1. Nature and Role of Futures Trading

Futures contracts are financial instruments dealing in commodities or other financial instruments for forward delivery or settlement, on standardized terms. They are traded on organized exchanges in which a clearing house interposes itself between buyer and seller and guarantees all transactions, so that the identity of the buyer or seller is a matter of indifference to the opposite party. The London Metal Exchange has long been the world's leading metals futures market and trades, *inter alia*, in futures contracts for copper, zinc, tin and lead, which are officially quoted for spot and three months delivery only.

Although the analysis of the feasibility conditions for futures trading awaits a comprehensive theoretical framework, it was customary until around 1973 to distinguish at least five conditions which were thought to be necessary for futures trading to be possible. Recent experience, however, has shown that some of these conditions are in fact not necessary. The first 'customary condition' is that there must be variation in the price of the actual commodity under consideration; second, there must exist economic agents with commitments in the actuals market; and third, it must be possible to specify a standard grade of the commodity and to measure deviations from that grade. As a result of the first two conditions, some economic agents will face a price risk and there will be a demand for hedging facilities. A futures market established specifically to meet purely speculative demands is possible but, as far as the present author is aware, is unknown. The third condition, together with standardization of delivery date and of delivery location and testing procedures, where relevant, means that a high degree of contract standardization is possible.[1]

Until recently it was customary to distinguish storability and deliverability as feasibility conditions. A consequence of the former of these two is that the forward premium could not exceed the marginal net cost of storage, and a consequence of deliverability is that the price of a futures contract at maturity and the cash price at that date would, theoretically, be brought to equality.

Recent experiences such as trading in share price indices (which can be neither stored nor delivered), and in finished live beef cattle (which may be delivered but are virtually non-storable) in Chicago and Sydney, have shown these two conditions to be unnecessary.[2]

Further conditions which are thought necessary for the establishment of futures trading are the presence of speculative capital (see Gray, 1960) and financial facilities for payment of margins and contract settlement (see Goss, 1972). Recently, Powers and Tosini (1977) have emphasized the infrastructure required, including financial, legal and communications systems. Moreover, they have placed renewed emphasis on the presence of speculative capital, drawing attention to the externalities generated by that capital and indeed by the exchange itself (pp. 981-2). The literature on feasibility of futures trading has distinguished between possibility and success of a market, and Gray (1966) has drawn attention to factors which may lead to a thin market even though the above conditions are fulfilled.

Because of its limited predictive ability, this 'shopping list' of commodity prerequisites has been superseded in recent years by attempts to develop a comprehensive framework to analyse futures market feasibility. Telser and Higinbotham (1977) argue that the degree of success of futures markets can be explained in terms of maximization of a net benefits function, and they found *inter alia* that the most actively traded commodities have the most variable prices. Veljanovski (Chapter 1 in this volume) shows that choice can be made among contractual arrangements on the basis of maximum net benefit, taking account of transactions costs. He argues that futures markets have a comparative advantage over spot markets in the temporary transfer of certain bundles of property rights between traders.

The major functions performed by futures markets are as follows: they facilitate stockholding; they facilitate the shifting of risk; they act as a mechanism for collection and dissemination of information; and they perform a forward pricing function. We shall consider the first three of these functions briefly, and the fourth in more detail.

First, futures markets facilitate stockholding because the forward premium acts as a guide to inventory control, and may be interpreted as a return on hedged stock (at least where the hedge is held to maturity of the future). The forward premium has been interpreted as a price of storage (Working, 1953a), and the holding of inventories at times of spot premium is explicable in terms of the convenience yield (Brennan, 1958).

Second, futures markets permit risk-shifting because they provide facilities for hedging. Hedging is defined as the holding of a futures market position in conjunction with an actuals position of opposite sign, in pursuit of expected gain, subject to a risk constraint. Hedging substitutes a basis risk for a price risk, and hedgers transfer all or part of their price risks (depending on whether they are fully hedged) to other market participants willing to bear those risks. This is so whether hedging is undertaken primarily for the purpose of risk-reduction (which Working (1953a) believed to be unimportant in practice) or for some other reason, such as to facilitate product pricing or enhance profitability of the overall stockholding operation. Hedging has also been studied as a means of reducing business risks in general, and hence as an instrument in the management of a total asset portfolio (Dusak, 1973).

The risk-reducing effect of futures trading can of course be obtained by other means of hedging, such as by use of forward contracts. Economic agents who hedge in futures markets do so because the net costs of that medium are less than the net costs of the alternatives. The costs of hedging include not only margins and transactions costs, which are now being studied as a function of market liquidity (Telser and Higinbotham, 1977; Telser, 1979) but also costs due to changes in price spreads. For example, a spot premium which narrows during the period of a short hedge imposes a cost on the hedger. Such costs are likely to be larger the smaller is the volume of trading, other things being equal. From such costs have to be subtracted the benefits of increased flexibility which futures contracts offer compared with forward contracts.[3]

The performance of futures markets as a hedging medium has been the subject of considerable empirical work. Generally speaking, futures markets have performed well from the routine hedging point of view (Yamey, 1951; Graf, 1953), in the sense of the supply of storage concept (Working, 1953b; Brennan, 1958) and also from the portfolio viewpoint (Rutledge, 1972; Ederington, 1979).

Thirdly, futures markets also act as centres for the collection and dissemination of information. If this information, including traders' expectations about the future, is fully reflected in current prices, then the price formation process is said to be efficient. Hence, futures markets have been subjected to weak-form tests for efficiency, seeking evidence of dependence in past prices, using runs tests, serial correlation tests, etc. (Larson, 1960; Stevenson and Bear, 1970). In some markets evidence of dependence has been found (Cargill and Rausser, 1975), while in others it has not (Praetz, 1975).

Tests have recently been employed to investigate whether certain markets are efficient in the sense of using all publicly available information as soon as it is published. This semi-strong form of the efficient markets hypothesis has been addressed by two different means, and has been rejected for US hogs, some currencies and some non-ferrous metals (see Leuthold and Hartmann, 1979; Hansen and Hodrick, 1980; and Goss, 1983). Futures markets also perform a forward pricing function, which is central to the empirical work reported in this chapter and is discussed in detail in the next section.

2. Forward Pricing Role of Futures Markets

The literature on futures markets has interpreted the forward pricing function as an extension of Working's (1949) 'price of storage' concept. If all available information is fully taken into account in the process of current price formation, then the best possible anticipation of the price relating to a later date is the current price. Working argued therefore that the current spot and futures prices are equally valid anticipations of the spot price at a subsequent date, and a current forward premium of $x is not a prediction that the spot price will rise by $x, but rather it is a market estimated carrying charge of $x. Similarly, a spot premium of $y is not a prediction of a fall in the spot price of $y, but is a market estimated inverse carrying charge of $y. This at least was the theory developed for continuously storable commodities (Working, 1942).

If spot and futures prices fully reflect all available information, then they may each be regarded as predictors of subsequent spot prices, although technically they are not forecasts, but are rationally formed prices relating to specific delivery dates. The hypothesis that futures prices are unbiased predictors of maturity date spot prices has been tested for both continuous and discontinuous inventory commodities, and also for non-inventory commodities. The evidence supports the view that futures prices are unbiased predictors for continuous inventory commodities such as corn, soybeans and coffee (Tomek and Gray, 1970; Kofi, 1973), but not for discontinuous inventory commodities such as potatoes (Kofi) or non-inventory commodities such as finished live beef cattle (Leuthold, 1974), or in the last case not with lags of more than three months prior to delivery.

The reasons for this phenomenon are still under discussion. Leuthold has linked the efficient prediction period for live beef with the typical hedging period. Kofi seeks an explanation in terms of the quality of information on demand and supply conditions. While there is some support for this hypothesis, the hypothesis that the predictive performance of futures prices varies directly with the degree of price administration can also be supported on the same evidence. Tomek and Gray attempt to account for this difference in predictive performance (at least in the case of potatoes) with the suggestion that the futures price represents expectations only (and not a price of storage). This explanation is perhaps incomplete because these expectations are always wrong and exhibit no learning process. Elsewhere, Gray (1972) has given a fuller explanation for the potatoes case.[4]

Other reasons suggested for this phenomenon are that the discontinuous and non-inventory markets are newer and have relatively smaller trading volumes. This hypothesis was tested by Giles and Goss (1981) for wool on the Sydney Futures Exchange, where the predictive performance of wool futures prices for 1963-7 (a youthful period for the exchange) was compared with that for 1968-78 and found to be inferior. Other suggestions advanced are that the absence or discontinuity of inventories itself constitutes a significant gap in the information flow, so that such markets are at a permanent disadvantage with continuous inventory markets, other things being equal. Moreover, it is possible that the absence of inventories increases the possibility of expectational error, because there is less opportunity for arbitrage between the spot and futures markets.

3. The Predictive Ability of Futures Prices for Copper, Zinc, Tin and Lead

The hypothesis considered in this chapter is that futures prices are unbiased predictors of subsequent spot prices. The implied relationship may be expressed in linear form as:

$$A_t = \alpha + \beta P_{t-i} + \varepsilon_t \quad (1)$$

where

A_t = spot (cash price)

P_t = three months futures price

i = 3 months lag

ε_t = random disturbance

t = time in months.

On the hypothesis $\alpha = 0$ and $\beta = 1$. Equation (1) was estimated by regression methods using monthly average data from *Metallgesellschaft* for copper, zinc, tin and lead for the sample period April 1966 to April 1984, with 55 non-overlapping observations. As in most other empirical work on this hypothesis, (1) was estimated by Ordinary Least Squares (OLS) for copper, tin and lead. If, however, all information bearing on A_t is not summarized in P_{t-i}, equation (1) will be under-specified and auto-correlation among the residuals is likely, as occurred in the case of zinc. Hence, the OLS standard errors would be understated. To allow for this phenomenon, the model for zinc was extended by assuming that:

$$\varepsilon_t = \rho\varepsilon_{t-k} + e_t \qquad (2)$$

where ρ = a parameter to be estimated

e_t = a well-behaved error term

k = 1

An iterative Cochrane-Orcutt procedure was employed to estimate α, β and ρ for zinc.

Moreover, the effect of auto-correlated errors and a lagged endogenous variable is that the OLS estimates of α and β will be both biased and inconsistent. Following Giles and Goss (1981), equation (1) (augmented by (2)) for zinc was therefore estimated by the instrumental variable technique with an AR1 correction using TSP 4.0 (Hall (1983)), in order to obtain consistent estimates.

As we saw in Section 2 above, if current prices fully reflect all available information then current spot prices may also be interpreted as predictors of subsequent spot prices. A variant of the main hypothesis tested here is that current spot prices are unbiased estimates of spot prices three months hence. The following relation has therefore been estimated:

$$A_t = \alpha' + \beta' A_{t-1} + \varepsilon'_t \qquad (3)$$

where i = 3

ε'_t = disturbance term.

Again, equation (3) was estimated by OLS for copper, tin and lead, and by IV with an AR1 correction for zinc because of the presence of serial correlation for that metal.

The parameter estimates for equations (1) and (3), augmented by equation (2) in the case of zinc, are given in Tables 7.1 and 7.2 respectively, together with the relevant standard errors, and values of $\bar{R}^2$ and Durbin Watson test statistics. From these estimates, it will be seen that on the basis of individual t tests of the hypotheses $\alpha = 0$ and $\beta = 1$, these separate hypotheses can be rejected for copper only at the 5 per cent level (but not at 1 per cent).

Yet the definitive test of the unbiasedness hypothesis in this case is a joint test of the hypothesis H: ($\alpha = 0, \beta = 1$). For copper, tin and lead this is an F test, and the calculated F-values for H: ($\alpha = 0, \beta = 1$) for these three metals are given in Table 7.1. When these values are compared with the critical 5 per cent $F_{2,60} = 3.15$ it is clear that the unbiasedness hypothesis cannot be rejected for any of these three metals. In the case of zinc, the appropriate test of the joint hypothesis is a χ^2 test with two degrees of freedom. The calculated χ^2 value for zinc for the hypothesis H($\alpha = 0, \beta = 1$) is given in Table 7.1; this compares with the critical 5 per cent $\chi^2(2)$ value of 5.99, at which level the unbiasedness hypothesis must be rejected (when compared with the critical 1 per cent $\chi^2(2)$ value of 9.21, the hypothesis cannot be rejected). Hence the case of zinc is marginal, although in line with the suggestion of Arrow (1982) that the more stringent significance levels should be reserved for

Table 7.1: Spot Prices Regressed on Lagged Futures Prices (1966-84)

	$\hat{\alpha}$	$\hat{\beta}$	$\hat{\rho}$	$\bar{R}^2$	DW	Observations
Copper (OLS)	117.498 (51.765)	0.849 (0.070)	—	0.729	1.898	55
Tin (OLS)	100.938 (111.342)	1.005 (0.023)	—	0.973	1.919	55
Zinc (IV)	47.883 (42.809)	0.868 (0.130)	0.367 (0.128)	0.669	1.784	52
Lead (OLS)	13.569 (10.331)	0.958 (0.039)	—	0.919	1.980	55

JOINT TEST STATISTICS (H: $\alpha - 0, \beta - 1$)

Calculated F-values

Copper: 2.577 Tin: 1.991 Lead: 0.873

Calculated χ^2 values
Zinc: 6.536

Table 7.2: Spot Prices Regressed on Lagged Spot Prices (1966-84)

	$\hat{\alpha}'$	$\hat{\beta}'$	$\hat{\rho}'$	$\bar{R}^2$	DW	Observations
Copper (OLS)	108.616	0.870	—	0.719	1.968	55
	(53.779)	(0.074)				
Tin (OLS)	117.366	0.997	—	0.967	1.881	55
	(123.164)	(0.025)				
Zinc (IV)	47.181	0.881	0.341	0.682	1.798	52
	(42.643)	(0.132)	(0.129)			
Lead (OLS)	16.879	0.951	—	0.921	2.004	55
	(10.127)	(0.038)				

JOINT TEST STATISTICS (H: $\alpha' = 0, \beta' = 1$)

Calculated F-values

Copper: 2.205 Tin: 1.169 Lead: 1.451

Calculated χ^2 values

Zinc: 6.908

larger samples, there may be grounds for preferring the 5 per cent level in this case. With respect to the hypothesis that spot prices are unbiased anticipations of spot prices three months later, as represented by equation (3), the outcomes are identical. The estimates reported in Table 7.2 suggest that the unbiasedness hypothesis cannot be rejected for copper, tin and lead, while for zinc this hypothesis can be rejected at the 5 per cent level (but not at 1 per cent).

The OLS results in Tables 7.1 and 7.2 are evidently free of first-order serial correlation, and the same would appear to be true of the IV estimates for zinc, although the DW statistics can only be informally interpreted with IV estimation. (A more precise test could be conducted along the lines suggested by Godfrey (1976).)

The results in this chapter support the conclusions reached in the original paper in *Applied Economics* for copper and tin and in a subsequent report for lead.[5] Agents in these markets using LME futures prices would have been as well off on average as if they had known the delivery date spot price in advance. In this respect the LME has facilitated the intertemporal allocation of economic resources.

Rejection of the unbiasedness hypothesis at the 5 per cent level for zinc does not necessarily imply that the zinc market is informationally inefficient, because of the other key assumptions on which that hypothesis is jointly conditional. In any case, the marginal result for zinc suggests that this case requires further research.

Ultimate rejection of the unbiasedness hypothesis for zinc, if that were to eventuate, may be explicable in terms of the risk non-neutrality of agents or discounting of the future, in terms of differences in the options available to agents under spot and futures contracts, or in terms of informational inefficiency in the zinc market.

In order to investigate further the informational efficiency of the zinc market, and indeed of these four non-ferrous metals markets, Appendix 1 considers the hypothesis that non-ferrous metals futures prices reflect as fully as possible publicly available information. It is assumed that this information set is measured by the immediately prior forecast errors for all four metals and the coefficients of equation (A1) were estimated by OLS. The hypothesis relating to informational efficiency is tested by the joint F-test that all coefficients ($\alpha, \beta_1, \ldots, \beta_4$) are zero. It will be seen that at the 5 per cent critical F value with (5, 49) degrees of freedom, this hypothesis can be rejected for zinc and copper, but not for tin and lead. At the 1 per cent level the hypothesis cannot be rejected for any of the metals.

The results for zinc in Appendix 1 are consistent with those in Table 7.1, suggesting that, for this metal, rejection of unbiasedness may be due, at least in part, to some inability to reflect information. For tin and lead also, non-rejection of unbiasedness is consistent with non-rejection of this version of the market efficiency hypothesis. In the case of copper, there would seem to be some ambiguity (at the 5 per cent level) in the two sets of results, because ability to reflect relevant information as fully as possible is an assumption on which the unbiasedness hypothesis is jointly conditional. This ambiguity disappears at the 1 per cent level.

To clarify the ambiguity in the results for copper, the question of multi-collinearity among the regressors in equation (A1) was considered. The hypothesis that $H_2{:}r_{ij} = 0$ (i, j=1, ..., 4, $i \neq j$) was tested against the alternative hypothesis $H_3{:}r_{ij} \neq 0$.

This test was conducted as a t-test of the significance of the partial correlation coefficients r_{ij} where

$$t_{i,j(\nu)} = \frac{r_{ij}\sqrt{n-k}}{\sqrt{1-r_{ij}^2}}$$

and $\nu = n-k$ degrees of freedom, k is the number of explanatory variables in (A1). These tests of significance of the collinearity among the various pairs of regressors showed that there is a significant relationship between the prior forecast errors for copper and zinc ($t_{1,3.24} = 3.8449$ compared with the critical value 5 per cent $t_{\nu=40} = 2.02$). None of the other relationships among the prior forecast errors is significant: there is some relationship between the prior forecast errors for tin and lead, but this is not significant ($t_{2,4.13} = 1.7494$).

The coefficients of equation (A1) for copper were therefore re-estimated with j = 2, 3, 4 only: that is, the prior forecast error for copper was deleted. These estimates are given in Appendix 2, together with calculated F statistics to test the hypothesis H_4:(α, $\beta_{2,3,4} = 0$). It will be seen that this version of the efficient markets hypothesis can be rejected at the 5 per cent level of significance but not at the 2.5 per cent level. The implication of these results is that the observed ambiguity of the outcomes for copper disappears at the 2.5 per cent level of significance. This suggests some slight informational inefficiency in the copper market.

The coefficients of equation (A1) were also re-estimated for zinc with j = 2, 3, 4, but the outcomes were the same as in Appendix 1, and so these results are not reported in Appendix 2. If equation (A1) is re-estimated for copper and zinc with the zinc prior forecast error deleted instead of that for copper, the market efficiency hypothesis cannot be rejected, so that deletion of the copper forecast error results in a more relevant specification of the set of publicly available information.

4. Conclusions

This chapter addresses the hypothesis that futures prices (and lagged spot prices) are unbiased predictors of delivery date spot prices, on the ground that they are rationally formed current prices incorporating all available information, including economic agents' expectations, and hence may be interpreted as market anticipations. OLS estimates of the hypothesized linear relationship were obtained for copper, tin and lead (IV with a correction for first-order auto-correlation for zinc). Joint tests of the hypothesis of zero intercept and unit slope suggest acceptance of the unbiasedness hypothesis for copper, tin and lead, and rejection of that hypothesis for zinc at the 5 per cent level of significance (but not at the 1 per cent level).

The implications of this result are that agents using London Metal Exchange copper, tin and lead futures prices for decision purposes are as well off on average as if they had known the subsequent cash price in advance. Rejection of this hypothesis for zinc, however, does not imply that this market is not performing its risk-reduction function satisfactorily or that it is informationally inefficient. In view of the marginal rejection of the unbiasedness hypothesis for zinc, the ability of futures prices for all four metals to reflect publicly available information was considered. It was assumed that an appropriate specification of that information set is the group of immediately preceding forecast errors for these four metals. The efficient markets hypothesis cannot be rejected for tin or lead, and this outcome is consistent with non-rejection of unbiasedness for these metals. For zinc the market efficiency hypothesis is rejected at the 5 per cent level but not at 1 per cent and this outcome is also consistent with the marginal rejection of unbiasedness for that metal. In the case of copper, there is some ambiguity in that the efficient markets hypothesis is rejected at the 5 per cent level. This ambiguity disappears at the 2.5 per cent level however, where the market efficiency hypothesis cannot be rejected.

Appendix 1: The Informational Efficiency of the London Metal Exchange

This Appendix is concerned with the ability of futures prices for copper, tin, zinc and lead on the LME to reflect publicly available information. It is assumed that an appropriate specification of that information set is comprised of the immediately prior forecast errors for these four non-ferrous metals. This version of the efficient markets hypothesis is then addressed by testing the hypothesis that the current forecast error for each metal is unrelated to the elements of this information set. The *rationale* for this procedure is that forecast errors contain information because of innovations which occur in the interval between the time when the futures price is formed and the delivery date of the contract. If, however, the market under consideration is efficient, this information will be utilized very rapidly and there should be no systematic relationship between the current forecast error for an individual metal and any of the immediately prior forecast errors. The existence of a systematic relationship would be evidence of a lag in the utilization of information. Hence the relevant estimating equation can be written

$$A_{t+k} - P_{t,t+k} = \alpha + \sum_{j=1}^{4} \beta_j (A_t - P_{t-k,t})_j + u_t \qquad \text{(A1)}$$

where $k = 3$

$j = 1, \ldots, 4$ for copper, tin, zinc and lead respectively.

The efficient markets hypothesis is tested by the joint test that the coefficients $\alpha, \beta_j = 0$.

This procedure was used by Hansen and Hodrick (1980) for currencies, and by Goss (1983) for non-ferrous metals on the LME for the period 1971-9, with overlapping observations. In this Appendix, however, the results are reported for equation (A1) for all four metals, for the sample period 1966-84 with 54 non-overlapping observations. The coefficients are estimated by OLS and there is no evidence of first-order serial correlation in any of the relationships. These estimates are given in Table A1, together with calculated F values to test the hypothesis that all coefficients $\alpha, \beta_1, \ldots, \beta_4 = 0$.

At the 5 per cent level of significance, this version of the efficient markets hypothesis must be rejected for copper and zinc, but cannot be rejected for tin or lead. At the 1 per cent level, the hypothesis cannot be rejected for any metal.

Table A1: Coefficient Estimates for Equation A1*

	$\hat{\alpha}$	$\hat{\beta}_1$	$\hat{\beta}_2$	$\hat{\beta}_3$	$\hat{\beta}_4$	$\bar{R}^2$	DW	Observations
Copper (OLS)	18.079	−0.330	−0.104	0.849	0.730	0.155	1.924	54
	(1.170)	(−1.687)	(−2.670)	(2.598)	(1.350)			
Tin (OLS)	123.778	0.214	−0.100	1.874	−0.047	0.015	2.027	54
	(1.935)	(0.264)	(−0.623)	(1.385)	(−0.021)			
Zinc (OLS)	10.396	−0.120	−0.045	0.631	−0.232	0.160	1.765	54
	(1.147)	(−1.047)	(−1.966)	(3.291)	(−0.733)			
Lead (OLS)	6.181	−0.084	−0.022	0.194	0.072	0.033	2.073	54
	(1.187)	(−1.279)	(−1.719)	(1.760)	(0.394)			

Notes: * T-values are in parentheses.

Calculated F-values to test H_1 ($\alpha, \beta^1, \ldots, \beta = 0$)

Copper: 2.829 Tin: 1.783 Zinc: 2.948 Lead: 1.291

Tabulated $0.05F_{5,40}$ − 2.45

Tabulated $0.01F_{5,40}$ − 3.51

Appendix 2: Informational Efficiency of the London Metal Exchange

Coefficient Estimates for Equation A1 (with j = 2, 3, 4)*

	$\hat{\alpha}$	$\hat{\beta}_2$	$\hat{\beta}_3$	$\hat{\beta}_4$	$\bar{R}^2$	DW	Observations
Copper (OLS)	18.279	−0.110	0.525	0.483	0.124	2.276	54
	(1.162)	(−2.781)	(1.949)	(0.912)			

Notes: * T-values are in parentheses.

Calculated F-values to test H_4: (α, $\beta_{2,3,4} = 0$)

Copper: 2.725

Tabulated $.05F_{4,40} = 2.61$

Tabulated $.025F_{4,40} = 3.13$

Notes

*Monash University, Australia. This is a revised version of a paper of the same title published in *Applied Economics*, 1981, 13, pp. 133-50, reprinted by permission of the editor and Chapman and Hall Ltd. The revisions follow the introduction of joint tests and extension of the sample period. I am grateful to David Giles, Max King and Mark Upcher for helpful comments, and to Olive Chin and Gulay Avsar for research assistance in preparing the revisions. Remaining errors are the sole responsibility of the author.

1. Homogeneity of course is sufficient but unnecessary to meet this condition. See also Houthakker (1959).

2. Recently in the literature on feasibility there has been a tendency for the 'commodity characteristics approach' to be absorbed by a maximization of net benefits approach in which both the costs and benefits of futures trading are functions *inter alia* of turnover, open positions and price variability (see especially Telser and Higinbotham, 1977). In the opinion of the present author this change has occurred because of the low predictive power of the earlier approach. [See also the chapter by Veljanovski in this volume. Ed.]

3. In fact, futures contracts are frequently used in conjunction with forward contracts.

4. The evidence on potatoes is not unambiguous. Yamey (1977) found that the relative inferiority of potato futures prices as predictors was greater during intra-seasonal periods (in the presence of inventories) than during inter-seasonal periods (when inventories were discontinuous).

5. Report prepared in 1982 by the present author for the Commodities Division, World Bank, Washington, DC.

References

Arrow, K.J. (1982) 'Risk Perception in Psychology and Economics', *Economic Inquiry*, vol. 22, 1-9.

Breeden, D.T. (1982) 'Statement' [on topics and methodologies for research in financial futures], *Review of Research in Futures Markets*, vol. 1(2), 175-8 (Chicago Board of Trade).

Brennan, M.J. (1958) 'The Supply of Storage', *American Economic Review*, vol. 48, 50-72.

Cargill, T.F. and G.C. Rausser (1975) 'Temporal Price Behavior in Commodity Futures Markets', *The Journal of Finance*, XXX, 4 (September), 1043-53.

Dusak, K. (1973) 'Futures Trading and Investor Returns: An Investigation of Commodity Market Risk Premiums', *Journal of Political Economy*, vol. 81, 1387-406.

Ederington, L.H. (1979) 'The Hedging Performance of the New Futures Markets', *Journal of Finance*, XXXIV, 1 (March), 157-70.

Fama, E.F. (1970) 'Efficient Capital Markets: A Review of Theory and Empirical Work', *Journal of Finance*, vol. 25, 383-417.

Giles, D.E.A. and B.A. Goss (1981) 'The Predictive Quality of Futures Prices, with an Application to the Sydney Wool Futures Market', *Australian Journal of Agricultural Economics*, vol. 25, 1-13.

Godfrey, L.G. (1976) 'Testing for Serial Correlation in Dynamic Simultaneous Equation Models', *Econometrica*, vol. 44, 1077-84.

Goss, B.A. (1972) *The Theory of Futures Trading*, London: Routledge and Kegan Paul.

— (1983) 'The Semi-Strong Form Efficiency of the London Metal Exchange', *Applied Economics*, vol. 15, 681-98.

Graf, T.F. (1953) 'Hedging — How Effective Is It?', *Journal of Farm Economics*, XXXV, 3 (August), 398-413.

Gray, R.W. (1960) 'The Characteristic Bias in Some Thin Futures Markets', *Food Research Institute Studies*, 1, (November), 298-312.

— (1966) 'Why Does Futures Trading Succeed or Fail? An Analysis of Selected Commodities', *Futures Trading Seminar*, vol. III, MIMIR: Madison.

— (1972) 'The Futures Market for Maine Potatoes: An Appraisal', *Food Research Institute Studies*, vol. 11, 313-41.

Hall, B.H. (1983), *Time Series Processor Version 4.0 Reference Manual*, TSP International, Stanford, California.

Hamburger, M.J. and E.N. Platt (1975) 'The Expectations Hypothesis and the Efficiency of the Treasury Bill Market', *The Review of Economics and Statistics*, 57, 190-9.

Hansen, L.P. and L.R. Hodrick (1980) 'Forward Exchange Rates as Optimal Predictors of Future Spot Rates: An Econometric Analysis', *Journal of Political Economy*, vol. 88, 829-53.

Houthakker, H.S. (1959) 'Scope and Limits of Futures Trading', *Allocation of Economic Resources*, M. Abramovitz *et al.*, Stanford University Press, pp. 141-59.

Kofi, T.A. (1973) 'A Framework for Comparing the Efficiency of Futures Markets', *American Journal of Agricultural Economics*, vol. 55 (November), 584-94.

Larson, A.B. (1960) 'Measurement of a Random Process in Futures Prices', *Food Research Institute Studies*, 1, 3 (November), 313-24.

Leuthold, R.M. (1974) 'The Price Performance on the Futures Market of a Non-storable Commodity: Live Beef Cattle', *American Journal of Agricultural Economics*, vol. 36 (May), 271-9.

Leuthold, R.M. and P.A. Hartmann (1979) 'A Semi-strong Form Evaluation of the Efficiency of the Hog Futures Market', *American Journal of Agricultural Economics*, 61, 3 (August), 482-9.

Powers, M.J. and P. Tosini (1977) 'Commodity Futures Exchanges and the

North–South Dialogue', *American Journal of Agricultural Economics*, 59, 5 (December), 977-85.
Praetz, P.D. (1975) 'Testing the Efficient Markets Theory on the Sydney Wool Futures Exchange', *Australian Economic Papers* (December), 240-9.
Rutledge, D.J.S. (1972) 'Hedgers' Demand for Futures Contracts: A Theoretical Framework with Applications to the United States Soybean Complex', *Food Research Institute Studies*, vol. 11, 237-56.
Stevenson, R.A. and R.M. Bear (1970) 'Commodity Futures: Trends or Random Walks?', *Journal of Finance*, XXV, 1 (March), 65-81.
Telser, L.G. (1979) 'Reasons for Having an Organized Futures Market', *Report 7925*, Center for Mathematical Studies in Business and Economics, University of Chicago.
Telser, L.G. and H.N. Higinbotham (1977) 'Organized Futures Markets: Costs and Benefits', *Journal of Political Economy*, 85, (5), 969-1000.
Tomek, W.G. and R.W. Gray (1970) 'Temporal Relationships Among Prices on Commodity Futures Markets: Their Allocative and Stabilizing Roles', *American Journal of Agricultural Economics*, 52, 3 (August), 372-80.
Working, H. (1942) 'Quotations on Commodity Futures as Price Forecasts', *Econometrica*, vol. 10, 39-52.
— (1949) 'The Theory of Price of Storage', *American Economic Review*, vol. 39 (December), 1254-62.
— (1953a) 'Futures Trading and Hedging', *American Economic Review*, vol. 43, 314-43.
— (1953b) 'Hedging Reconsidered', *Journal of Farm Economics*, vol. 35, 544-61.
Yamey, B.S. (1951) 'An Investigation of Hedging on an Organised Produce Exchange', *The Manchester School of Economics and Social Studies*, vol. XIX (September), 305-19.
— (1977) 'Continuous Inventories, Futures Prices and Self-fulfilling Prophecies', mimeo, London School of Economics.

8 AN ANALYSIS OF GOLD FUTURES PRICES IN LARGE AND SMALL MARKETS

C. Rae Weston and Ross McDonnell*

Gold, for example, is traded in many countries and currencies; where daily quotations are available, gold prices in different locations are invariably within transaction costs of equality. (Richard Roll, 'Violations of Purchasing Power Parity and their Implications for Efficient International Commodity Markets', UCLA, May 1978, p. 1)

1. Introduction

It is the purpose of this chapter to investigate the relevance of the above proposition to the gold futures prices in large and small gold futures markets. Despite a number of tests made concerning the relationship between spot prices across various markets (Booth and Kaen, 1979), very little work has been done on the connection between the futures markets relationships (an exception is Brendan Brown, 1977).

Writing of the gold futures markets in November 1979 the *Australian Financial Review* said, 'There is a market open somewhere in the world practically 24 hours a day ... The world clock shows that the gap in official markets is four hours between the close of the New York Comex and the opening of the Sydney Futures Exchange' (26 November 1979).

By comparison with the New York Comex, both the Winnipeg Commodity Exchange and the Sydney Futures Exchange are markets of much smaller size, so that even to the extent that they fill in the time gap, they may not have the same depth as the Comex market and market imperfections may arise. There are, in particular, differences between the Sydney Futures Exchange (SFE) arrangements and those of the other two markets which may be sufficient to reduce the ability of SFE trading to reflect

*Massey University and Australian Commercial Computing Pty Ltd.

only the moves in the Comex market. First, the size of the contract is different (50 troy ounces in SFE, as opposed to 100 troy ounces); second, the presence of exchange control regulations in Australia may deter potential offshore operators in the SFE, while there is not the same limit in the other markets (the Australian authorities are in fact sufficiently paranoid about speculation to have limited the recently introduced currency futures markets in US dollars to residents only); and third, within the Australian market, clients who are neither Exchange members nor members of the Clearing House, may only be unsecured creditors with respect to deposits paid by them to a broker; by comparison, clients' funds appear to be fully covered by the Clearing House provisions of the Comex market.

The purpose of this chapter is to examine the daily data of gold futures prices from three markets — Winnipeg, New York and Sydney — over the period April 1978 to April 1979 in order to investigate: (i) the comparative efficiency of the markets; (ii) the coherence between the markets; and (iii) the comparative response of individual markets to the release of external information.

There are interesting differences between the three markets; for example, Winnipeg, the first of these gold futures markets in time, was then a centre of investor interest, but has more recently been of reduced importance due to the opening of the US gold futures markets. Both Winnipeg and Sydney (the gold contract of the latter opened in April 1978) have much more localized markets than New York; previously Sydney had offered wool futures and cattle futures, and interest in that gold futures market was very slow to develop. That is, Sydney in its first months of gold futures trading was a small thin market, Winnipeg, a small but well-established market, while New York was a large well-developed market.

The availability of futures trading in gold on successive international markets over approximately 20 hours of a 24-hour day reduces the possibility that market closing changes the speed of adjustment of prices, although there is still a gap at weekends. Granger and Morgenstern, however, (1971, pp. 122-9), in discussing the effect of night and weekend closing of a market, note three possible hypotheses: first, that the opening price on day t will be the closing price on day t−1 regardless of the time that passes between them, if price changes are only generated by the operation of the market itself; second, that the mechanism that generates the prices may operate quite independently of whether the market is open or not; and third, that the mechanism generating prices will still operate when the market is closed, but at a lower speed (where speed is measured by the variance per unit time of the first difference of the price series). The possible relevance of each of these hypotheses will be discussed in relation to the results presented in the remainder of the chapter.

2. Methodology and Data

Methodology

The statistical analysis reported in this chapter falls naturally into two parts: first, a test of the weak form of market efficiency; and second, a spectral analysis of the structure of each of the market series considered and the relationship between the series. It is of assistance in applying the latter analysis if it is possible to establish that the distribution of gold futures prices is stationary. Accordingly, as the first part of our analysis of the applicability of the weak form of market efficiency, we examine the distribution properties of changes in the daily gold futures prices in the markets considered.

For each of the markets considered the mean, standard deviation, skewness and kurtosis are reported and the Kolmogorov–Smirnov two-sample test is used to test whether the distribution of price changes ought to be regarded as stationary. Next, serial correlation coefficients are estimated. If statistically significant auto-correlations are not identified it is likely that dependency does not exist in the time series. In the absence of a time dependency it is appropriate to apply the runs test in order to determine whether the observed number of runs approximates the expected number.

Spectral analysis is based on the Cramer Decomposition Theorem which provides the result that a stationary series X_t with a discrete index set $t = 0, 1, 2, \ldots$, and mean u can be represented as:

$$X_t - u \quad = \quad \int_{-\Pi}^{\Pi} \exp(iwt)\, d\,Z(w)$$

where

$$w \quad = \quad \text{angular frequency}$$

$$w = 2\Pi f$$

and

$$dz(w) = \text{an independent increment process.}$$

This decomposition theorem implies that any stationary series may be decomposed and studied on a cycle-by-cycle basis. In our analysis we use the auto-spectrum to isolate cycles in the series, because the value of the auto-spectrum at any frequency is a measure of the contribution of that particular frequency to the total variance of a series. While we are interested in the strength of the relationship between any two series, that is the coherence, the phase angle allows us to consider the leads and lags between the series.

Data

The raw data for this study are the per ounce prices for gold futures traded on the Winnipeg, Sydney and New York markets converted to the US exchange rate (although some use is made later of the unadjusted prices for the New York–Sydney market pairs). As our prime interest lies in identifying the relationships between the prices on large and smaller markets, we analyse the Winnipeg–New York and Sydney–New York pairings. The log of the first differences of the per ounce gold futures prices is used in the subsequent analysis.

There is, of course, a problem in identifying a continuous series of prices, from daily futures trading, that will be comparable across markets. We have available for the three markets high and low prices for sales during each trading day for all of the contract months traded in each market. In addition, we have the closing prices on the New York market and the opening bids and offers for the Sydney market. We are reluctant to use the bid and offer data because our investigations revealed that these bear no consistent relationship to the prices at which actual trades are made. We do, however, in the last test reported for the New York–Sydney market relationships, take the closing price on the US market and the opening bid on the Australian market in order to explore the timing connections.

For the remainder of the tests reported, we use the average of the highs and lows for each future quoted on both markets (for each pair) on each trading day. That is, we concentrate on the paired futures. Two separate methods were undertaken in attempting to construct continuous series: the first is to identify all of those futures quoted on both markets on each day and to take those in sequence. This produces too lumpy a sequence and we abandoned this at an early stage.

The second method, which is that applied in this chapter, is to identify a single pairing of futures traded on each day; that is, we may take the first quoted future traded in both markets each day to form a continuous sequence, or the second quoted future, or the third quoted future, and so on. We report here results for both the first and second traded futures.

3. Results

The New York and Winnipeg Markets

There is only one hour difference between these two markets, a time-difference that our data do not allow one to distinguish. In Table 8.1 we report the summary statistics for the distribution of daily log price changes for the first quoted future in both markets. The New York results reveal a negative skewness that is significant at the .01 level, while the Winnipeg results reveal a slight positive

Table 8.1: Distribution Statistics for Log Daily Price Change in First Quoted Future (April 1978-April 1979)

		New York and Winnipeg		
Statistic		New York		Winnipeg
Mean		0.0012		0.0012
Deviance		0.0151		0.0147
Skewness		−0.1518		0.0700
Kurtosis		1.3832		1.9984
Correlation			0.9388	
Runs Test: first quoted month: all paired futures				
Normalized total runs		0.5952		0.3205
Kolmogorov–Smirnov Two-sample Test				
2 sample	One side	0.1873		0.2402
		0.3020		0.3020
	Two side	0.3721		0.4737
1st with last section		0.5873		0.5873
	One side	0.0787		0.0787
	Two side	0.1574		0.1574

skewness significant at the .10 level. The kurtosis statistics reveal a tendency to a platykurtic distribution in both cases.

The runs test is the simplest test of whether the past history of these price changes may be used to predict their future movements, that is, whether the description 'random walk' is relevant. The rationale of the runs test is that unless there is a time dependency within the data span, both the observed length and the number of runs ought to approximate the expected number. If the normalized total runs lie between 0 and 1, a weak test of market efficiency is confirmed and we are able to make this confirmation for both markets.

In order to apply spectral analysis to these data we need evidence of stationarity in the data.

Application of the Kolmogorov–Smirnov one-sample test suggests that the distributions are normal. The Kolmogorov–Smirnov two-sample test allows us to test stationarity; and the results reported in Table 8.1 suggest that the two samples (and the first section with last section comparison) are from the same distribution and, therefore, stationary.

Table 8.2: Distribution Statistics for Log Daily Price Change in Second Quoted Future (April 1978-April 1979)

		New York and Winnipeg		
Statistic		New York		Winnipeg
Mean		0.0011		0.0011
Variance		0.0151		0.0149
Skewness		−0.0358		0.0595
Kurtosis		1.6835		
Correlation			0.9817	
Runs Test: second quoted month: all paired futures				
Normalized total runs		0.2274		0.7731
Kolmogorov–Smirnov Two-sample Test				
2 sample	One side	0.1873		0.1072
		0.4494		0.5321
		0.2780		0.2962
	Two side	0.3721		0.2142
		0.8188		0.9107
		0.5441		0.5770
1st with last section				
	One side	0.0787		0.1431
	Two side	0.1574		0.2854

Stationarity, which is confirmed by these results, allows us to proceed to spectral analysis without any further filtering of the data. Figure 8.1 plots the spectrums for the two markets. The pattern revealed is strong evidence against the random walk hypothesis. Because we are only observing one quoted future, the earliest, we include in our results those tests for the second quoted future as well. Table 8.2 reports results that are similar to Table 8.1. Reference to Figure 8.2 suggests that the main peaks in the frequencies, revealed in Figure 8.1, are confirmed. Clearest of the peaks is that at three days.

New York–Sydney

There is a larger time difference between these markets, owing to the fact that Sydney time is 16 hours ahead of New York time. Further, the Sydney futures trading in gold opened on the first day of our time period. Accordingly, we might expect trade to be thinner on this market than on the New York market. Australian

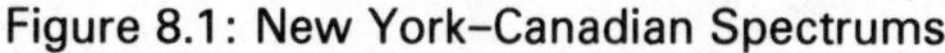
Figure 8.1: New York–Canadian Spectrums

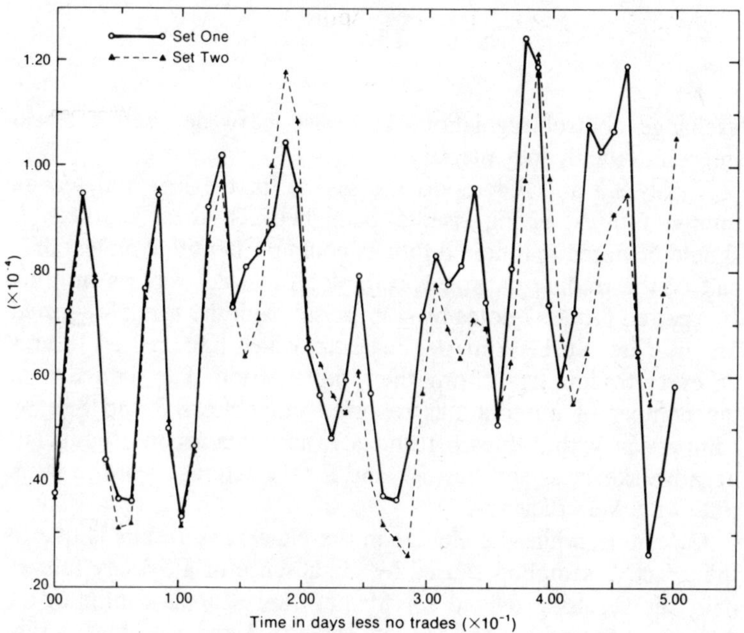

Figure 8.2: New York–Canadian Spectrums

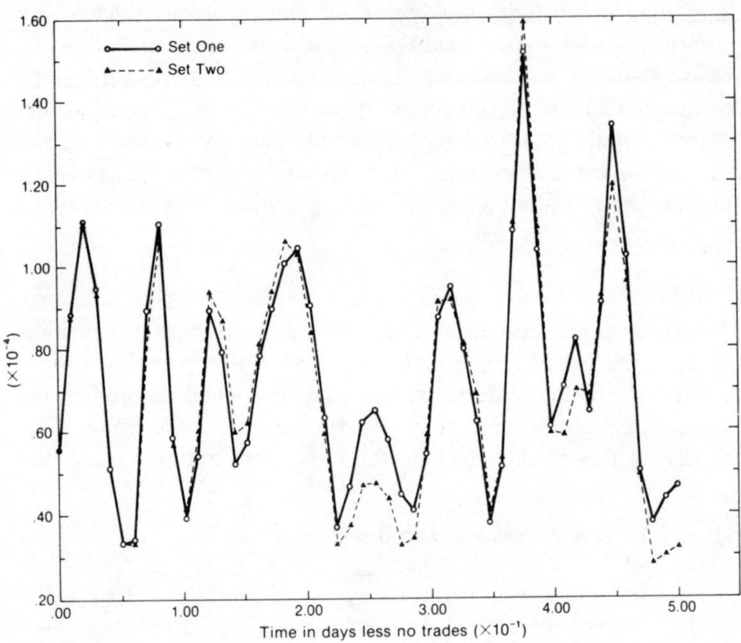

exchange control regulations may also have deterred overseas interest in the Sydney market.

Tables 8.3 and 8.4 report the results for the first and second quoted futures, giving rise to pairs between these markets. It should be noted that paired futures could be identified on less than half of the trading days; for example, Table 8.4 reports on only 107 paired futures quotes by comparison with the results reported for the New York–Winnipeg markets, which have paired futures on every trading day during the sample period. The reduction in the number of observations reported in Tables 8.3 and 8.4, by comparison with Tables 8.1 and 8.2, accounts for the significant negative skewness and kurtosis and for the refutation of the weak test of market efficiency.

Of course, while the change in the New York results is due to the selective sampling caused by the absence of a Sydney futures pair, the results provided for Sydney represent as continuous a series as it is possible to identify. Tables 8.3 and 8.4 reveal a dis-

Table 8.3: Distribution Statistics for Log Daily Price Change in First Quoted Future (April 1978-April 1979)

Statistic		New York and Sydney New York		Sydney
Mean		0.0023		0.0009
Variance		0.0249		0.0154
Skewness		−3.8430		−2.9706
Kurtosis		31.8844		23.2452
Correlation			0.7911	
Runs Test: first quoted month: all paired futures				
Normalized total runs		−1.1443		−0.2861
Kolmogorov–Smirnov Two-sample Test				
2 sample	One side	0.2047		0.1311
	Two side	0.4059		0.2617
1st with last section				
	One side	0.0642		0.1404
	Two side	0.1283		0.2801

Table 8.4: Distribution Statistics for Log Price Change in Second Quoted Future (April 1978-April 1979)

Statistic		New York and Sydney New York		Sydney
Mean		0.0026		0.0028
Variance		0.0253		0.0255
Skewness		1.9709		1.7574
Kurtosis		8.4639		12.4601
Correlation			0.8249	
Runs Test: daily log price changes: paired futures				
Normalized total runs		−2.0812		−1.6187
Kolmogorov–Smirnov Two-sample Test				
2 sample	One side	0.1515		0.2837
	Two side	0.3020		0.5544
1st with last section				
	One side	0.0678		0.0424
	Two side	0.1356		0.0848

parity in the skewness results; that is, positive skewness is seen in the first quoted future series, in contrast to significant negative skewness in the case of the second quoted future. The kurtosis figures reflect a strongly leptokurtic curve for the distribution. Both series also fail the runs test.

With the smaller number of observations it is unreasonable to put any serious reliance on the results of spectral analysis, so we merely note from that analysis that the main frequency cycle revealed by the US–Canadian results is not identifiable.

Before categorizing the Sydney market as inefficient on the basis of these results, it is reasonable to explore the possible role of the exchange rate in these figures. Figures 8.3 and 8.4 and Table 8.5 report on the second quoted future series with the data unadjusted for the exchange rate. The results reported for the exchange rate–adjusted data in fact confirm those reported in Table 8.5.

One further test incorporating Sydney market data, which would enable us to examine the spectral results in particular a little

Figure 8.3: New York–Sydney: Log of Prices [unadjusted]

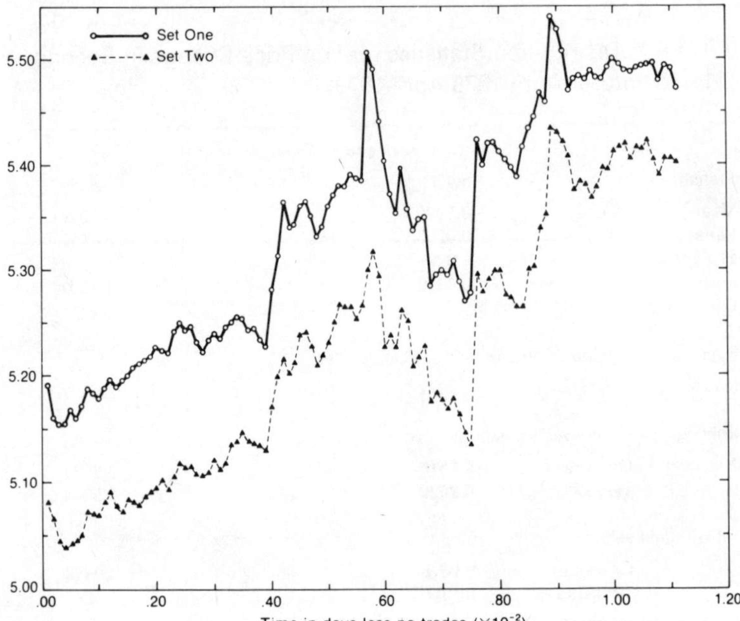

Figure 8.4: New York–Sydney: First Difference of Log Prices [unadjusted]

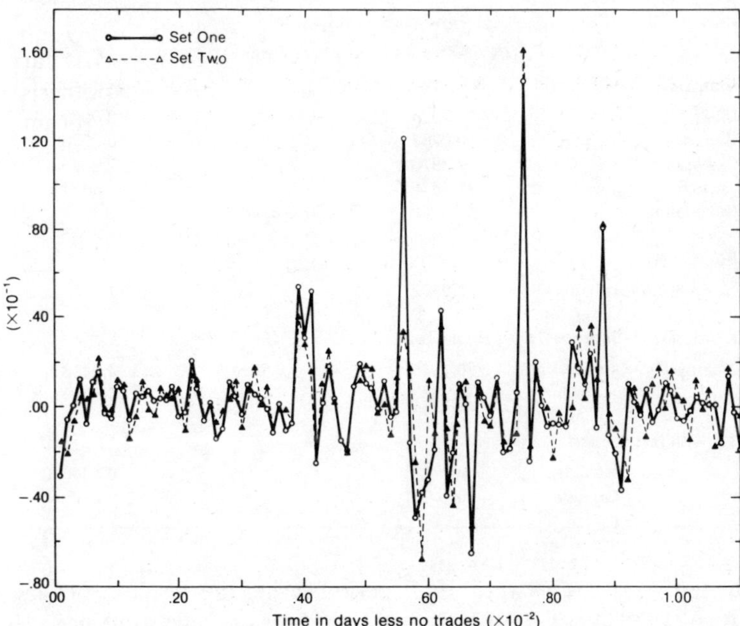

less tentatively is reported in Table 8.6. Those results use a combination of the US closing price and the Sydney opening bid to form a series of paired futures. This has the effect of more than doubling the number of observations in the series to 225. In this case the figures are adjusted for the exchange rate. The skewness for the Sydney series is reduced now to much nearer normal; however, the kurtosis statistic reveals a strongly leptokurtic curve for the distribution. The runs test is now successful and the Kolmogorov–Smirnov one- and two-sample tests do not reject the hypotheses of normality and stationarity. It is, in these circumstances, more appropriate to consider the results of spectral analysis. Once more, as with the New York–Winnipeg spectrums, there is a significant frequency cycle at three days but it is not the clearest cycle here. Again, as for the New York–Winnipeg spectral analysis, there is considerable evidence that there are sufficient cycles to justify a conclusion of non-randomness. In current work we attempt to test for the possibility of profitable trading strategies

Table 8.5: Distribution Statistics: Second Quoted Future (April 1978-April 1979)

		New York and Sydney (Not adjusted for exchange rate)		
Statistic		New York		Sydney
Mean		0.0026		0.0029
Variance		0.0263		0.0238
Skewness		2.3870		2.6479
Kurtosis		11.1875		17.5821
Correlation			0.8138	
Runs Test				
Normalized total runs		−2.0522		−1.1401
Kolmogorov–Smirnov Two-sample Test				
2 sample	One side	0.1346		0.4413
	Two side	0.2686		0.8080
1st with last section				
	One side	0.0713		0.1089
	Two side	0.1425		0.2175

in the April 1979-April 1980 period, using the results from the April 1978-April 1979 period to identify reasonable strategies.

It is important to note that the results incorporating the Sydney opening bids use this artificial non-traded price as a proxy for trades which, our earlier results suggest, are not in fact made. We may conclude from the contrast in the results, using bids as opposed to traded prices, that the traded market is inefficient and the distribution of price changes is skewed. The opening bid series imparts a smoothness to the trading which does not exist in fact.

One further difference between the two sets of Sydney results is the presence of an expected time lag in the close-opening bid results, a lag not reflected in the earlier results. This is inferential evidence that the two markets run independently of each other.

External Effects and Gold Futures Prices

There are two influences that external effects, for example the Carter budget package to support the US dollar announced on 1 November 1978, might have on the price series investigated in this chapter. First, in the case of the New York–Sydney paired futures, it may well be that price determination in both markets is coin-

Table 8.6: Distribution Statistics for Log Daily Price Changes for the US Closing Price with Opening Bid Sydney: Second Quoted Future (April 1978-April 1979)

		New York and Sydney (exchange rate adjusted)	
Statistic		New York	Sydney
Mean		0.0014	0.0006
Variance		0.0161	1.1393
Skewness		−0.0510	0.0108
Kurtosis		1.1329	25.0967
Correlation		0.2367 (with one day lag = 0.5647)	
Runs Test: US closing price with opening bid Sydney: second quoted future			
Normalized total runs		0.5292	0.2117
Kolmogorov–Smirnov Two-sample Test			
2 sample	One side	0.0567	0.1431
	Two side	0.1133	0.2854
1st with last section			
	One side	0.0787	0.0787
	Two side	0.1574	0.1574

cident only in reaction to events occurring outside the markets. There is sufficient unexplained correlation between these two markets to suggest that the usual processes of arbitrage may not be working, on the Sydney side at least.

Second, for all three markets, the presence of external events may well be the influence that accounts for the unexpected degree of kurtosis in the results.

These two influences would allow us to account for some of the inefficient elements that, according to our results, may be present in these markets. The allegation is that there are external effects that bias the normal pattern of price determination in these markets.

4. Conclusions

Evidence from several sources, reporting investigation of daily or weekly gold prices, supports the results of the present study that inefficient elements may be present in gold markets. For example,

Solt and Swanson (1981) examine weekly spot gold price data and conclude that the market is not efficient; Bird (1983), analysing daily price data from the London gold market between 1972 and 1982, not only suggests that the random walk hypothesis ought to be rejected, but also that there are sufficient dependencies to allow profitable exploitation. Weston (1983) reports levels of correlation between spectrums of spot markets for the April 1979 to August 1980 period that suggest arbitrage may not be effective between these markets. For example, in one pair of markets, only a 60.30 per cent correlation between the spectrums of the spot prices in London and Zurich was found. Elsewhere in the same study, spectral tests for the presence of cycles in spot gold and in gold futures prices, for the period April 1979 to August 1980, revealed no evidence of short-term cycles.

It seems reasonable to conclude that the results reported in this chapter, to the extent that they suggest the presence of inefficient elements in the gold markets, are consistent with other evidence from gold markets generally.

References

Bird, Peter J.W.N. (1983) 'The Weak Form Efficiency of the London Gold Market', Discussion Paper in Economics, Finance and Investment, no. 99, University of Stirling, July.

Booth, G. Geoffrey and Fred R. Kaen (1979) 'Gold and Silver Spot Prices and Market Information Efficiency', *The Financial Review*, Eastern Finance Association, Spring.

Brown, Brendan (1977) 'The Forward Sterling Market and its Relation to Arbitrage between the Silver Market in London, Chicago and New York', *Oxford Economic Papers*, vol. 29.

Cook, W.G. (1980) 'Taxation of Commodity Futures', Conference of Taxation Institute of Australia (NSW Branch).

Fama, Eugene F. (1970) 'Efficient Capital Markets: A Review of Theory and Empirical Work', *Journal of Finance*, May.

Foster, F.G. and Stuart, A. (1954) 'Distribution-Free Tests in Time-Series Based on the Breaking of Records', *Journal of the Royal Statistical Society* (b), Part 1.

Granger, C.W. and O. Morgenstern (1971) *Predictability of Stock Market Prices*, Massachusetts: Heath Lexington.

Grossman, Sanford and Joseph E. Stiglitz (1976) 'Information and Competitive Price Systems', *American Economic Review*, 66, 2 (May).

Hilliard, Jimmy E. (1979) 'The Relationship between Equity Indices on World Exchanges', *Journal of Finance*, 34, 1 (March).

Holthausen, Duncan M. and John S. Hughes (1978) 'Commodity Returns and Capital Asset Pricing', *Financial Management* (Summer).

Hooten, J. (1978) 'Futures Trading in Gold', *The Bankers' Magazine of Australasia* (June).

Koutsoyiannis, A. (1982) 'A Short-run Pricing Model for a Speculative Asset, With Data for the Gold Bullion Market', *Waterloo Economic Series*, 126, University of Waterloo, Ontario.

Roll, Richard (1978) 'Violations of Purchasing Power Parity and their Implications for Efficient International Commodity Markets', UCLA Study Center in Managerial Economics and Finance, (May).

Solt, M.E. and P.J. Swanson 'On the Efficiency of the Markets for Gold and Silver', *Journal of Business*, 54 (July).

Weston, Rae (1983) *Gold: A World Survey*, London: Croom Helm; New York: St Martin's Press

Winnipeg Commodity Exchange (1979) *By-Laws and Regulations for Gold Futures and Options on Gold Futures*, Winnipeg, Manitoba.

9 THE DISTRIBUTION OF RETURNS IN SYDNEY WOOL FUTURES

Keven Rainbow and Peter D. Praetz*

This chapter studies the empirical frequency distribution of daily returns on the wool contract on the Sydney Futures Exchange for the period December 1969 to December 1978. The aim is to determine whether these returns can reasonably be approximated by a normal distribution, since consistency with such a distribution has desirable economic and statistical properties.

Section 1 summarizes research into the empirical aspects of return distributions. Section 2 discusses the theory of competing distributions and the inferential measures which distinguish between them. Section 3 presents the empirical results and discusses possible problems with the data. Section 4 looks at the implications of the results which are consistent with non-normal distributions. Section 5 examines the limitations of this study and suggests avenues for further research. Section 6 provides a brief conclusion.

1. Some Recent Research on Return Distributions

The question of the determination of the distribution that fits a return series must be addressed before inferences may be drawn about statistical tests on those data. There appears to be little evidence available on the distribution of returns on futures markets and even less information about returns on the Sydney Futures Exchange. There has, however, been substantial and continuing research on the empirical frequency distribution of stock market returns. The evidence from this latter area may be helpful because both futures and stock markets are free exchanges, with similar economic forces underlying price movements, and so the distributions of returns may be expected to be similar, and often have been assumed to take the same form. Furthermore, because data

* Monash University, Australia.

are more readily available for stock markets than for futures markets, empirical research on the distribution of returns is more complete in that area. This evidence will be reviewed briefly now.

This area was recently discussed by Praetz and Wilson (1978). The studies reviewed there used daily, weekly and monthly share prices and indices over differing time periods, and tested for consistency with different statistical distributions. Evidence had been found which variously supported a normal distribution, a student t-distribution, non-normal members of the stable Paretian family of distributions, a compound events model and a log normal model. Some of these tests were deficient because the authors failed to test for alternative distributions. In their research with Australian share price data Praetz and Wilson specifically compared the normal distribution with the t-distribution of differing degrees of freedom, and the non-normal stable distribution with various exponents. On the basis of several statistical tests their conclusion was (p. 86):

> This paper has found no evidence to support stable Paretian distributions as a representation for stock price returns and portfolios. The case for their retention now is very weak. Student t distributions provide a better fit to the data as well as being easier to handle statistically. Even normality is not such a bad representation for portfolios.
>
> ... non-stationarity in the returns generating process clearly seems to be the most likely explanation of the typical distribution shape that we have found.

Interest in this topic was stimulated by Mandelbrot (1963), who rejected the accepted normality assumption and suggested rather the non-normal stable distributions. This paper will be discussed later in this section. Fama (1965) took up the challenge of Mandelbrot with an extensive study of daily stock returns, for stable distribution with differing exponents. Fama (p. 68) concludes:

> Even a casual glance ... is sufficient to show that the estimates of α produced by the three different procedures are consistently less than 2 (that consistent with a normal distribution). In combination with the results produced by the frequency distri-

butions and the normal–probability graphs, this would seem to be conclusive evidence in favour of the Mandelbrot hypothesis.

In an attempt to find the reason for the departure from normality, Fama (pp. 55-60) tested for different distributions for the different days and periods of the week and for non-stationarity in the parameters of the underlying distribution. The results did not support normality. He found no weekend effect; that is, no difference between Monday (close) to Tuesday (close) for example, and Friday (close) to Monday (close). He also found no difference in the behaviour of the distribution with changes in the mean of the distribution. However, when considering non-stationarity he did not test for changes in the variance of the distribution.

Praetz (1969) found stability in the means of distributions of stock returns over time, but concluded (p. 132) 'we would reject the hypothesis that the variance of price changes is constant from year to year'. It seems, therefore, that Fama (1965) may not have tested for the appropriate non-stationarity effect. Praetz (1972) took account of the change in variance and concluded (p. 49):

> Osborn's Brownian motion theory of share price changes is modified to account for the changing variance of the share market. This produces a scaled t-distribution which is an excellent fit to series of share price indices. This distribution is the only known simple distribution to fit changes in share prices. It provides a far better fit to the data than the stable Paretian, compound process and normal distribution.

For this reason the t-distribution was included in the Praetz and Wilson (1978) study. Among papers in this area, for example, Press (1967), Officer (1972) and Osborn (1974), a major contribution has been made by Blattberg and Gonedes (1974). They too favoured the student t-distribution (p. 275):

> We inferred from our results that the student model provides a better empirical description than the stable model. This does not mean that the rates of return do in fact follow a student model. It only indicates that the latter provides a better empirical fit than the stable model. The student model has fat tails as does

> the stable model, but converges to normality for large sum sizes. The stable model does not converge to normality.

Although little research has been done on the distribution of returns in futures markets, some attention has been paid to the serial correlation of price changes. Praetz (1975) has summarized the results on this latter issue which generally were consistent with independence of price changes.

The lack of attention to the distribution of returns in futures markets is surprising because the study by Mandelbrot (1963) which stimulated interest in return distributions was on cotton prices rather than stock market returns.

One of the characteristics of non-normal stable distributions is infinite variance; that is, the sum of independent, identically distributed, random variables does not converge to a finite limit but continues to grow with larger and larger sample sizes.

Mandelbrot (p. 308) found:

> The tails of the distributions of price changes are in fact so extraordinarily long that the sample second moments typically vary in an erratic fashion. For example, the sample second moment ... does not seem to tend to any limit even though the sample size is enormous by economic standards, and even though the series to which it applies is presumably stationary.

Mandelbrot employed sample sizes varying from 1 to 1,300 observations. He also made graphical tests which supported his basic conclusion that (p. 319) 'long series of monthly price changes should therefore be represented by *mixtures* of stable Paretian laws; such mixtures remain Paretian'.

The literature began therefore with some evidence for stable Paretian, non-normal distributions. Cootner (1964), however, queried this evidence. He suggested that actual cotton prices are affected *inter alia* by the level of inventories, which varies throughout the harvest year with a consequent effect on the price variance; when stocks are large, price changes are small and so too is their variance, but when stocks are small, price changes are large with a large variance. He added (p. 334):

> This can happen in spot prices because these changes cannot be arbitraged away — they would occur in a perfect market. Brownian motion or its Paretian equivalent is only reasonable for prices of futures, and even in this area it will not hold without modification if one accepts ... [the] evidence that futures that expire near the end of the season are more variable than those which expire earlier ... this suggests that the 'Paretian' behaviour of cotton spot price changes may really be a result of nonstationarity.

Thus we are left with conflicting evidence on the distribution of price changes in futures markets.

Kendall (1953) has also examined this issue. He observed that it was the change, not the absolute value, which constitutes the basic element in price determination, and made two significant findings. First, he found (p. 89) the changing variance that other authors have found, and second, for Chicago wheat futures, he found that the distributions were near normal (p. 91).

Clark (1973) used a subordinated stochastic process (i.e. subordinated to a normal distribution) as a model for speculative prices with a general class of finite-variance distributions for price changes. He studied cotton futures price changes, with the process directed by operational time which was lognormally distributed, and concluded (pp. 146-7):

> There is, then, a strong case for normality of price change when it is adjusted for operational time ... All of the results are very strong evidence in favour of the finite-variance subordination model. They also point out that the marginal distribution (unconditional on operational time) of price changes should be lognormal-normal rather than stable.

Hunt (1974) found evidence of a weak seasonal pattern in daily Sydney wool futures returns during the period 1964-73, but a more recent investigation by Fisher and Tanner (1978) failed to find such a pattern. Although on balance the evidence from both stocks and futures markets does not support the stable distribution, it is still to be determined which distribution fits futures price changes the best.

2. Inferential Considerations for Return Distributions Theory

In this chapter we compare the family of stable Paretian and student t-distributions.

Stable Paretian distributions are described by Mandelbrot (1963) and Fama (1963, 1965). They have characteristic function (t) given by

$$\phi(t) \quad = \quad \exp\{idy - c|y|^{\alpha}(1 + iby \tan(\alpha\pi/2)/|y|)\}$$

where: d is a location parameter and the mean if $\alpha > 1$; $b(-1 \leqslant b \leqslant 1)$ is a measure of skewness; c is the scale parameter; and the exponent $\alpha(0 \leqslant a \leqslant 2)$ measures probability in the tails of the distribution of returns. With $b = 0$ we have symmetry; $\alpha = 2$ gives the normal distribution; and when $\alpha = 1$ and $b = 0$ we have the Cauchy distribution. When α is in the interval $0 < \alpha < 2$, the extreme tails of the stable Paretian distributions are higher than those of the normal distribution, and the total probability in the extreme tails is larger the smaller the value of α. Furthermore, these distributions are higher than the density function of the normal distribution in the neighbourhood of their location parameter's common value, zero. Thus for $\alpha < 2$, stable distributions have higher densities around the mean and the tails and lesser densities in the middle than the normal. The most important consequence of this is that the variance exists (is finite) only in the extreme case of $\alpha = 2$. The mean, however, exists as long as $\alpha > 1$. The disagreement between the hypothesis of the normal distribution and Mandelbrot's hypothesis is over the value of the characteristic exponent α.

Stable Paretian distributions have two important properties: (i) stability or invariance under addition (the distribution of sums of independent, identically distributed, stable Paretian variables is itself stable Paretian and, except for origin and scale, has the same form as the distribution of the individual summands, i.e. α and b are constant); (ii) these distributions are the only possible limiting distributions for sums of independent, identically distributed, random variables.

The stability property is important because the price changes of a futures contract for any time interval can be regarded as the sum of the changes from transaction to transaction during the interval.

Thus price changes of daily, weekly and monthly stable Paretian variables will follow a stable Paretian distribution of the same form. If stable Paretian variables have a finite variance, the limiting distribution of their sum will be the normal distribution. If the basic variables have infinite variance, the limiting distribution must be stable Paretian with $0 < \alpha < 2$.

The student t-distributions, developed as return distribution models by Praetz (1972) and Blattberg and Gonedes (1974) have distribution function f(y),

$$f(y) \quad = \quad (1 + (y-\mu)^2/\sigma^2(2m-2)]^{-m-\frac{1}{2}}$$

$$\Gamma(m+\tfrac{1}{2})/\Gamma(m)\sigma\{2(m-2)\pi\}^{\frac{1}{2}}$$

where: y has mean μ and variance σ^2; $\Gamma(m)$ is the gamma function; and f(y) has a t distribution on 2m degrees of freedom, except for a scale factor of $[m/(m-1)]^{\frac{1}{2}}$. This model follows by combining the normal model for returns with an inverted gamma distribution; this models the stochastic variance to account for the non-stationarity in variance reported above. The student t-distribution has fatter tails than the density function of a conventional standardized normal random variable, and it is higher than the standard normal density in the neighbourhood of their common mean, zero, when scaling is done by σ^2.

For the student model with degrees of freedom greater than 2, the distribution of sums of random variables converges to the normal distribution as the number of observations increases; that is, the classical central limit theorem applies.

Parameter estimation proceeds by using the sample mean ($\bar{x}$) and sample standard deviation (s) to separate returns into 16 separate class intervals. Stable Paretian probabilities are given in Fama and Roll (1968) for $\alpha = 1.0, 1.1, \ldots 1.95, 2.0$. Student t probabilities are calculated for degrees of freedom $T = 3$ to 31 and both sets are compared with empirical relative frequencies, giving a chi-squared statistic. The best α and T are estimated from the minimum of the chi-squared values.

There are 12 chi-squared degrees of freedom, four being lost due to three estimated parameters ($\bar{x}$, s and either α or $T = 2m$) and one constraint (for the sum of expected and observed being equal), so an overall goodness-of-fit is tested by the χ^2_{12} statistic.

The normal distribution test loses three degrees of freedom since there is no α or T, and so this hypothesis is tested by the χ^2_{13} statistic.

The test for skewness and kurtosis is defined by Pearson (1930) as $b_1 = m_3^2/m_2^3$ (skewness), and $b_2 = m_4/m_2^2$ (kurtosis), where $m_j = \Sigma_i(x_i - \bar{x})^j/N$. With a normal and independent sample, x_i, of size N and with constant variance, $(b_1\ N/6)^{1/2}$ and $(b_2 - 3)(N/24)^{1/2}$ are unit normal deviates. Statistics for skewness and kurtosis are somewhat imperfect as large sample sizes are needed, but the sample of 299 observations per contract in this study should be adequate for that purpose. The final test conducted was the Studentized Range (SR) where SR = range/standard deviation. The SR was found by Fama and Roll (1971) to be the best of a number of goodness-of-fit tests of normality against non-normal stable alternatives.

3. Results

The data for this study consist of daily closing prices from beginning of December 1969 to beginning of December 1978 on all wool contracts traded on the Sydney Futures Exchange. Because it is desirable to have as many observations as possible, the data were organized in the following way.

Observations from trading in the maturity month of each contract were deleted because in that period the futures price is affected by delivery month influences. Trading in each contract begins 18 months before it is delisted, but in the first few months most contracts exhibited little open interest and little trading. In order to avoid the 'non-trading' effect likely to result from this scant turnover, observations were deleted from the first two months' trading for each contract. Thus data were employed from 15 months' trading for each of 40 contracts. In order to facilitate computation the number of observations was standardized at 299 price changes (300 daily closing buyer prices) for each contract. (This standardization was achieved by deletion of observations at the end of the contracts' trading life, where necessary.) There is a slight seasonal pattern only in wool futures prices, and no adjustment was made for this, in accordance with the views of Cootner (1964), noted above. Nevertheless, two adjustments were made to the data. First, there was a change from imperial to metric measurement of quantities in wool-handling during the sample period, and prices in the early part of the period were converted from cents per pound to cents per kilogram, so that all price data employed are on this latter basis. Second, because *rates* of return were investigated by most previous studies on this topic, to facilitate comparison price relatives were calculated, and from these, rates of return were derived as follows:

$$\tilde{R}_{it} = \tilde{P}_{it}/P_{it-1} - 1 = \text{return on contract i over day t}$$

where $\tilde{}$ denotes a random variable, i = 1, . . . , 40 and t = 2, . . . , 300.

Although tests were conducted both with and without natural log transformation of returns, the former results are preferred. This is first because the change in log prices is the yield, under continuous compounding, from holding a security, and second because the variability of simple price changes of a security is an increasing function of the price of that security (Fama, 1965; Praetz, 1969). It should be noted that any positive skewness of returns will be reduced by this transformation (see Fama, 1976, p. 31). Results for the log of returns only are presented here.

The various rate of return statistics are presented in Table 9.1, including statistics for skewness (g_1), kurtosis (g_2), mean ($\bar{R}$), standard deviation (S), studentized range (SR), chi-squared statistics for the t and stable Paretian distributions (χ^2_t and χ^2_{sp}), first-order serial correlation coefficient r_1 and the number of serial correlation coefficients n_r out of the first twelve which are significant at the 1 per cent level.

The r_1 values vary from .19 to −.30 and only five are significant at the 1 per cent level of ± .15. Even the largest −.30 only accounts for 9 per cent of the variance of prediction for a simple auto-regressive model. The r_1 and n_r values are included as a check on market efficiency and, more important, as a diagnostic for data errors. The low values of both statistics are encouraging because they suggest the data are free of gross errors (see Praetz, 1976).

Table 9.2 contains the actual frequency distribution of returns in standardized class interval units, and the frequency expected under normality for two contracts, March 1974 and July 1978.

Table 9.3 contains percentages (and numbers in brackets) of contracts which are significant at the 1, 5 and 10 per cent levels of chi-squared goodness-of-fit tests of the t, stable Paretian and normal distributions, kurtosis (g_2), skewness (g_1) and studentized range (SR). The results are discussed below, using a 1 per cent level of significance due to the possible violation of test assumptions and the large number of contracts studied.

It will be seen from Table 9.3 that the t-distribution is far superior to the stable Paretian because on the former hypothesis only 25 per cent of the sample (10 contracts) result in a significant

Table 9.1: Rate of Return Statistics*

Contract	g_1	g_2	$\bar{R}(\times 10^4)$	S(%)	SR	χ^2_t	χ^2_{sp}	r_1	n_r
Mar 71	.45	7.0	−15	1.41	9.9	27	92	.18	2
May 71	.63	3.8	−12	1.36	8.5	27	63	.10	1
July 71	.60	2.8	−11	1.23	6.8	27	51	.15	1
Oct 71	.66	3.4	−11	1.25	7.4	13	46	.11	0
Dec 71	.68	4.0	− 9	1.29	7.8	20	48	.03	0
Mar 72	.11	2.8	0	.98	9.0	19	40	.00	0
May 72	.23	1.2	5	.83	7.1	6	10	.19	3
July 72	.24	1.5	10	.91	7.2	13	22	.11	0
Oct 72	−.26	1.9	13	1.00	8.0	8	21	−.03	0
Dec 72	.54	14.9	22	2.15	13.1	54	158	.00	4
Mar 73	−.04	10.5	37	2.34	11.5	21	89	.05	0
May 73	.24	4.8	31	2.84	9.4	30	85	.09	2
July 73	.53	9.4	36	3.40	11.9	27	94	−.08	0
Oct 73	−.20	2.2	28	3.44	7.1	20	31	.06	1
Dec 73	−.03	1.7	20	3.28	7.4	11	21	.11	0
Mar 74	.09	1.2	10	2.89	6.9	12	16	.13	0
May 74	.13	2.0	0	2.78	6.8	22	37	.06	0
July 74	.25	2.1	− 1	2.42	7.8	10	20	.03	1
Oct 74	.61	2.4	−12	1.85	7.5	8	15	.08	1
Dec 74	.67	3.6	−10	1.76	8.3	18	30	.12	1
Mar 75	.05	3.3	−11	1.39	8.9	16	27	.07	1
May 75	.20	4.0	− 8	1.12	9.8	13	28	.06	0
July 75	.38	4.3	− 5	1.10	9.7	8	27	.06	2
Oct 75	.12	6.3	− 5	1.00	10.8	9	39	.09	0
Dec 75	−.34	2.7	0	.81	7.6	20	40	.11	0
Mar 76	−.52	3.7	− 3	.81	9.0	18	47	.02	0
May 76	.26	5.9	2	.74	10.7	13	34	−.07	0
July 76	−.24	1.2	2	.68	7.1	12	15	.05	0

Oct 76	−.31	0.8	3	.64	6.2	16	21	−.01	0
Dec 76	.06	2.6	3	.69	9.0	11	18	−.04	0
Mar 77	2.60	22.4	7	.77	11.7	16	35	.10	0
May 77	1.47	9.9	4	.69	10.0	21	32	.11	0
July 77	.32	3.1	1	.66	8.8	18	27	.05	0
Oct 77	1.11	7.9	2	.58	10.5	16	27	.10	0
Dec 77	.39	29.1	2	.54	16.4	13	81	−.17	1
Mar 78	.46	2.7	− 1	.49	8.3	30	58	−.02	0
May 78	.30	2.5	− 2	.40	8.4	23	38	.08	0
July 78	.06	1.8	− 1	.37	8.2	38	42	.01	0
Oct 78	−.17	0.3	− 1	.32	5.8	39	44	−.07	0
Dec 78	.11	20.4	0	.43	14.3	74	185	−.30	1

Note: * Values of statistics for skewness (g_1), kurtosis (g_2), mean ($\bar{R}$), standard deviation (S), studentized range (SR), chi-squared values for t and stable-Paretian distributions (χ^2_t and χ^2_{sp}), and serial correlation measures (r_1 and n_r) for 299 daily wool future returns for 40 contracts with maturities from March 1971 to December 1978.

Table 9.2: Actual and Expected (Normal) Frequency Distribution of Daily Returns

Frequency Class	Actual (−)	Expected (Normal)	Actual (+)
(a) March 1974			
0 to ½	66	57.2	64
½ to 1	44	44.8	46
1 to 1½	21	27.5	23
1½ to 2	11	13.2	6
2 to 2½	4	5.0	5
> 2½	4	1.5	5
(b) July 1978			
0 to ½	55	57.2	73
½ to 1	41	44.8	47
1 to 1½	23	27.5	18
1½ to 2	16	13.2	17
2 to 2½	2	5.0	1
> 2½	2	1.5	4

Table 9.3: Goodness of Fit Tests*

Test	χ^2 Significance Level (%)		
	1	5	10
t	25 (10)	30 (12)	45 (18)
Stable Paretian	75 (30)	77½ (31)	87½ (35)
Normal	72½ (29)	82½ (33)	90 (36)
Kutosis	97½ (39)	97½ (39)	97½ (39)
Skewness (+)	37½ (15)	42½ (17)	55 (22)
Skewness (−)	2½ (1)	7½ (3)	12½ (5)
Studentized range (+)	80 (32)	90 (36)	95 (38)
Studentized range (−)	0 (0)	0 (0)	0 (0)

Note: * Percentages (and numbers in brackets) of contracts significant at 1, 5 and 10 per cent levels for chi-squared goodness-of-fit measures for testing the t, stable Paretian and normal distributions, kurtosis, skewness and studentized range.

χ^2 value compared with 75 per cent (30) on the latter hypothesis. Kurtosis is very strong with only one contract not significant. Some positive skewness also emerges with 15 contracts significant. This is reflected in the studentized range results, which also reject normality at the positive end for 32 contracts.

From Table 9.2 it is clear that the actual frequencies are more peaked than the expected normal frequencies and give the appearance of possibly having fatter tails; the typical result for actual frequencies from stocks is of fat tails, the distribution being more peaked near zero and having lower frequencies in between.

It is possible that data errors may be responsible for some of the results indicated above — very few errors are needed in a data base to produce significant results (see Beedles and Simkowitz, 1978) — and such errors appear to exist in even the best large data bases. After an examination of the top quality data bases of US stocks, Rosenberg and Houglet (1974, p. 1306) stated:

> Since the errors are relatively large, each higher power causes the effect of the errors to grow proportionally larger. The errors affect the means by factors of less than 1/1000, the variances by factors as great as 5/3, the skewness by factors as great as 11, and the kurtosis by factors as great as 18 — indeed, the errors ... virtually determine the skewness and kurtosis.

The extent to which such errors affect the data employed here is unknown. Both skewness and kurtosis are strongly significant for some individual contracts, and data errors may be responsible for this result. On the other hand, data errors tend to result in negative first-order serial correlation, which is absent in the results presented here. A further possible explanation of the skewness and kurtosis found may be the 'non-trading' effect of low volumes in the early part of the life of the contracts.

Rosenberg and Houglet (1974) have suggested the exclusion of outlying observations as a means of reducing skewness and kurtosis, although if this procedure results in support for the normal distribution there is an implication that the results are preconceived. In this study, experimentation with data reduced by the elimination of outliers improved the relative performance of the normality hypothesis, but did not change the nature of the results (experiments with reduced data are not reported here).

4. Economic and Statistical Implications

The economic and statistical implications of returns which conform to a stable distribution have been well documented by Fama (1963, 1965) and Blattberg and Gonedes (1974). Following Fama (1965, pp. 93-8), these may be stated as:

1. In a Gaussian market, if the sum of a large number of price changes across a long time period is very large, it is likely that each individual price change during the time period is negligible when compared to the total change. In a market that is stable Paretian with $\alpha < 2$, however, the size of the total will more than likely be the result of a few very large changes that took place during much shorter sub-periods. In other words, whereas the path of the price level of a given security in a Gaussian market will be fairly continuous, in a stable Paretian market with $\alpha < 2$ it will usually be discontinuous.

   The discontinuous nature of a stable Paretian market has the implication that such a market is inherently more risky than a Gaussian market. The variability of a given expected yield is higher in a stable Paretian market, than it would be in a Gaussian market, and the probability of large losses is greater. Moreover, in a stable Paretian market with $\alpha < 2$ speculators cannot usually protect themselves from large losses by means of such devices as 'stop-loss' orders.

2. In practical terms 'infinite' variance means that the sample variance and standard deviation of a stable Paretian process with $\alpha < 2$ will show extremely erratic behaviour for very large samples. That is, for larger and larger sample sizes the variability of the sample variance and standard deviation will not tend to dampen nearly as much as would be expected with a Gaussian process.

In this situation the mean-variance concept of an efficient portfolio loses its meaning. Moreover, the asymptotic properties of the parameters in classical least-squares regression analysis are strongly dependent on the assumption of finite variance in the distribution of the residuals.

If the stable Paretian distribution were upheld, the Capital Asset Pricing Model could not be applied to these data.

On the other hand, the student distribution has some advantages, in that this model allows the use of well-defined density functions, whereas well-defined density functions for the stable model exist in only two cases, where $\alpha = 1$ and $\alpha = 2$. Moreover, the parameters for the student model may be estimated from the closed form solution of its likelihood function. This is not possible for the stable distributions, which require approximations, and it is not possible to estimate α from statistical theory.

5. Limitations of this Study

No single study can prove returns conform to a particular distribution; the best it can do is provide evidence for or against a particular hypothesis. The results here, of course, are specific to this set of data, and our understanding of returns in the wool futures market would be improved by extending the sample period. *A priori* it was expected that natural log transformations would improve the fit of the distributions tested here to the data. The results appear to support this contention because, for all tests, the transformation reduced the significance of departures from the models fitted.

One of the reasons for departure from normality using daily data is the 'weekend' effect mentioned earlier. If one attempts to fit one distribution (e.g. the normal distribution) to all the data, when some of the data come from different distributions, a poor fit for the distribution hypothesized is to be expected. This point was not investigated for these data although it may have no effect on the results, as in the case reported by Fama (1965, pp. 55-6). It has been suggested in the stock market literature that the use of daily rates of return may be inappropriate because such returns are all affected by market-wide influences. It has been suggested that these market-wide influences should be eliminated and a distribution fitted to the residuals. Officer (1971) examined this alternative with daily stock prices and found it to make virtually no difference to the results, mainly because the cross-sectional correlation among daily returns is close to zero.

It was mentioned in Section 2 above that stable distributions are invariant under addition. That is, daily, weekly and monthly returns would follow the same form of distribution if they were in fact stable variables. Fama (1976, p. 33) pointed out, however, in relation to stock prices, that monthly returns are closer to normality than daily returns. This possibility may be explored with futures market data, but was not tested here.

Tests other than those reported in this chapter may be used to find the model that best fits the data. Fama (1965) employed normal probability graphs, double-log and probability graphs, range analysis and the sequential variance method used by Mandelbrot (1963). Blattberg and Gonedes (1974) used a maximum likelihood estimation procedure, and more recently Greene and Fielitz (1977) used a technique to detect long-term dependence, which they claim leads to the conclusion that the distribution of security returns is non-normal stable Paretian as opposed to Gaussian. Saniga and Hayya (1977) have also proposed goodness-of-fit tests to discriminate between non-normal symmetric stable distributions on the basis of skewness and kurtosis.

In addition to the models mentioned above which have been tested, Oldfield, Rogalski and Jarrow (1977) have suggested a new process, an auto-regressive jump process, which may be fitted to stock returns.

The search for an appropriate distribution could thus continue far beyond the limits of this study.

6. Conclusion

This chapter has attempted briefly to review the literature of fitting distributions to market returns, to explain the grounds for research interest in this topic, as well as to provide some evidence on the distribution of daily returns on the wool contract on the Sydney Futures Exchange.

The rival hypotheses addressed are that the student t, normal and stable Paretian distributions best describe the returns on the Sydney wool futures contract for the period December 1969 to December 1978, with 299 sample price changes for each of 40 contracts. Using a chi-square test, the student t distribution clearly outperforms the normal and stable Paretian distributions, and tests for skewness and kurtosis provide further evidence against normality. The first-order serial correlation coefficients do not indicate any significant market inefficiency in the use of past price information, nor do they indicate any serious data errors.

References

Beedles, W.L. and M.A. Simkowitz (1978) 'A Note on Skewness and Data Errors', *Journal of Finance*, 33, 288-92.

Blattberg, R. and N. Gonedes (1974) 'A Comparison of the Stable and Student Distributions as Statistical Models for Stock Prices', *Journal of Business*, 47, 244-80.

Clark, P.K. (1973) 'A Subordinated Stochastic Process with Finite Variance for Speculative Prices', *Econometrica*, 41, 135-55.

Cootner, P. (1964) 'Comments on the Variation of Certain Speculative Prices', in P. Cootner (ed.), *The Random Character of Stock Market Prices*, revised edn, Cambridge, Massachusetts: MIT Press.

Fama, E.F. (1963) 'Mandelbrot and the Stable Paretian Hypothesis', *Journal of Business*, 36, 420-9.

— (1965) 'The Behaviour of Stock-Market Prices', *Journal of Business*, 38, 34-105.

— (1976) *Foundations of Finance*, Oxford: Basil Blackwell.

Fama, E.F. and R. Roll (1968) 'Some Properties of Symmetric Stable Distributions', *Journal of the American Statistical Association*, 63, 817-36.

— (1971) 'Parameter Estimates for Symmetric Stable Distributions', *Journal of the American Statistical Association*, 66, 331-8.

Fisher, B. and C. Tanner (1978) 'In Search of Hunt's Short-run Price Cycles in the Sydney Wool Futures Exchange', *Australian Journal of Agricultural Economics*, 22, 129-34.

Greene, M.T. and B.D. Fielitz (1977) 'Long-term Dependence in Common Stock Returns', *Journal of Financial Economics*, 4, 339-50.

Hunt, B. (1974) 'Short-run Price Cycles in the Sydney Wool Futures Market', *Australian Journal of Agricultural Economics*, 18, 133-43.

Kendall, M.G. (1953) 'The Analysis of Economic Time-Series ... Part 1: Prices', in P. Cootner (ed.), pp. 85-99.

Mandelbrot, B. (1963) 'The Variation of Certain Speculative Prices', in P. Cootner (ed.), pp. 307-32.

Officer, R.R. (1971) 'A Time Series Examination of the Market Factor of the New York Stock Exchange', PhD diss., University of Chicago.

— (1972) 'The Distribution of Stock Returns', *Journal of American Statistical Association*, 67, 807-12.

Oldfield, B.S. Jr., R.J. Rogalski and R.A. Jarrow (1977) 'An Autoregressive Jump Process for Common Stock Returns', *Journal of Financial Economics*, 5, 389-418.

Osborn, D.R. (1974) 'The Distribution of Price Changes on the Sydney Stock Exchange', *Australian Journal of Statistics*, 16, 44-9.

Pearson, E.S. (1930) 'A Further Development of Tests for Normality', *Biometrika*, 22, 239-49.

Praetz, P.D. (1969) 'Australian Stock Prices and the Random Walk Hypothesis', *Australian Journal of Statistics*, 11, 123-39.

— (1972) 'The Distribution of Share Price Changes', *Journal of Business*, 45, 49-55.

— (1975) 'Testing the Efficient Markets Theory on the Sydney Wool Futures Exchange', *Australian Economic Papers*, 14, 240-9.

— (1976) 'Some Effect of Errors on the Independence and Distribution of Stock Price Returns', *Australian Journal of Management*, 1 (2), 79-83.

Praetz, P.D. and E.J. Wilson (1978) 'The Distribution of Stock Market Returns: 1958-1973', *Australian Journal of Management*, 3, 79-90.

Press, S.J. (1967) 'A Compound Events Model for Security Prices', *Journal of Business*, 40, 317-25.

Rosenberg, B. and M. Houglet (1974) 'Error Rates in CRSP and Compustat Data Bases and their Implications', *Journal of Finance*, 29, 1303-10.

Saniga, E.M. and J.C. Hayya (1977) 'Simple Goodness-of-Fit Tests for Symmetric Stable Distributions', *Journal of Financial and Quantitative Analysis*, 276-89.

10 CONJECTURED MODELS FOR TRENDS IN FINANCIAL PRICES, TESTS AND FORECASTS

Stephen J. Taylor*

1. Introduction

The prices of many financial assets, including stocks, commodities and currencies, change several times during a day. Much published research claims that the day-to-day changes in financial prices are either random or differ from a random process in a negligible manner, which cannot be exploited by speculators. Another viewpoint is that prices contain trends but, previously, there has not been much published evidence to support the idea of trends. Statistical tests have been done upon the prices of (i) stocks traded in London (Dryden, 1970; Cunningham, 1973), America (Fama, 1965; Granger and Morgenstern, 1971), Australia (Praetz, 1969) and Scandinavia (Jennergren and Korsvold, 1974); (ii) commodities traded in America (Labys and Granger, 1970; Dusak, 1973; Cargill and Rausser, 1975) and Australia (Praetz, 1975); and (iii) international exchange rates (Cornell and Dietrich, 1978). This chapter gives the first detailed analysis of the daily prices of commodities traded at the large markets in London.

It will be argued that price changes have appeared random because the alternative hypothesis of trends has been described vaguely. Explicit trend models are conjectured and tested, with conclusions which point to the existence of trends in the markets studied. Some applications of the models are given. A time series of *daily* prices will be denoted by $\{z_t\}$. The return from holding the asset from day t−1 to day t is defined by $x_t = \log(z_t/z_{t-1})$. The logarithmic transformation is now conventional (Fama, 1965, pp. 45-6) and it is the best choice from the Box–Cox set of transformations (Taylor and Kingsman, 1979).

A variety of models have been used to describe the apparent random behaviour of financial prices. The *random walk* model

*Department of Operational Research, Lancaster University, England. This paper won the Society's Frances Wood Memorial prize for the session 1979-80 (section 7 of original paper (pp. 358-60) has been omitted in this chapter).

states that the daily returns are uncorrelated and have constant mean:

$$x_t = \mu + e_t, \quad E(e_t) = 0, E(e_t e_{t+i}) = 0 \ (i \neq 0). \tag{1.1}$$

Inflationary factors will cause certain prices to drift upwards. This possibility can be modelled by the *positive random walk*:

$$x_t = \mu_t + e_t, \tag{1.2a}$$

$$\mu_t \geqslant 0, \tag{1.2b}$$

$$E(e_t) = 0, E(e_t e_{t+i}) = 0 \ (i \neq 0), \quad \text{cov}(\mu_s, e_t) = 0 \quad (\text{all } s,t). \tag{1.2c}$$

Equations (1.2c) state that the drift terms $\{\mu_t\}$ are all uncorrelated with a white-noise series $\{e_t\}$. A special case of (1.2) is the so-called 'weak form' of the *efficient market* model, which states that prices accurately reflect all past price information and reward rational investors for accepting risk (Fama, 1970; Jensen, 1978). Let RF_t be the return from risk-free investments and let RP_t be the risk premium. The statistical representation of the model will be written:

$$(1.2a,b,c), \quad \mu_t = RF_t + RP_t, RP_t \geqslant 0. \tag{1.3}$$

Models (1.2) and (1.3), and (1.1) for $\mu \geqslant 0$, are special cases of the sub-martingale process (Fama, 1970):

$$E(x_t | \text{all } x_{t-i}, i \geqslant 1) \geqslant 0. \tag{1.4}$$

This model, and the preceding special cases, can be assessed by evaluating trading rules, since (1.4) implies that any method which buys and sells the asset over a specified period, using knowledge of the past prices alone, is inferior to the strategy of buying at the beginning of the period and selling at its conclusion. Some trading rules have been claimed to perform well (Leuthold, 1972), but significance test procedures have only recently been published (Praetz, 1979b). Cargill and Rausser (1975) and Praetz (1976) emphasize the importance of applying tests to trading rule results.

Price-trend models were first described in statistical notation in Taylor and Kingsman (1978). Formal models are essential, if a price-trend hypothesis is to be investigated thoroughly. Otherwise, evidence for trends can only be obtained from trading-rule analyses, which lack a satisfactory methodology. We define formal models by (1.2a), (1.2c) *and* a stochastic process for $\{\mu_t\}$.

The simplest example considered is a step-process, in which μ_t equals either μ_{t-1} with probability p, or a new independent value with probability 1−p. In this example, the trend μ_t is constant on each of a sequence of time intervals, each interval having random duration. For each interval, $\log(z_t)$ is expected to 'move' by a constant amount each day and this is what we mean by trend. We do not assume that μ_t is non-negative (as in 1.2b) and, in a trend model, μ_t is not interpreted as an inflation term or as a risk-adjusted, expected return. Rather, we interpret μ_t as a response to changes in the anticipated demand for, and supply of, the asset; it is then reasonable to permit $\mu_t \leqslant 0$. Kingsman (1974) offers some insight into the econometric character of demand and supply models for commodities. We cannot hope to identify the beginnings and ends of specific trends. Instead, we conjecture trend models, make theoretical deductions and then test appropriate hypotheses.

The structure of the chapter, and the major ideas and results, are as follows. Section 2 contains various processes for the trend $\{\mu_t\}$, of varying complexities. Our processes are characterized by the correlation structure implied for the trend, namely $\mathrm{cor}(\mu_t,\mu_{t+i}) = p^i (0 < p < 1, \text{ all } i)$. Section 3 describes fluctuations in the variance of the returns $\{x_t\}$. Standard auto-correlation tests are invalid if the fluctuations are ignored. We describe a method of rescaling the returns, to obtain a series whose variance is approximately constant. Also, stochastic processes for the series $\{\mathrm{var}(x_t)\}$ are conjectured.

Section 4 focuses on the primary argument against price trends: the alleged absence of auto-correlation in the returns. Denoting the theoretical auto-correlation by $\rho_i = \mathrm{cor}(x_t,x_{t+i})$, we define a null hypothesis H_0: $\rho_i = 0(\text{all } i > 0)$, corresponding to the random walk model. We derive an alternative hypothesis, $H_1 : \rho_i = Ap^i(\text{all } i > 0, A > 0, 0 < p < 1)$, from the price-trend models. In the past, H_0 has been tested against a *general* alternative hypothesis, using test statistics whose power is not high when the *specific* hypothesis H_1 is valid. It is therefore possible that many reported conclusions are erroneous. A new test statistic is given and evaluated on eight (hitherto untested) commodity series and an exchange-rate series. The random walk model is rejected for most series at the 5 per cent significance level, and tests of the positive random walk and efficient market models are also presented. In particular, exchange rates are not random walks.

Having established the plausibility of the models, Section 5 describes estimates of the model parameters. The maximum autocorrelation $\rho_1 = Ap$, is typically less than 0.04. Section 6 gives an optimal linear forecasting method for price-trend models. Although accurate forecasts of future returns are not possible, a reasonable correlation between the forecast and the trend-component is demonstrated. Section 7 presents conclusions and Section 8 discusses desirable directions for further research on price trends in financial time series.

2. Price-trend Models

2.1 Constant Variance Models

A price-trend model of a price series $\{z_t\}$ is defined by

$$\left.\begin{aligned} \log(z_t) - \log(z_{t-1}) &= x_t = \mu_t + e_{t'} \\ E(e_t) = 0,\ E(e_t e_{t+i}) &= 0\ (i \neq 0), \\ \operatorname{cov}(\mu_s, e_t) &= 0 \quad (\text{all } s,t) \end{aligned}\right\} \tag{2.1}$$

in conjunction with a stochastic process for the trend component $\{\mu_t\}$. Initially, it is supposed that the daily returns $\{x_t\}$ have constant variance. Let σ^2 denote $\operatorname{var}(e_t)$,v^2 denote $\operatorname{var}(\mu_t)$, and $\bar{\mu} = E(\mu_t)$.

Our simplest example of a trend process is obtained by assuming that:

(1) the trend values are determined by the current information about demand and supply;
(2) new information arrives randomly at the market;
(3) there is new information on a proportion $1-p$ of the trading day, $0 < p < 1$;
(4) the trend value changes only when new information becomes available;
(5) when the trend value changes, the new value is independent of all past values.

These assumptions define the trend process:

$$\left.\begin{aligned} \mu_t &= \mu_{t-1}, \quad \text{probability p,} \\ &= \bar{\mu} + \eta_t, \quad 1 - p. \end{aligned}\right\} \qquad (2.2)$$

Throughout this section $\{\eta_t\}$ denotes a series of identically distributed random variables, having zero means, with each η_t independent of the past trend values $\{\mu_s, \text{all } s<t\}$. Equations (2.1) and (2.2) define what we call *the basic trend model.*

The mean duration of the trends defined by (2.2) is denoted by m and equals:

$$\sum_{i=1}^{\infty} i(1-p)\,p^{i-1} = (1-p)^{-1} \text{ trading days.}$$

We expect, *a priori*, that $1 - p$ and $R = v^2/\sigma^2$ will both be small.

Some assumptions are necessary if the concept of price trends is to be tested by statistical methods. The preceding assumptions are asserted to be plausible and enable us to write a stochastic process for $\{\mu_t\}$, from which the auto-correlation in the returns series $\{x_t\}$ caused by price trends can be predicted.

The assumptions can, however, be relaxed in several ways without affecting the subsequent auto-covariance tests. First, it is arguable that the effect of new information upon the price decreases over the days following its announcement. Accordingly the *damped trend model* is given by deleting assumption (4) and replacing (2.2) by:

$$\left.\begin{aligned} \mu_t - \bar{\mu} &= \kappa(\mu_{t-1} - \bar{\mu}), \quad \text{probability p,} \\ &= \eta_t, \quad 1 - p \end{aligned}\right\} \qquad (2.3)$$

The trend term, in this process, decays towards the mean level $\bar{\mu}$ until a new trend starts. Alternatively, it can be argued that the size of a new price trend depends on the preceding trends. An *auto-regressive trend model* can be obtained by deleting assumption (5) and using the trend process:

$$\left.\begin{aligned} \mu_t - \bar{\mu} &= \mu_{t-1} - \bar{\mu}, \quad \text{probability p,} \\ &= \phi(\mu_{t-1} - \bar{\mu}) + \eta_t, \quad 1 - p \end{aligned}\right\} \qquad (2.4)$$

Processes (2.3) and (2.4) retain the third assumption, that the events causing the trends occur on a proportion $1 - p(0 < p < 1)$ of the trading days. A *continuous-events trend model* relaxes this assumption, as follows:

$$\mu_t - \bar{\mu} \quad = \quad \phi(\mu_{t-1} - \bar{\mu}) + \eta_t. \tag{2.5}$$

The constant ϕ then equals the proportion of the total price movement, due to the term η_t, which occurs after day t. Note that, in (2.5) the η's need not have a continuous probability distribution but may have a positive probability that η_t equals zero, corresponding to nil new trend information.

All the preceding processes are special cases of:

$$\left.\begin{aligned} \mu_t - \bar{\mu} &= \kappa(\mu_{t-1} - \bar{\mu}), && \text{probability p,} \\ &= \phi(\mu_{t-1} - \bar{\mu}) + \eta_t, && 1 - p \end{aligned}\right\} \tag{2.6}$$

since $\kappa = 1$ and $\phi = 0$ gives (2.2), $\kappa < 1$ and $\phi = 0$ gives (2.3), $\kappa = 1$ and $\phi \neq 0$ gives (2.4), and $\kappa = 0$, $p = 0$, gives (2.5). Furthermore, (2.6) is a special case of:

$$\mu_t - \bar{\mu} \quad = \quad \alpha_t(\mu_{t-1} - \bar{\mu}) + \eta_t \tag{2.7}$$

with the conditions: (i) the α_t are independent random variables, (ii) α_t and η_s are independent whenever $s \neq t$, (iii) $E(\eta_t|\alpha_t) = 0$; also, in general, $\text{var}(\eta\delta_t|\alpha_t)$ depends on α_t). This trend process defines our *general trend model*: assumptions (1) and (2) still apply, but the other assumptions are not used. The term η_t measures the impact of any new information on day t whilst α_t, which is not independent of η_t, measures the importance of the past trend information in the determination of the current trend value.

2.2 Fluctuating Variance Models

In practice the daily returns x_t have a time-dependent variance $\sum_t^2 = \text{var}(x_t)$, as will be discussed in Section 3. We add to the trend models the further assumptions that both $\text{var}(\mu_t)$ and $\text{var}(e_t)$ are time-dependent quantities and also that the ratio $R = \text{var}(\mu_t)/\text{var}(e_t)$ is constant over time. Thus, we conjecture that the size of price trends is proportional to the amount of market activity, taking $\text{var}(e_t)$ to be a measure of the trading activity on day t.

The trend processes are modified for the situation of fluctuating variance by writing μ_t/Σ_t wherever μ_t was previously written and by defining $\bar{\mu}$ to now be $E(\mu_t/\Sigma_t)$. As an example, the basic model is then:

$$\begin{aligned} \mu_t/\Sigma_t &= \mu_{t-1}/\Sigma_{t-1}, && \text{probability } p, \\ &= \bar{\mu} + \eta_t, && 1 - p \end{aligned}$$

giving:

$$\left.\begin{aligned} \mu_t &= (\Sigma_t/\Sigma_{t-1})\,\mu_{t-1}, && \text{probability } p, \\ &= \bar{\mu}\,\Sigma_t + \eta_t\,\Sigma_t, && 1 - p \end{aligned}\right\}$$

3. Remarks on Variance Fluctuations

3.1 The Problem

The random walk models will be tested against the price-trend models in Section 4, by considering sample auto-correlation coefficients. Statistical theory states that the variance of an auto-correlation coefficient r_i is approximately $1/n$ for the first differences of n observations from a random walk, *if* the first differences have *constant* variance. However, it appears that the variances of daily returns from financial assets always fluctuate. It is therefore necessary to discuss the fluctuating variance property of daily returns.

An example of variance fluctuations is given in Table 1 of Taylor and Kingsman (1978). It is shown that sample variances of daily returns, calculated from annual sets of sugar prices, have ranged from 0.08×10^{-3} to 1.22×10^{-3}. Other articles which describe variance fluctuations include Praetz (1969), Fielitz (1971) and Westerfield (1977) for stock prices and Clark (1973), Rutledge (1976) and Taylor and Kingsman (1979) for commodity prices. Some researchers have described a relationship between the variance of returns and trading volume. Volume data were not available for this study, so this relationship could not be used in the quest for a constant variance series.

3.2 Estimation

Suppose that observed returns $\{x_t\}$ are the realizations of random variables $\{X_t\}$, denote var(X_t) by $\sum_t^2$ and define u_t to be $x_t / \sum_t$. We assume that $\sum_t^2$ is finite; see Hagerman (1978) for recent evidence on the finiteness of the variance. If the variances $\sum_t^2$ were known, auto-correlation coefficients could be calculated from the unit-variance series $\{u_t\}$ and the standard large-sample theory would be applicable. However, $\sum_t^2$ cannot be observed. Nevertheless, estimates $\hat{\sum}_t$ can be obtained with the purpose of applying auto-correlation methods to the series $x_t / \hat{\sum}_t$. The author prefers to estimate the mean absolute deviation:

$$a_t \quad = \quad E|X_t| \quad = \quad \textstyle\sum_t \text{ multiplied by a constant,}$$

rather than $\sum_t$, and to calculate the auto-correlations from $x_t/\hat{a}_t$. An exponentially weighted moving average of the past absolute price changes gives a suitable estimate, viz.:

$$\hat{a}_t \quad = \quad \gamma \sum_{i=0}^{\infty} (1-\gamma)^i |x_{t-1-i}| \quad = \quad (1-\gamma)\,\hat{a}_{t-1} + \gamma |x_{t-1}|. \quad (3.1)$$

This method of estimation assumes that the variances $\sum_t^2$ change gradually. It is found that maximum likelihood estimates of γ are always close to 0.1 for commodity prices. A detailed account of the estimation procedure is given in Taylor and Kingsman (1979).

3.3 Variance Processes

We will calculate auto-correlation coefficients from the *rescaled returns*, $y_t = x_t/\hat{a}_t$. To assess the validity of this novel procedure, it is advisable to check it on simulations of the series $\{x_t\}$ using appropriate variances $\{\sum_t^2\}$. It is thus helpful to find stochastic processes for $\{\sum_t^2\}$ which give $\hat{\gamma}$ approximately equal to 0.1; this subject is of independent interest also.

The series $\{\hat{a}_t\}$ has been plotted for series of copper and sugar prices, with the following tentative conclusions about $\{\sum_t\}$:

(1) the series is stationary;
(2) the median value is approximately 0.016;
(3) the distribution about the median is skewed towards the right;
(4) an approximate 95 per cent confidence interval for $\sum_t$ is from $0.016/\sqrt{8}$ = 0.006 to $0.016\sqrt{8}$ = 0.045; note that

$100\sum_t$ is approximately the standard deviation of the percentage price change, $100(z_t - z_{t-1})/z_{t-1}$.

Conclusions (3) and (4) led us to consider processes for the logarithm of $\sum_t$. It is arguable that the plots of $\{\hat{a}_t\}$ can be modelled by either continuous or discrete processes. The simplest continuous process consistent with the plots is the AR(1) model:

$$\log(\textstyle\sum_t/0.016) = \phi\log(\textstyle\sum_{t-1}/0.016) + \varepsilon_t \qquad (3.2)$$

with var $\{\log(\sum_t)\} = \text{var}(\varepsilon_t)/(1 - \phi^2) = (0.25 \log 8)^2$ and $\{\varepsilon_t\}$ white noise. An appropriate simple discrete process is the Markov chain:

$\sum_t$ has states (0.008, 0.016, 0.032) and transition matrix,

$$\begin{bmatrix} 1-\pi & \pi & 0 \\ \pi/2 & 1-\pi & \pi/2 \\ 0 & \pi & 1-\pi \end{bmatrix}$$

Extensive simulations have shown that estimates $\hat{\gamma} \simeq 0.1$ occur when $\phi = 0.98$ or $\pi = 0.02$. For these values, the correlation between $\log(\sum_t)$ and $\log(\sum_{t+i})$ is $(0.98)^i$; this is also the approximate correlation between $\sum_t^2$ and $\sum_{t+i}^2$.

4. Auto-correlation Results

4.1 Theoretical Auto-correlations

a. Random walk models: Various random walk models were described in Section 1. The model (1.1) has constant mean and zero auto-correlations at all non-zero lags. This is denoted by *the random walk hypothesis*:

$$H_0 : \rho_i = 0, \quad \text{all } i > 0. \qquad (4.1)$$

Models (1.2) and (1.3) are of the form: $x_t = \mu_t + e_t$, $\{e_t\}$ is white noise, every pair μ_s and e_t are uncorrelated. Any model of this form has theoretical auto-correlations:

$$\rho_i \quad = \quad \frac{\text{cov}\,(\mu_t,\mu_{t+i})}{\text{var}(\mu_t) + \text{var}(e_t)} \tag{4.2}$$

Clearly $|\rho_i| < \text{var}(\mu_t)/\text{var}(e_t) = \delta$, say. The constraints, (i) $\mu_t \geqslant 0$, (ii) μ_t has an interpretation as an inflation or mean-return term, ensure that $\text{var}(\mu_t)$ is small. For example, if μ_t is always equivalent to an annual return of between 0 and 28 per cent, then $0 \leqslant \mu_t \leqslant 0.001$ and a reasonable bound for $\text{var}(\mu_t)$ is obtained from the respective uniform distribution, viz. $(0.001)^2/12$. If also $\text{var}(e_t) \geqslant (0.005)^2$, δ is no more than $(0.001)^2/\{12 \times (0.005)^2\} = 1/300$. We define further null hypotheses by:

$$H_{0p}: |\rho_i| \leqslant \delta_p, \quad \text{all } i > 0, \quad \mu_t \text{ is consistent with inflation (model 1.2)}, \tag{4.3}$$

$$H_{0e}: |\rho_i| \leqslant \delta_e, \quad \text{all } i > 0, \quad \mu_t \text{ is consistent with an efficient market (model 1.3)}. \tag{4.4}$$

b. Price-trend models: Initially suppose that $\text{var}(x_t)$ is constant and recall the notation $v^2 = \text{var}(\mu_t)$, $\sigma^2 = \text{var}(e_t)$. The general price-trend model, defined by (2.7), has

$$\text{cov}(\mu_t,\mu_{t+i}) \quad = \quad \{E(\alpha_t)\}^i v^2. \tag{4.5}$$

Denoting $E(\alpha_t)$ by p, and substituting (4.5) in (4.2), we obtain:

$$\rho_i \quad = \quad p^i v^2/(v^2 + \sigma^2). \tag{4.6}$$

We note that the coefficients depend on p and the ratio $v^2/\sigma^2 = R$ alone; they are all positive; they are small if $R < 1$; the values decline slowly if p is almost 1; *all* the price-trend models discussed in Section 2 have the *same* form of theoretical auto-correlation.

The last remark indicates that it is impossible to distinguish between the different trend processes by considering auto-correlation coefficients. At present there is no feasible method of identifying the separate processes; this is unimportant in practice, as will be shown in the section on forecasting. We define *the price-trend hypothesis* to be:

$$H_1: \rho_i = Ap^i, \quad \text{some } A > 0, \quad 0 < p < 1, \quad \text{all } i > 0 \tag{4.7}$$

and henceforth interpret the parameter p in the context of the basic trend model (equation (2.2)), so that $m = (1 - p)^{-1}$ will refer to the mean duration of the trends.

When $var(x_t)$ fluctuates, equation (4.6) is valid if the ratio $R = var(\mu_t)/var(e_t)$ is constant; this condition is the pragmatic assumption stated in Section 2.2.

c. An ARMA model: The auto-correlations of an ARMA(1,1) process:

$$x_t - px_{t-1} = \xi_t - q\xi_{t-1}, \quad \{\xi_t\} \text{ white noise,} \tag{4.8}$$

have $\rho_{i+1} = p\rho_i$, for all $i > 0$ (Granger and Newbold, 1977, p. 27). It can be shown that an ARMA(1,1) process has the auto-correlations $\rho_i = Ap^i$ if q is chosen to be the solution of:

$$q^2 - q\left\{\frac{1 + (1 - 2A)p^2}{(1 - A)p}\right\} + 1 = 0 \tag{4.9}$$

which satisfies $0 < q < 1$. This result gives a simple method of finding the optimal linear forecasts for the price-trend models.

4.2 *Test Statistics*

Previous tests of the random walk hypothesis have been performed without reference to a specific alternative hypothesis. Some researchers have implicitly done this by evaluating:

$$Q_k = n \sum_{i=1}^{k} r_i^2,$$

where the r_i are the sample auto-correlation coefficients of n daily returns and k is chosen subjectively; for H_0 true, Q_k is asymptotically distributed as χ^2_k. Other researchers have assessed individual r_i's using two-tailed tests. The former method lacks power and the latter is haphazard, so that both are unsatisfactory.

By considering the likelihood-ratio statistic for tests of H_0 against H_1, using as 'data' $\{r_1, r_2, \ldots, r_k\}$, the author has shown (Taylor, 1980) that a suitable set of statistics for accurately recorded prices is given by:

$$T_{k,\phi} = \sum_{i=1}^{k} \phi^i r_i \quad (0 < \phi < 1) \tag{4.10}$$

These statistics take advantage of the prediction, in H_1, that the r_i's have monotonically decreasing positive expectations.

Errors often occur in price-series data. Their primary effect is to decrease r_1, since an error in z_t causes errors in x_t and x_{t+1}, one of which will be positive and the other negative. As test power can be lost because of errors in the data, a better set of test statistics is, in practice:

$$U_{k,\phi} = \sum_{i=2}^{k} \phi^i r_i \quad (0 < \phi < 1). \tag{4.11}$$

It is necessary to choose k, ϕ and the significance level α before performing a test. Optimal choices of k and ϕ require a prior opinion about the trend parameters A and p. The author's opinions, which largely derive from an earlier analysis of copper and sugar prices (Taylor, 1978), have been used in a selection procedure which culminated in the recommendations $k = 30$ and $\phi = 0.92$ (Taylor, 1980).

For a constant-variance random walk, $\sqrt{(n)}r_i$ has asymptotic distribution N(0,1) and, for $i \neq j$, r_i and r_j are asymptotically independent (Anderson and Walker, 1964). Therefore, when H_0 is true:

$$U^* = \left(\sum_{i=2}^{30} 0.92^i r_i\right) / \left(\sum_{i=2}^{30} 0.92^{2i} n^{-1}\right)^{1/2}$$

$$= 0.4649 \sqrt{n} \sum_{i=2}^{30} 0.92^i r_i \tag{4.12}$$

is asymptotically distributed as N(0,1). The test is one-tailed, with H_0 rejected when U^* exceeds a critical value determined by the significance level. In fact, $E(r_i) < 0$ and $\text{var}(r_i) < n^{-1}$ when H_0 is true, so that a conservative test is expected when the asymptotic results are used (Taylor, 1980). Figure 10.1 indicates tentative

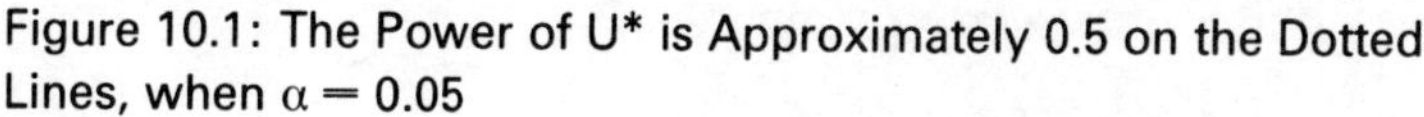

Figure 10.1: The Power of U* is Approximately 0.5 on the Dotted Lines, when $\alpha = 0.05$

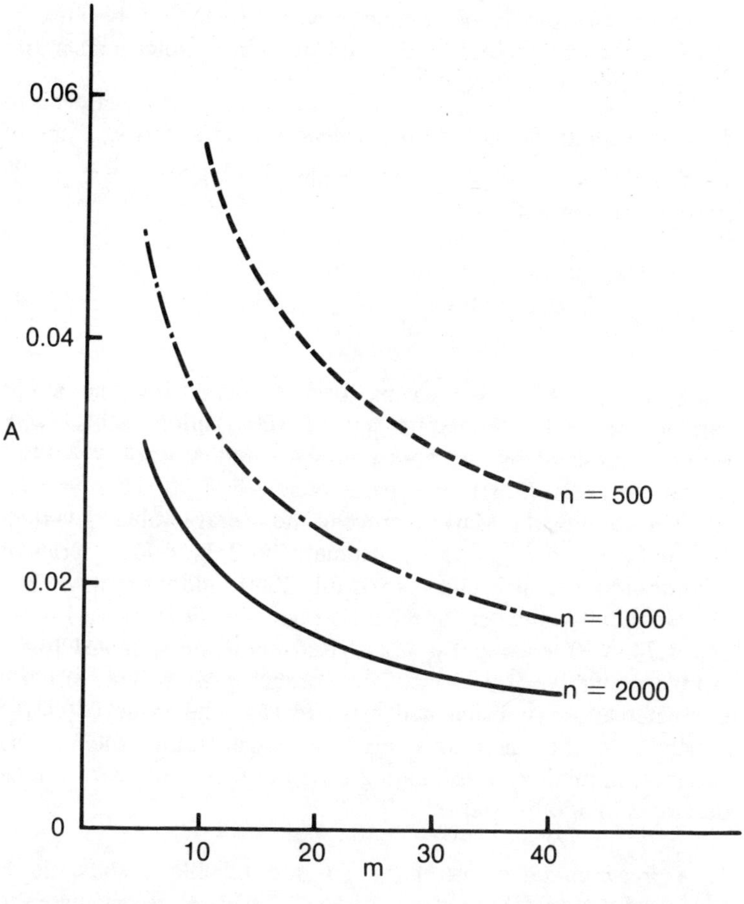

estimates, derived from simulations, of the parameter regions for which the power of the recommended test exceeds one-half when $\alpha = 0.05$.

The hypotheses H_{0p} and H_{0e} can be tested against H_1 by estimating appropriate upper bounds δ_p and δ_e and then calculating:

$$U_p^* \quad = \quad 0.4649 \sqrt{n} \sum_{i=2}^{30} 0.92^i (r_i - \delta_p)$$

$$= U^* - (4.480\sqrt{n})\,\delta_p,$$

and $$U_e^* = U^* - (4.480\sqrt{n})\,\delta_e. \tag{4.13}$$

These statistics should be compared with N(0,1) and, because δ_p and δ_e are overestimates of the null hypothesis auto-correlation, the tests are conservative.

4.3 Defining the Sample Auto-correlation Coefficients

a. An unreliable method: The sampling variance of the standard auto-correlation definition:

$$r_i = \sum_{t=1}^{n-i} (x_t - \bar{x})(x_{t+i} - \bar{x}) / \sum_{t=1}^{n} (x_t - \bar{x})^2, \tag{4.14}$$

where $\bar{x} = (x_1 + \ldots + x_n)/n$ has been estimated for fluctuating-variance series by simulating sets of 100 random walks, with variances defined by the auto-regressive and Markov processes (equations (3.2), (3.3)), with parameters $\phi = 0.98$ and $\pi = 0.02$ respectively. For the Markov process, the average value of $\text{var}(r_i)$, over the lags $i = 1, \ldots, 50$, is estimated at $1.34/n$ for a series of 1,000 random returns and $1.46/n$ for 2,000 random returns. The corresponding estimates for the auto-regressive process are $1.47/n$ and $1.74/n$. Consequently, tests based upon the standard large-sample result, $\text{var}(r_i) \simeq 1/n$, are unreliable when the variance fluctuates and r_i is calculated as in (4.14). The value of $\text{var}(r_i)$ depends on the lag i and the process generating the returns variance. A method of estimating $\text{var}(r_i)$ directly from data will be described in another paper.

b. A recommended method: To get reliable results, it is suggested that rescaled returns, $y_t = x_t/\hat{a}_t$, are used to calculate the coefficients, with $\hat{a}_t$ defined inductively by (3.1) and with $\gamma = 0.1$. The series $\{y_t\}$ has an approximately constant variance if the variances Σ_t^2 change gradually or rarely, as in the auto-regressive and Markov processes respectively. Initial estimates of a_t are required; the choice:

$$\hat{a}_{20} = \frac{1}{20} \sum_{t=1}^{20} |x_t|$$

is suitable and then, for a series of n_1 returns, the coefficients are calculated from:

$$r_i = \sum_{t=21}^{n_1-i} (y_t - \bar{y})(y_{t+i} - \bar{y}) / \sum_{t=21}^{n_1} (y_t - \bar{y})^2, \tag{4.15}$$

where $\bar{y} = (\sum y_t)/(n_1 - 20)$. The term n in U*, and elsewhere, now denotes the effective number of returns, $n = n_1 - 20$. Definition (4.15) has been assessed by simulating sets of 100 random walks, with n = 1,000 or 2,000, and with variances which are either constant or auto-regressive with $0.9 \leqslant \phi \leqslant 0.995$ or Markov with $0.005 \leqslant \pi \leqslant 0.05$. In every case, $var(r_i)$ was estimated to be less than 1/n and 5 or less of the 100 random walks had significant values of U* at the 5 per cent level. In particular, the recommended definition gives acceptable results when the variance is either constant or fluctuates rapidly ($\phi = 0.9$ or $\pi = 0.05$).

It is therefore recommended that returns are rescaled before calculating the auto-correlation coefficients.

c. Futures data: When a time series of prices is constructed from commodity futures contracts, the prices are taken from consecutive annual contracts. For example, the prices of 13 December sugar futures contracts have been used to define a series of prices from 1961 to 1973 inclusive, by taking the prices of the December 1961 contract from January 1961 to November 1961 inclusive, then the prices of the December 1962 contract from December 1961 to November 1962, and so on. To define r_i for futures data, separate initial values of $\hat{a}_t$ are calculated for each contract. Also, when evaluating $\sum (y_t - \bar{y})(y_{t+i} - \bar{y})$, the summation is limited to those times t for which y_t and y_{t+i} are rescaled returns from the same contract.

4.4 Empirical Tests of the Random Walk Hypothesis

Eleven series of daily prices have been used to test the random walk hypothesis against the alternative price-trend hypothesis. A summary of the series definitions, the number of positive auto-correlation coefficients and the values of the test statistics are given in Table 10.1; a table of coefficients, at lags 1-30, is available from the author. The order of events in the auto-correlation analysis was

Table 10.1: Empirical Values of the Auto-correlation Test Statistics

Commodity	Inclusive Years	n	Positive Coefficients at Lags 1-10	11-20	21-30	U*	U^*_e	U^*_p
Copper 1	1966-74	2,119	8	8	7	4.84	4.46	4.15
Sugar	1961-73	3,165	10	8	6	5.29	4.82	4.45
Copper 2	1974-8	1,076	7	6	6	1.86	1.59	1.37
Cocoa	1971-6	1,407	8	6	7	3.47	3.16	2.91
Coffee	1971-6	1,450	10	8	5	4.60	4.28	4.03
Lead	1970-8	2,250	8	9	6	3.50	3.10	2.79
Silver	1970-4	1,078	7	7	3	2.88	2.61	2.37
Tin	1970-8	2,250	7	6	5	1.49	1.09	0.78
Zinc	1970-8	2,250	8	6	6	2.18	1.78	1.47
Maize	1971-6	1,436	6	4	5	1.52	1.20	0.96
Sterling/$	1974-8	1,028	8	8	7	2.78	*	*

as follows: copper and sugar prices were shown not to be random walks by evaluating Q_{50} and then the price-trend parameters A and p were estimated (Taylor, 1978); the estimates contributed to the process of selecting a new test statistic, which ended in the decision to decide future tests by evaluating U* in conjunction with a 5 per cent significance level; the test was then evaluated on further price series, all of which had not been tested previously for non-randomness.

a. Tests on data previously analysed: The copper prices studied in Taylor (1978) are a series of 2,140 daily prices of the spot (immediate delivery) contract. These and all the other prices, with the single exception of the maize series, are for the commodity traded at the London market. The copper series has small negative coefficients at lags 1 and 2 followed by 16 consecutive positive coefficients and U* equals 4.84.

Sugar prices are quoted for as many as eight contracts, for immediate delivery and for delivery in up to seven specified future months. The series analysed takes daily closing prices from 13 consecutive December contracts, as described in Section 4.3. The first 30 coefficients are plotted as Figure 10.2(a); the first 12 are all positive and U* equals 5.29.

b. Tests on new metals data: A further 1,076 copper prices have been appended to the original file and, for these U* equals 1.86. As this number exceeds the 5 per cent critical point (1.65), it is concluded that copper prices were *not* random between 1975 and 1978. The statistic Q_{50}, used for the previous tests, equals 31.96 for the later copper prices. Thus U* gives a significant conclusion for these prices but Q_{50} does not, illustrating the superior power of the former statistic. Figure 10.2(b) shows the coefficients for the complete series of 3,216 prices.

Spot prices of lead, silver, tin and zinc were originally available for 1,099 days, with respective values of U* equal to 0.96, 2.88, 1.00 and 1.68. Two of these figures are statistically significant but the other two exceed the 20 per cent critical value, which suggested that the prices could be non-random. Consequently, a further 1,172 prices were collected and appended to the original files. This was only possible for lead, tin and zinc and gave new values of U* equal to 3.50, 1.49 and 2.18. Each value of U* has been increased by extending the series, and lead and zinc prices are asserted *not* to be random walks.

The metal markets do not determine their prices independently. However, for lead, silver, tin and zinc, the correlations between their daily rescaled returns are all positive and less than 0.5. It can be shown that if the returns of two series have correlation τ and H_0 applies, then the respective U* statistics have correlation τ^2. Consequently, the test statistics for the metals are correlated in a slight and unimportant manner.

c. Tests on new agricultural data: A series of 1,433 cocoa prices has been constructed from 6 September futures contracts, using the method described for sugar prices. Likewise, a series of 1,476 coffee prices has been obtained from 6 November futures contracts. For cocoa, U* = 3.47, whilst for coffee, U* = 4.60. The test values prove conclusively that cocoa and coffee prices are *not* random walks. Once more the coefficients are usually positive at low lags, indicating that the price-trend hypothesis is a feasible description of these series. Indeed, the first 14 coefficients are all positive for the coffee prices.

From 6 December contracts for maize traded on the Chicago market, a series of 1,457 prices has been assembled. This series has U* = 1.52, which is not statistically significant.

Figure 10.2(a): Sugar Autocorrelation Coefficients. [Lines are 95 Per Cent Confidence Limits ± 1.96/√n]. (b) Copper Autocorrelation Coefficients

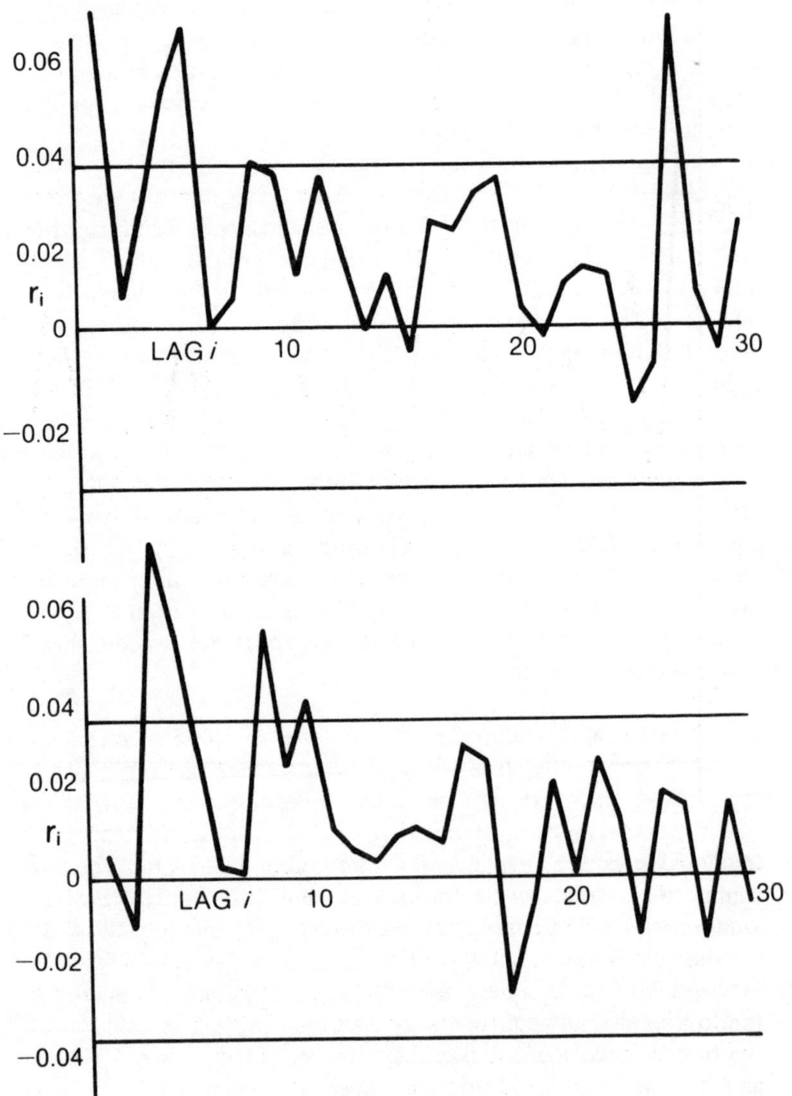

Figure 10.2(c): Exchange Rate Autocorrelation Coefficients

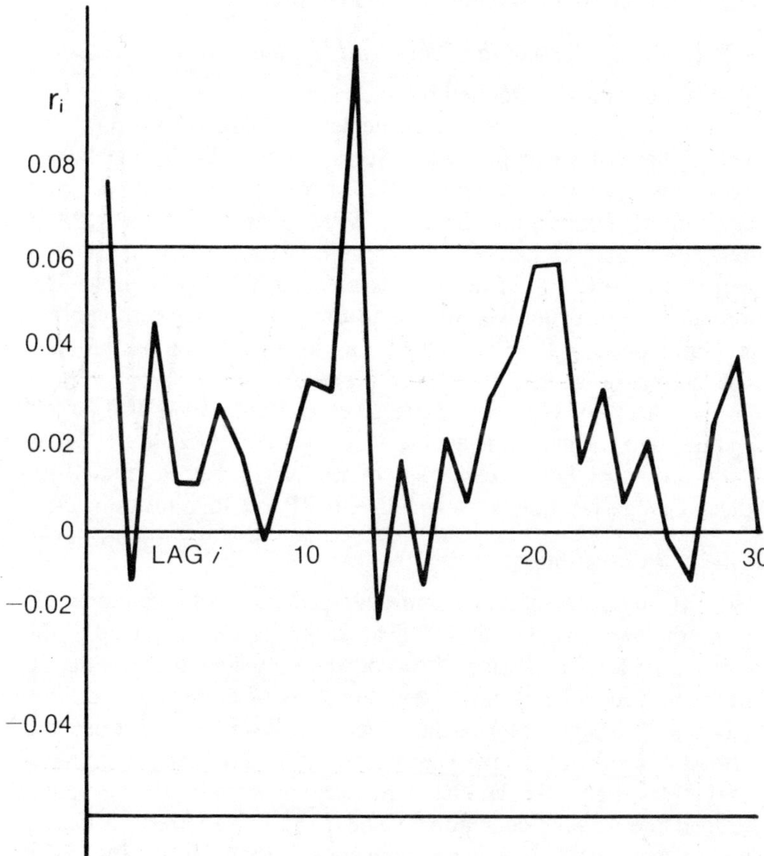

d. Tests on exchange-rate data: The rate of exchange of sterling against the dollar has been obtained from the IMF publication *International Financial Statistics,* for the 1,049 trading days between 1 November 1974 and 19 December 1978. This series has $U^* = 2.78$ and it is concluded that the exchange rate is *not* a random walk. The coefficients are plotted as Figure 10.2(c); 40 of the first 50 and 31 of the next 50 coefficients are positive. Cornell and Dietrich (1978) tested exchange-rate series for an earlier period. Using Q_8, they did not reject the random walk hypothesis. For our series, Q_8 equals 8.83 and so this test criterion would not give a significant result; also $Q_{30} = 36.24$ and $Q_{50} = 62.84$. Thus U^* is substantially more powerful than Q for detecting price-trend behaviour, not only in theory but also in practice.

4.5 Empirical Tests of the Other Null Hypotheses

To test H_{0p} and H_{0e}, defined by (4.3) and (4.4), we take $\delta_p = 3.33 \times 10^{-3}$, $\delta_e = 1.86 \times 10^{-3}$ and calculate U_p^* and U_e^* from (4.13). The choice of δ_p is explained in Section 4.1, whilst δ_e is obtained by assuming a risk-free return (RF_t) of between 5 and 13 per cent per annum (Dimson and Brealey, 1978), a risk-premium (RP_t) of between 0 and 12 per cent per annum (Fama, 1976, p. 14) and $\text{var}(e_t) \geqslant (0.005)^2$; further details are available on request. The bound δ_e is particularly generous to the efficient market hypothesis, since Dusak (1973) claims that agricultural commodities have risk premia far smaller than those for stocks.

The values of U_e^* and U_p^* are given in Table 10.1. The largest changes are for the sugar series, which has $n = 3165$, $U^* - U_e^* = 0.47$ and $U^* - U_p^* = 0.84$. Test values have not been entered for the exchange-rate series, since RF_t and RP_t are then meaningless.

4.6 Test Conclusions

We have tested eight new commodity price series for randomness, using the new test statistic U^*. Six test values are significant at the 5 per cent level and each of the other two values exceeds the 10 per cent point (1.28) of the test. For tests of the efficient market model, U_e^* is significant at the 5 per cent level for five series and always exceeds the 15 per cent point (1.04). Likewise, four values of U_p^* are significant at the 5 per cent level and all the values exceed the 25 per cent point (0.68); these latter tests probably have a true significance level much smaller than the nominal 5 per cent figure. It is concluded that the random walk model and its variants are not adequate descriptions of the process generating commodity prices. This conclusion applies also to exchange rates. Instead, the preponderance of positive coefficients suggests that a price-trend model gives a better description of observed prices.

4.7 Other Tests

After completing the calculations of U^* for all the data, ten other test statistics were evaluated, to compare the performances of established methods with the U^* test. A summary of the comparisons is given, in terms of the number of 'fair test' series (the 11 series given in Table 10.1, excepting the sugar and first copper series) significant at the 5 per cent level. With this criterion, U* scores 7 out of 9. Full details of the comparisons are given in Taylor (1980).

The unsophisticated statistic r_1, often used in the past, is significant for four series, both for one- and two-tailed tests. It outperforms Q_{10}, Q_{30} and Q_{50}, which all score three or less, for the one-tailed test.

Spectral tests are based on estimates of the spectral density function (Granger and Newbold, 1977, ch. 2). The theoretical spectral density for the price-trend models, multiplied by 2π and divided by the returns variance, is

$$g(\omega) = 1 - A + \frac{A(1-p^2)}{1 + p^2 - 2p\cos\omega} \tag{4.16}$$

The function $g(\omega)$ has a single, thin peak, at $\omega = 0$. A random walk would have a flat spectrum, $g(\omega) = 1$ for all ω, but tests for a flat spectrum are technically difficult (Praetz, 1979a). Our estimated spectra were calculated at 26 frequencies, $\omega_j = j\pi/25$ ($j = 0, \ldots, 25$), using the Parzen window and the first 100 sample auto-correlations. A test using the number of significant peaks at the frequencies $\{\omega_j\}$, which with one exception was always three or less, scored one. A score of zero was obtained by a test for a weekly cycle ($\omega = 0.4\pi$). The only successful spectral statistic was $\hat{g}(0)$, which scored 7; all the series have a sharp peak at $\omega = 0$, as predicted by equation (4.16).

The non-parametric runs test, by which Dryden (1970) and Jennergren and Korsvold (1974) obtained a significantly small number of runs, scored only one, for the one-tailed test.

We summarize the comparisons in the claim that U* is, in practice, more powerful than most other test procedures. Examination of the estimated spectral density at 'zero frequency' appears to be powerful also.

5. Parameter Estimates

The price-trend parameters, A and p, have been estimated by the numbers $\hat{A}$ and $\hat{p}$ which minimize:

$$S(A',p') = n \sum_{i=k_1}^{k_2} (A'p'^i - r_i)^2 \qquad (5.1)$$

which measures the agreement between the estimated theoretical auto-correlations, $\hat{\rho}_i = A'p'^i$, and the observed auto-correlations r_i over a selected range $k_1 \leqslant i \leqslant k_2$. Conditional on a choice p′, S is minimized by $\hat{A}_p' = \sum p'^i r_i / \sum p'^{2i}$. The minimum of S can then be found from a set of values $S_{m'} = S(\hat{A}_{p'},p')$, defining $m' = (1 - p')^{-1}$.

Estimates are given in Table 10.2 and are plotted on Figure 10.3. We chose $k_1 = 2$ when there was a possibility of a data-errors problem and $k_1 = 1$ otherwise, with $k_2 = 50$ for all but one series. The estimates should be considered provisional and *no* claims are made about their accuracy. It has been observed that $m'(\hat{A}_{p'})^2$ is approximately constant for a given series. The two dotted lines on Figure 10.3 denote this quantity equal to 0.003 and 0.032; the lines define approximate boundaries for the parameters of price-trend models, for commodities traded at the London markets. We note that the estimates Â are small, as expected for series which

Table 10.2: Parameter Estimates

Commodity	$\hat{A}$	$\hat{m}$	k_1	k_2	S[a]	Q[b]
Copper 1	0.0339	18	1	50	62.98	83.07
Sugar	0.0403	18	1	50	55.62	97.87
Copper 2	0.0336	8	1	50	28.00	31.96
Cocoa	0.0470	13	1	50	45.35	63.41
Coffee	0.1199	6	1	50	38.48	85.71
Lead[c]	0.0257	40	2	50	44.09	69.10
Silver	0.0372	15	2	50	52.88	61.64
Tin	0.0119	20	2	50	36.49	39.14
Zinc[c]	0.0175	40	2	50	38.70	50.27
Maize	0.0129	30	2	50	54.64	57.72
Sterling/$[d]	0.0340	56	*	*	*	*

Notes: [a] S denotes the minimum value of S(A′,p′).

[b] $Q = n \sum_{k_1}^{k_2} r_i^2$.

[c] $\hat{m}$ truncated.

[d] Estimates obtained by considering clipped data also and various k_2.

Figure 10.3: Parameter Estimates

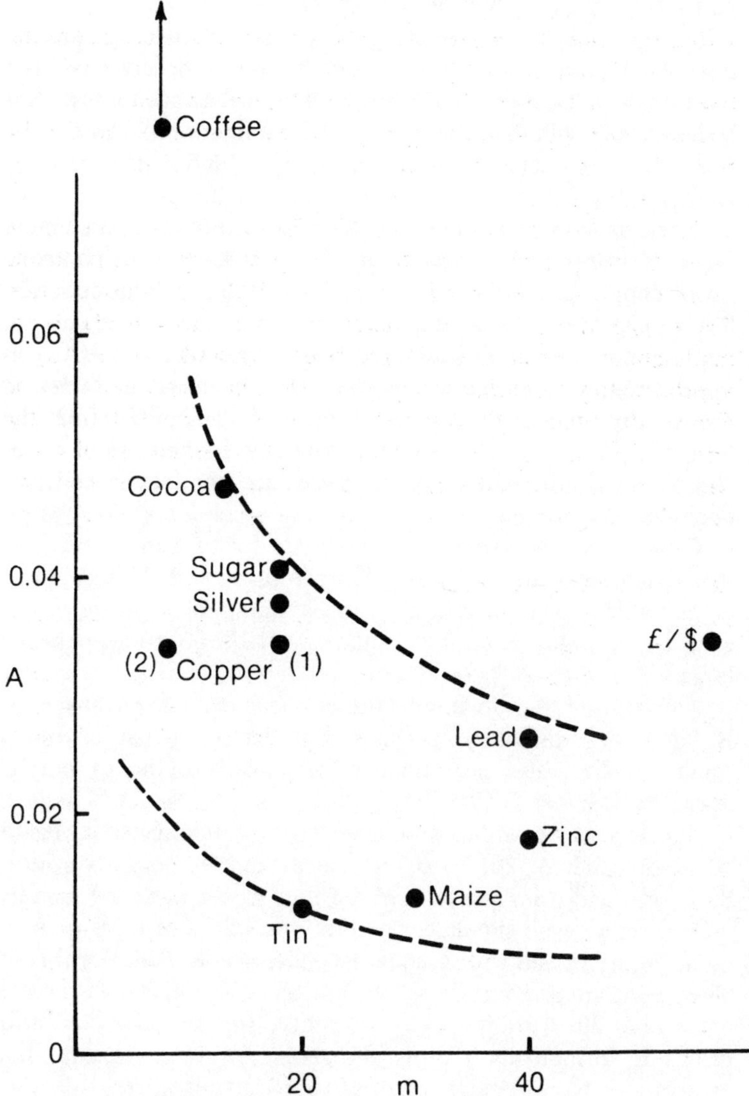

masquerade remarkably well as random walks. Nevertheless, the estimates are the order of ten times the quantities δ_p and δ_e, which strongly suggests that the expected value of x_t, conditional on the past returns x_{t-i} $(i>0)$, is often negative.

For the lead, zinc and exchange-rate series, $S_{m'}$ decreases as the possible mean duration, m′, increases from 2 to 60 days. To keep the estimates for the metals similar, $\hat{m} = 40$ has been chosen for lead and zinc with $\hat{A}$ given by $\hat{A}_{0.975}$. The former and latter copper prices have estimated mean durations of 18 and 8 days respectively. However, a mean of 18 days is possible for the latter prices as $S_{18} = 28.74$ is little more than $S_8 = 28.00$. For comparison, the former prices have $S_{18} = 66.67$ and $S_8 = 69.93$. For the complete set of copper prices from 1966 to 1978 inclusive, estimates $\hat{A} = 0.0315$ and $\hat{m} = 16$ are obtained.

Generally, the agricultural commodities have smaller mean trend durations than the metals; the coffee estimate of six days is particularly small. The sugar estimate of 18 days differs from the estimate of 34 days calculated in Taylor (1978), because of minor changes in the definitions of the series and the auto-correlation coefficients.

Large values of m are not implausible for exchange rates. An analysis of the actual returns and the returns modified by 'clipping' eight outliers gave an estimated mean duration of 56 days. For such a large value of $\hat{m}$, the estimate $\hat{A} = 0.0340$ is unexpectedly large.

The method of estimation is the only one currently available. It is far from satisfactory, because S is extremely flat about its minimum and thus the estimates, particularly of m, cannot be accurate.

The accuracy of $\hat{m}$ has been assessed by simulating series for m equal to either 5, 20, 35 or 50, calculating $S_{m'}$ for these mean durations, and using the least of the four values to define $\hat{m}$. Sets of 100 series were simulated for the four values of m, with $A = 0.04(20/m)^{1/2}$, and with n equal to either 1,000, 1,400 or 2,200. The results are given in Table 10.3 and show that $\hat{m}$ is not accurate when $m \geqslant 20$. Also, it appears that increasing the series length n does not substantially improve the accuracy. For a given m′, the estimate $\hat{A}_{p'}$ has a standard error of approximately $\{2/(m'n)\}^{1/2}$.

Table 10.3: Parameter Estimation: Simulation Results

n = 1,000

	Estimate of m			
Actual m	5	20	35	50
5	73	20	1	6
20	18	41	13	28
35	18	33	14	35
50	13	14	16	57

n = 1,400

	Estimate of m			
Actual m	5	20	35	50
5	86	9	1	4
20	17	54	11	18
35	9	29	24	38
50	14	21	13	52

n = 2,200

	Estimate of m			
Actual m	5	20	35	50
5	86	12	0	1
20	12	55	18	15
35	5	27	22	46
50	4	17	21	58

6. Forecasting

The auto-correlation tests show that daily price series are not random walks and it appears that the prices are described better by a price-trend model. We therefore consider forecasts of future returns and prices derived by assuming that the returns $\{x_t\}$ are generated by a process with theoretical auto-correlations $\rho_i = Ap^i$. It is further assumed that the returns have unconditional expectations equal to zero.

6.1 Linear Forecasts (Theory)

a. Forecasting the next return: Initially it is assumed that the variance of the returns is constant. Forecasts made at time t of the next return x_{t+1} are denoted by $\hat{x}_{t+1}$ and assessed by calculating their mean-squared-error (MSE):

$$F = E(x_{t+1} - \hat{x}_{t+1})^2. \tag{6.1}$$

When $x_t = \mu_t + e_t$, $var(\mu_t) = v^2$ and $var(e_t) = \sigma^2$, the random walk forecast, $\hat{x}_{t+1} = 0$, has $F = v^2 + \sigma^2$. Furthermore, for all forecasts, $F \geqslant \sigma^2$, and the lower bound can only be attained if the next trend value is always known. The maximum proportional reduction in MSE from the random walk forecast is thus $v^2/(v^2 + \sigma^2) = A$, which has already been shown to be a small number.

We now restrict attention to the forecasts which are linear in the past returns:

$$\hat{x}_{t+1} = \sum_{i=0}^{\infty} w_i x_{t-i}.$$

The optimal set $\{w_i\}$ is determined by the theoretical auto-correlations $\{\rho_i\}$. Consequently the particular type of trend model (basic, damped, auto-regressive or something more general) is unimportant: to obtain optimal forecasts it is only necessary to know $A = var(\mu_t)/\{var(\mu_t) + var(e_t)\}$ and $p = E(\alpha_t)$; c.f. equations (2.7), (4.5) and (4.6). It also follows that the optimal $\{w_i\}$ can be obtained from the associated ARMA(1,1) model, defined by equations (4.8) and (4.9).

Algebraic manipulation of equation (4.8) shows that the optimal linear forecast is:

$$f_{t,1} = \sum_{i=0}^{\infty} (p-q)q^i x_{t-i}, \tag{6.2}$$

where q is the root of the quadratic equation (4.9) between 0 and 1. The optimal linear forecast is similar to an exponentially weighted moving-average, but differs by having a sum of weights $(\sum w_i)$ equal to $(p-q)/(1-q)$. The updating formula is:

$$f_{t,1} = qf_{t-1,1} + (p-q)x_t \tag{6.3}$$

and the MSE of the forecasts can be shown to equal

$$F_{min,1} = (v^2 + \sigma^2) \left\{ 1 - \frac{Ap(-q)}{1-pq} \right\} \qquad (6.4)$$

A forecast of the next price is given by $\hat{z}_{t+1} = z_t \exp(f_{t,1})$.

Table 10.4 shows, for the values of A and m estimated for the 11 price series, (1) A, (2) m, (3) $p = 1 - 1/m$, (4) 'the discount rate' q, (5) the sum of weights, $\sum w_i$, (6) the percentage reduction in MSE, $100Ap(p-q)/(1-pq)$, (7) the proportion of the maximum reduction in MSE obtained using linear forecasts, $p(p-q)/(1-pq)$. The first copper series has median entries in columns 5-7. Thus, typically, the sum of weights is one-third, the reduction in MSE is less than 1 per cent and linear forecasts attain less than one-quarter of the maximum reduction associated with the price-trend model.

The low sum of weights is essentially due to the fact that v^2 is much less than σ^2. This can be illustrated by considering the basic trend model with normally distributed e_t's and μ_t's when, if the trend μ_t started M days earlier, the maximum likelihood estimate of x_{t+1} equals $p\sum x_{t-i}/(M + \sigma^2/v^2)$, with the sum over $i = 0, \ldots M-1$, giving $\sum w_i = Mp/(M + \sigma^2/v^2)$.

b. Predicting tomorrow's trend: When forecasting the next return or price, it is clear that only negligible improvements (using the MSE criterion) can be made upon the random walk forecast. At first sight it therefore appears that the forecasts can have no practical value. The relatively large random terms, e_t, are the cause of the low reduction in MSE, so that forecasts of $x_{t+1} = \mu_{t+1} + e_{t+1}$ cannot be accurate. However, in a decision-making situation it is important to identify correctly the sign of tomorrow's trend μ_{t+1}, whether it be positive or negative, rather than to predict x_{t+1}. Thus, the correlation between $f_{t,1}$ and μ_{t+1} is arguably a more practical measure of the forecasts' usefulness than the reduction in MSE.

Regarding $\{f_{t,1}\}$ and $\{x_{t+1}\}$ as series of random variables:

$$\text{cov}(f_{t,1}, x_{t+1}) = \text{var}(f_{t,1}) = \text{var}(x_t) - F_{min,1}$$

(Granger and Newbold, 1977, pp. 122-3), and it can then be shown that:

Table 10.4: Theoretical Results for Forecasts of the Next Return

Series	(1) A	(2) m	(3) p	(4) q	(5) $\sum w_i$	(6) Percentage Reduction in MSE	(7) Proportion of Maximum Possible
Copper 1	0.0339	18	0.9444	0.9182	0.32	0.63	0.19
Copper 2	0.0336	8	0.8750	0.8482	0.18	0.31	0.09
Lead	0.0257	40	0.9750	0.9565	0.43	0.69	0.27
Silver	0.0372	15	0.9333	0.9044	0.30	0.64	0.17
Tin	0.0119	20	0.9500	0.9397	0.17	0.11	0.06
Zinc	0.0175	40	0.9750	0.9615	0.35	0.37	0.21
Sugar	0.0403	18	0.9444	0.9141	0.35	0.84	0.21
Cocoa	0.0470	13	0.9231	0.8873	0.32	0.76	0.18
Coffee	0.1199	6	0.8333	0.7501	0.33	2.22	0.19
Maize	0.0129	30	0.9667	0.9559	0.24	0.18	0.14
Sterling/$	0.0340	56	0.9821	0.9609	0.54	1.26	0.37

$$\text{cov}(f_{t,1},\mu_{t+1}) \quad = \quad \text{var}(f_{t,1}) \quad = \quad \frac{p(p-q)v^2}{1-pq} \tag{6.5}$$

and

$$\text{cor}(f_{t,1},\mu_{t+1}) \quad = \quad \left\{\frac{p(p-q)}{1-pq}\right\}^{1/2}. \tag{6.6}$$

The standard deviation of $f_{t,1}$ for the price-series estimates is v multiplied by the numbers in column 7 of Table 10.4. The respective correlations between the forecast $f_{t,1}$ and the unobservable trend μ_{t+1} are given in column 1 of Table 10.5. Eight of the eleven correlations exceed 0.4. It must be noted that the correlations assume that the parameters A and p are estimated perfectly.

We denote var($f_{t,1}$) by v_*^2 and cor($f_{t,1}$,μ_{t+1}) by r, so that $v_* = rv$. If it is assumed that the joint distribution of $f_{t,1}$ and μ_{t+1} is bivariate normal:

$$\begin{aligned} P(\mu_{t+1} > 0 | f_{t,1} = kv_*) &= P(N(kr,1-r^2) > 0) \\ &= \Phi\left(\frac{kr}{\sqrt{(1-r^2)}}\right) \end{aligned} \tag{6.7}$$

where Φ is the cumulative distribution function of the standardized normal distribution. The probability (6.7) is given in columns 2 and 3 of Table 10.5, for k = 1,2 respectively. These probabilities are encouragingly large. They suggest that it is often possible to predict correctly whether the trend is positive or negative.

c. Forecasting over a general time horizon: Further algebra shows that the optimal linear forecast of x_{t+N},$N>0$, made at time t, is:

$$f_{t,N} \quad = \quad p^{N-1}f_{t,1}$$

and the optimal linear forecast of $S_{t,N} = \log(z_{t+N}/z_t) = x_{t+1} + \ldots + x_{t+N}$, made at time t, is:

$$\hat{S}_{t,N} \quad = \quad \sum_{i=1}^{N} f_{t,i} \quad = \quad (1-p^N)f_{t,1}/(1-p) \tag{6.8}$$

Table 10.5: Theoretical Results for Predictions of the Trend

	(1)	(2)	(3)	(4)
		$P(\mu>0)$		
Series	r	k=1	k=2	Expected Change (%) k=1, $\sigma = 0.016$
Copper 1	0.43	0.70	0.86	2.3
Copper 2	0.30	0.63	0.75	0.5
Lead	0.52	0.76	0.92	5.4
Silver	0.42	0.68	0.82	2.0
Tin	0.25	0.61	0.71	0.9
Zinc	0.46	0.72	0.88	3.9
Sugar	0.46	0.72	0.88	2.7
Cocoa	0.43	0.70	0.86	2.0
Coffee	0.43	0.70	0.86	1.5
Maize	0.37	0.67	0.81	2.0
Sterling/$	0.61	0.83	0.97	10.3

so that z_{t+N} can be forecast by $z_t \exp(\hat{S}_{t,N})$. If a return $\hat{\mu} = f_{t,1}$ is forecast over the next day, then a total return of $(1 + p + \ldots + p^{N-1})\,\hat{\mu}$ is predicted over the next N days. Letting N tend to infinity shows that the predicted total return is $\hat{\mu}/(1-p) = m\hat{\mu}$. Thus, when $f_{t,1} = kv_*$, it is predicted that the trend will, on average, change $\log(z_t)$ by:

$$m(kv_*) \quad = \quad mkrv \quad = \quad mkr\sigma\,\{A/(1-A)\}^{1/2} \qquad (6.9)$$

Column 4 of Table 10.5 illustrates the value of (6.9) when k = 1 and $\sigma = 0.016$. The figures are approximately the expected long-term percentage price change when first the trend estimate equals the standard deviation of its generating random variable and secondly the daily price changes have standard deviations of about 1.6 per cent of the price. These figures must be interpreted with care, since they are sensitive to the estimates of A and m. The median entry in column 4 is 2.0 per cent. As commodity investors usually pay only a 10 per cent margin, a naive interpretation of the 2 per cent figure states that an investor could frequently take decisions for which the expected return on capital invested was 20 per cent.

It can be shown that the variance of $S_{t,N}$ is:

$$V_N = \operatorname{var}\left(\sum_{i=1}^{N} x_{t+i}\right) = N(v^2 + \sigma^2) + 2mpv^2\left(N - \frac{1-p^N}{1-p}\right) \tag{6.10}$$

and that the reduction in the MSE of $S_{t,N}$ obtained using linear forecasts equals:

$$W_N = \left(\frac{1-p^N}{1-p}\right)^2 \operatorname{var}(f_{t,1})$$

which can be evaluated using (6.5). The percentage reduction in MSE is $100W_N/V_N$; typical values will be compared in Section 6.2 with the reductions obtained in practice.

d. Modifications for fluctuating-variance series: Suppose now that $\sum_t^2 = \operatorname{var}(x_t)$ fluctuates with time. If the ratio $R = \operatorname{var}(\mu_t)/\operatorname{var}(e_t)$ is constant, as conjectured in Section 2.2, the optimal linear forecast of $u_{t+1} = x_{t+1}/\sum_{t+1}$ is $\hat{u}_{t+1} = \sum(p-q)q^i u_{t-i}$. Forecasting x_{t+1} by $\sum_{t+1}\hat{u}_{t+1}$ gives, after some rearrangement:

$$\hat{x}_{t+1} = (\textstyle\sum_{t+1}/\sum_t)\{q\hat{x}_t + (p-q)x_t\} \tag{6.11}$$

as the optimal linear forecast of x_{t+1}. In practice every $\sum_t$ is unknown at all times. We define 'Forecast 1' by replacing the ratio $\sum_{t+1}/\sum_t$ by $\hat{a}_{t+1}/\hat{a}_t$, where the term $\hat{a}_t$ is an estimate of $E|X_t|$ made at time $t-1$ and is defined by equation (3.1). This forecast can also be obtained by applying the theory for constant-variance series to the rescaled returns, $y_t = x_t/\hat{a}_t$. The updating equations are:

$$\left.\begin{aligned} \hat{a}_{t+1} &= (1-\gamma)\,\hat{a}_t + \gamma|x_t|, \\ \hat{x}_{t+1} &= (\hat{a}_{t+1}/\hat{a}_t)\{q\hat{x}_t + (p-q)x_t\} \end{aligned}\right\} \tag{6.12}$$

and we recommend $\gamma = 0.1$. We define 'Forecast 2' by deleting the multiplier $\hat{a}_{t+1}/\hat{a}_t$ from equation (6.12) which, essentially, ignores the variance fluctuations.

To forecast $S_{t,N} = \log(z_{t+N}/z_t)$ it is necessary to estimate future variances $\sum_{t+i}^2$, $2 \leqslant i \leqslant N$. The only viable procedure is to use the relationship between $\hat{S}_{t,N}$ and $\hat{S}_{t,1}$ established for constant-variance series, viz. equation (6.8).

6.2 Empirical Accuracy of the Forecasts

Two assessments have been made of the empirical accuracy of the linear forecasts. The first analysis checks whether the theoretically optimal forecasts achieve the predicted reductions in MSE when they are used on price data. The parameter estimates obtained in Section 5 are used, although in practice these estimates would not have been available until the whole series were observed. A second analysis considers forecasts based on some parameter estimates that could have been available.

Series of forecasts $\{\hat{S}_{t,N}\}$ are assessed by calculating the weighted error sum-of-squares:

$$\sum_{t} (S_{t,N} - \hat{S}_{t,N})^2/\hat{a}_t^2. \tag{6.13}$$

The summation is over all times t which are divisible by N. We denote this quantity by F_0 when $\hat{S}_{t,N} = 0$ is the random walk forecast, by F_1 when $\hat{S}_{t,N}$ is the optimal linear forecast, and calculate the percentage reduction in MSE as $100(F_0 - F_1)/F_0$ per cent. The weighted least-squares method once more nullifies the problems caused by the fluctuating variance of the returns.

The percentage reductions in MSE predicted by the theory and the reductions actually achieved are given for 'Forecast 1' in Table 10.6, for N = 1, 5, 10 and 20. When N = 1, there is a consistent and close agreement between the theoretical and actual reductions and several reductions are statistically significant. For further horizons N, there is an increase in both the theoretical and actual reductions. Again there is a good agreement and the differences between the theoretical and actual reductions are consistent with the relatively small sample sizes. 'Forecast 1' outperforms 'Forecast 2' for four series, is inferior for four series and has essentially the same results for the remaining three series.

In the second analysis, the five series of more than 2,000 prices were each subdivided and estimates of A and p were obtained from the first sub-series and used to calculate the forecasts for the second sub-series. The comparison between the reductions expected after analysing the first sub-series and those actually obtained over the second sub-series is given in Table 10.7, again

Table 10.6: Reductions in MSE (%), Theoretical (T) and Actual (A)

	Forecast Horizon (Days)							
	1		5		10		20	
Series	T	A	T	A	T	A	T	A
Copper 1	0.63	0.64	2.26	2.99	3.11	5.79	3.29	5.82
Copper 2	0.31	0.33	0.84	0.79	0.89	0.28	0.65	0.27
Lead	0.69	0.67	2.83	2.32	4.54	4.11	6.15	6.11
Silver	0.64	0.29	2.18	3.40	2.86	4.94	2.20	6.57
Tin	0.11	0.31	0.43	1.47	0.64	1.58	0.77	1.72
Zinc	0.37	0.38	1.56	2.18	2.58	3.40	3.63	3.83
Sugar	0.84	0.96	2.96	3.57	4.00	4.38	4.15	6.37
Cocoa	0.86	1.22	2.72	3.70	3.33	4.94	2.99	3.04
Coffee	2.22	2.57	4.27	3.21	3.52	1.65	2.05	0.65
Maize	0.18	0.22	0.74	1.46	1.19	2.32	1.61	0.20
Sterling/$	1.26	1.11	5.19	2.83	8.36	7.80	11.53	14.84

Table 10.7: Percentage Reductions for Second Analysis, Theoretical Predictions (T) from First Sample, Actual Computed for Second Sample (A)

		Forecast Horizon (Days)							
		1		5		10		20	
Series	Dates	T	A	T	A	T	A	T	A
Copper	1966-74	0.63		2.26		3.11		3.29	
	1974-8		0.27		0.54		0.01		2.14
Lead	1970-4	0.28		1.21		2.01		2.87	
	1975-8		0.79		2.70		3.75		5.63
Tin	1970-4	0.11		0.35		0.43		0.37	
	1975-8		0.11		0.72		0.90		1.16
Zinc	1970-4	0.43		1.80		2.95		4.12	
	1975-8		−0.18		−0.23		−0.86		−2.80
Sugar	1961-7	0.95		3.52		5.07		5.79	
	1968-73		0.82		2.98		4.79		9.93

for 'Forecast 1'. The prior expectations are exceeded for lead and tin, are not attained for copper and zinc, and are approximately matched for sugar. Overall it appears that prices could have been forecast marginally better by using the price-trend models instead of random walk theory.

7. Conclusions

We have defined, tested and studied a new set of statistical models for financial time series. These models include a price-trend term μ_t. By specifying formal stochastic processes for μ_t, it is possible to calculate the theoretical auto-correlation in daily returns due to the conjectured type of trend behaviour. It is then possible to perform statistical tests of the random walk and related hypotheses against a price-trend hypothesis.

The sample evidence from long series of commodity and currency prices is overwhelmingly against the random walk and related hypotheses. It is concluded that such models are not adequate descriptions of the process generating the data investigated. We emphasize that clearcut conclusions were obtained, and could only have been obtained, by two innovations. First, the consequences of fluctuations in the variance of the returns were neutralized. Without this action, the asymptotic sampling theory appealed to in many earlier articles is seriously invalid. Secondly, a new and powerful test statistic was used, to avoid the fate of the established test statistics: a frequent false acceptance of the random walk hypothesis, as enumerated in Section 4.7. The price-trend models successfully explain the observed preponderance of positive auto-correlations coefficients and therefore appear to give a more accurate description of the prices.

It is possible to estimate and interpret the price-trend parameters, to obtain optimal linear forecasts and to assess naive investment rules. Thus, conveniently, the models are mathematically tractable. It is necessary, of course, to distinguish between a model of the prices' stochastic process and their 'true' stochastic process. It would be oversimplistic to say that a price-trend model generates observed prices. Nevertheless, it is asserted that the price-trend models describe certain statistical features of observed prices which the random walk models cannot explain. Also, it is considered that the price-trend models are consistent with the market forces of supply and demand.

Although there is very little auto-correlation in the markets, typically less than 0.04 at all non-zero lags, the economic efficiency or otherwise of the markets studied remains an open question.

8. Further Research

The conclusions are, at present, only applicable to the London commodity markets and one international currency market. It is possible that they apply to several other financial markets. Researchers are therefore encouraged to test further price series for price-trend behaviour. It would be particularly interesting to test stock price series. The author recommends that long series are studied, consisting of at least 1,000 and preferably more than 2,000 prices, to give a high test power when a price-trend model is valid (cf. Figure 10.1). Daily returns must be checked for fluctuating variance and, if necessary, appropriate action should be taken, as illustrated in Section 4.3. The test statistic U*, defined in Section 4.2, is recommended for a test of the random walk hypothesis against the price-trend hypothesis.

There is probably considerable scope for improvement in the method of parameter estimation. It is hoped that the established theory of estimation for ARMA processes can be utilized. For practical applications, it would be useful to assess the implications of basing forecasts and investment decisions upon incorrect estimates of the trend parameters.

Research continues into the efficiency of the futures markets. Trading rules are being constructed, using the prices before 1977, and will be assessed by their performance on the prices from January 1977 to a later date, probably December 1979.

The conclusions have important consequences for commodity stabilization policies and it is hoped that the time-series results will be used to make stabilization research more realistic.

Finally, the models would be enhanced if the trend terms μ_t and their stochastic processes were to be linked with an econometric description of price determination.

References

Anderson, T.W. and A.M. Walker (1964) 'On the Asymptotic Distribution of the Autocorrelations of a Sample from a Linear Stochastic Process', *Annals of Mathematical Statistics*, 35, 1296-303.

Cargill, T.F. and G.C. Rausser (1975) 'Temporal Price Behaviour in Commodity Futures Markets', *Journal of Finance*, 30, 1043-53.

Clark, P.K. (1973) 'A Subordinated Stochastic Process Model with Finite Variance for Speculative Prices', *Econometrica*, 41, 135-55.

Cornell, W.B. and J.K. Dietrich (1978) 'The Efficiency of the Market for Forward Exchange Under Floating Exchange Rates', *Review of Economics and Statistics*, 60, 111-20.

Cunningham, S.W. (1973) 'The Predictability of British Stock Market Prices', *Applied Statistics*, 22, 315-31.

Dimson, E. and R.A. Brealey (1978) 'The Risk Premium on UK Equities', *Investment Analyst*, 52, 14-18.

Dryden, M.M. (1970) 'A Statistical Study of UK Share Prices', *Scottish Journal of Political Economy*, 17, 369-89.

Dusak, K. (1973) 'Futures Trading and Investor Returns: An Investigation of Commodity Market Risk Premiums', *Journal of Political Economy*, 81, 1387-406.

Fama, E.F. (1965) 'The Behaviour of Stock Market Prices', *Journal of Business*, 38, 34-105.

— (1970) 'Efficient Capital Markets: A Review of Theory and Empirical Work', *Journal of Finance*, 25, 383-417.

— (1976) *Foundations of Finance*, Oxford: Basil Blackwell.

Fielitz, B.D. (1971) 'Stationarity of Random Data: Some Implications for the Distribution of Stock Price Changes', *Journal of Financial and Quantitative Analysis*, 6, 1025-34.

Granger, C.W.J. and O. Morgenstern (1971) *Predictability of Stock Market Prices*, Massachusetts: Heath Lexington.

Granger, C.W.J. and P. Newbold (1977) *Forecasting Economic Time Series*, New York: Academic Press.

Hagerman, R.L. (1978) 'More Evidence on the Distribution of Security Returns', *Journal of Finance*, 33, 1213-21.

Jennergren, L.P. and P.E. Korsvold (1974) 'Price Formation in the Norwegian and Swedish Stock Markets — Some Random Walk Tests', *Swedish Journal of Economics*, 76, 171-85.

Jensen, M.C. (1978) 'Some Anomalous Evidence Regarding Market Efficiency, an Editorial Introduction', *Journal of Financial Economics*, 6, 95-101.

Kingsman, B.G. (1974) 'Forecasting and Research for Supply Markets-Commodity Buying Systems', *Long Range Planning*, 7, 24-38.

Labys, W.C. and C.W.J. Granger (1970) *Speculation, Hedging and Commodity Price Forecasts*, Massachusetts: Heath Lexington.

Leuthold, R.M. (1972) 'Random Walks and Price Trends: The Live Cattle Futures Markets', *Journal of Finance*, 27, 879-89.

Praetz, P.D. (1969) 'Australian Share Prices and the Random Walk Hypothesis', *Australian Journal of Statistics*, 11, 123-39.

— (1975) 'Testing the Efficient Markets Theory on the Sydney Wool Futures Exchange', *Australian Economics Papers*, 14, 240-9.

— (1976) 'On the Methodology of Testing for Independence in Futures Prices', *Journal of Finance*, 31, 977-9.

— (1979a) 'Testing for a Flat Spectrum on Efficient Market Price Data', *Journal of Finance*, 34, 645-58.

— (1979b) 'A General Test of a Filter Effect', *Journal of Financial and Quantitative Analysis*, 14, 385-94.
Rutledge, D.J.S. (1976) 'A Note on the Variability of Futures Prices', *Review of Economics and Statistics*, 58, 118-20.
Taylor, S.J. (1978) 'Time Series Properties and Models of Commodity Prices', PhD Thesis, Lancaster University.
— (1982) 'Tests of the Random Walk Hypothesis Against a Price-Trend Hypothesis', *Journal of Financial and Quantitative Analysis*, 17, 37-61.
Taylor, S.J. and B.G. Kingsman (1978) 'Non-stationarity in Sugar Prices', *Journal of the Operational Research Society*, 29, 971-80.
— (1979) 'An Analysis of the Variance and Distribution of Commodity Price-changes', *Australian Journal of Management*, 4, 135-49.
Westerfield, R. (1977) 'The Distribution of Common Stock Price Changes: An Application of Transaction Times and Subordinated Stochastic Models', *Journal of Financial and Quantitative Analysis*, 12, 743-66.

INDEX